D1476738

HITLER'S STRATEGIC BOMBING OFFENSIVE

ON THE EASTERN FRONT

HITLER'S STRATEGIC BOMBING OFFENSIVE ON THE EASTERN FRONT

BLITZ OVER THE VOLGA, 1943

DMITRY DEGTEV AND DMITRY ZUBOV

AIR WORLD

AIR WORLD

HITLER'S STRATEGIC BOMBING OFFENSIVE ON THE EASTERN FRONT
Blitz Over the Volga, 1943

First published in Great Britain in 2021 by Air World Books,
an imprint of Pen & Sword Books Ltd, Yorkshire – Philadelphia

ISBN: 978 1 52678 989 1

Typeset by SJmagic DESIGN SERVICES, India.
Printed and bound in the UK by CPI (UK), Croydon, CR0 4YY.

Pen & Sword Books Ltd incorporates the imprints of Pen & Sword Archaeology,
Air World Books, Atlas, Aviation, Battleground, Discovery, Family History, History,
Maritime, Military, Naval, Politics, Social History, Transport, True Crime, Claymore
Press, Frontline Books, Praetorian Press, Seaforth Publishing and White Owl

For a complete list of Pen & Sword titles please contact:

PEN & SWORD BOOKS LTD
47 Church Street, Barnsley, South Yorkshire, S70 2AS, UK.
E-mail: enquiries@pen-and-sword.co.uk
Website: www.pen-and-sword.co.uk

Or

PEN AND SWORD BOOKS,
1950 Lawrence Roadd, Havertown, PA 19083, USA
E-mail: Uspen-and-sword@casematepublishers.com
Website: www.penandswordbooks.com

Contents

Acknowledgements

The authors would like to express their gratitude for the help and assistance provided by the military historian Sergey Bogatyrev, the Luftwaffe historian Mikhail Zefirov, and Walter Waiss of the Kampfgeschwader 27 archive (Boelcke Archiv).

Introduction

During the Second World War, the Luftwaffe conducted two major strategic operations aimed at destroying the industrial and the economic capabilities of the opponents of the Third Reich. One of these, the Blitz, which was directed against the United Kingdom from the autumn of 1940 through to the spring of 1941, is well known. Day and night, German bombers headed out over the English Channel and attacked British cities and factories. Through these raids alone, Hitler hoped to undermine the military power of Great Britain and force it to seek terms for surrender. While the Blitz undoubtedly resulted in great destruction and many thousands of casualties, it did not deliver the intended result. The reason for this failure, however, lies chiefly not in German equipment or technology, which at that time was excellent, but in the incompetent leadership of the Third Reich.

As the geographic area of the war expanded, the Luftwaffe found itself drawn into an increasing number of missions to support the Wehrmacht's troops in widely different parts of Europe and Africa. As the burden on the aircrews increased, and losses mounted, attacks by German bombers on key strategic targets became fewer in number and less concentrated. Consequently, the results of the bombing operations gradually lessened. Parallel attempts to create strategic aviation forces and introduce heavy bombers suffered a natural collapse, a situation directly related to the nature of the Nazis' system of command and control.

In 1942 and 1943, the Third Reich itself began to suffer under the weight of the strategic bomber offensive unleashed by the RAF and the USAAF. In June 1943, the Luftwaffe decided to utilise its experiences of being on the receiving end of the British and American assault and strike back. It duly conducted its second large-scale strategic operation of the war, but this time the target was not Britain.

The situation in the war had changed dramatically. On the Eastern Front Hitler's forces found themselves facing the sheer might and resourcefulness

INTRODUCTION

of Stalin's Red Army. To try and stem the seemingly endless supply of the enemy's weapons and war materiel to the front, the Luftwaffe drew up plans to launch a new offensive at the Soviet war industries located along the Volga River.

The attacks took place on the eve of Operation *Zitadelle* – the campaign undertaken against Russian forces in the Kursk salient that initiated the Battle of Kursk. The Luftwaffe's headquarters staff hoped to destroy the main factories involved in the production of tanks, aircraft and fuel. For these complex and risky night missions all the Junkers Ju 88 and Heinkel He 111 bombers available to Hitler in the East were used.

The operation, mysteriously called *Carmen II*, lasted for a month and covered a vast target area that stretched from the Rybinsk reservoir (often informally called the Rybinsk Sea) to the Caspian Sea. Yet, despite it being the Luftwaffe's largest single campaign on the Eastern Front, little is known about the operation.

In this book, we set out to explore a completely new chapter in the history of the Third Reich's air war on the Eastern Front, and in doing so provide comprehensive answers to many important questions. What targets, for example, were attacked during the operation? How did the German bombers operate at the limit of their range? What was the Russian response? What damage did the Soviet war industries suffer, and, most importantly, how did this ultimately affect Operation *Zitadelle*?

Dmitry Degtev and Dmitry Zubov,
Russian Federation, 2020

Chapter 1

The Führer's Nazgûl

'The Russians are coming'

In early 1943, despite the recent disaster at Stalingrad, Adolf Hitler was relatively optimistic. The encirclement of the 6th Army seemed temporary, and new units, primarily the II SS Panzer Corps, were due to arrive on the Eastern Front. The captured regions in the Caucasus had to be evacuated, the armies of the allies of the Third Reich on the Don were defeated, but on other parts of the huge front, at Leningrad, Demyansk and Rzhev, German troops firmly held their positions. The situation in North Africa had also been stabilised. Submarines in the Atlantic continued to sink British and American ships, and the devastating raids of British bombers on German cities were still sporadic. Hitler's vast empire, stretching from the Bay of Biscay and the Mediterranean Sea to the Arctic Ocean, Lake Ladoga and the Black Sea, still looked to be in good shape.

The main thing was to stop the Russian offensive in the south at any cost and to gain a foothold in the new impregnable positions before quietly preparing for another summer offensive. The Führer's hopes were for new tanks, new bombers, jet fighters and missiles. Hitler wanted to stall for time, and then attack his enemies with all the power of the 'Wunderwaffe'.

But the situation continued to deteriorate. On 31 January, the Paulus army in Stalingrad unexpectedly surrendered without waiting for fresh blockade-relieving strikes and the promised uninterrupted supply by air. At the same time, the Luftwaffe suffered huge losses: 488 aircraft of all types, including 165 He 111 bombers used for cargo delivery. Most of them were destroyed during take-off and landing in terrible weather, or abandoned on snow-covered airfields. Among the losses were fifteen of the new He 177 'Greifs' from I./FKG 50, which were designed for air strikes in England and the Urals but debuted as transport aircraft. More than 1,100 pilots joined the list of missing and dead, which was three times more than during the whole offensive on the Caucasus and Stalingrad.

At the same time, the Red Army continued to advance. Having broken through the defensive line of Army Group B, the troops of the Bryansk and Voronezh fronts advanced rapidly to the west, bypassing the German group in Orel from the south. On 8 February the most important railway and aviation hub at Kursk was liberated.

On 6 February an Fw 200 C-4/U1 Condor with the code 'CE+1B' on the fuselage landed in Zaporozhye. It was the Führer's personal plane, which was to take the commander of Army Group South, Generalfeldmarschall Erich von Manstein, to the Wolfschanze(Wolf's Lair) headquarters in East Prussia. Hitler's conversation with him lasted from 17.00 to 21.00, accompanied by a meal. The Führer called for fanaticism and insisted on the need to hold the position at all costs, not allowing the Russians to reach the Dnieper. After that the Generalfeldmarschall spent the night in one of bunkers, and in the morning he was flown back to Ukraine.

On 9 February, T-34 tanks broke into Belgorod, and a week later red flags were hoisted over the centre of Kharkov, a city that Hitler himself called nothing less than 'the key to Ukraine'. Inspired by this success, the Soviet command drove their units further south-west in the direction of Zaporozhye and Dnepropetrovsk. Ahead loomed a tempting goal– not to let the Germans withdraw beyond the Dnieper! On 17 February a frightened Hitler flew in his Fw 200 to the headquarters of the Army Group South in Zaporozhye to assess the situation on the spot and meet Manstein again. The front was being held just 100km from the airfield, where the Condor landed at 06.00. Manstein later recalled:

> I welcomed the opportunity to report to him personally my idea, and that he could personally verify the seriousness of the situation. Still, it was difficult to ensure the safety of his stay in such a large industrial city of Zaporozhye (especially because the enemy was approaching the city). Besides, he said he'd be here for a few days. He took up his quarters in our office with his retinue, which included the chief of the General Staff and General Jodl (as always Hitler took with him his personal chef). The entire surrounding area had to be hermetically sealed off.[1]

At the moment of the Führer's arrival there was a comical episode, showing all the duplicity of the Nazi regime. I./KG 51 commander Hauptmann Klaus Häberlen recalled:

Three days before we stopped the Russian tank breakout, there was a sudden great commotion at the airfield. It began because Zaporozhye had a visit from the commander-in-chief of the Wehrmacht Adolf Hitler. A short time later, after many orders given directly by him had led to terrible losses, he was nicknamed Gröfaz by our pilots ['the greatest commander of all time', a mocking term]. As the Fw 200 Condor was coming in, I got into my elegant Ford V8,[2] which had been everywhere with me since Paris, and drove to the scene to watch the Führer's arrival up close. As I approached the mission control building, I bumped into General Pflugbeil,[3] who, instead of his big, camouflaged Mercedes, was sitting in a Kubelwagen. He looked at me dumbfounded and could only say: 'Häberlen, how can you roll up in such a car, here, where the Führer will land. For God's sake, you can't show up here in a car like that.'

As I drove away, I was able to see Generalfeldmarschall Manstein arrive, as well as other important 'birds' – none in the cars they usually drove. They could understand it anyway they wanted, but I didn't. Why shouldn't we, those who put our lives on the line every day, drive beautiful trophy cars?[4]

German military leaders who, despite the difficult situation at the front, used to drive around in luxury limousines, wanted to show Hitler that they lived in Spartan conditions at the front, and that they only used German-made army vehicles. They were afraid to show the Führer that they were drowning in luxury.

The reluctance of Pflugbeil and Manstein to show the true conditions in which they lived could be understood. Even during heavy fighting, they lived in comfort, slept in clean beds, took baths, and rode through the occupied cities in luxury limousines. Luftwaffe officers including Häberlen also kept up with their chiefs. Unlike the infantrymen and tankmen who lived in damp trenches, dugouts and barracks, the pilots were based far from the front line and in between flights they went on excursions, visited cinemas and casinos and drove their own cars.

However, 'Gröfaz' himself, despite promoting a modest and simple lifestyle, lived in his Führerhauptquartier, on which funds sufficient to equip several infantry divisions were spent on its construction and security.

Manstein's concern for the Führer's safety was not misplaced. At the entrance to Zaporozhye, Hitler was recognised and welcomed by soldiers and locals. There were almost no German troops in the city, so the security cordon of the quarter in which the Führer stopped was, in addition to his personal protection squad, provided by a guard company of the army group headquarters and several anti-aircraft units. On the evening of 17 February, the Führer arrived at Manstein's headquarters and discussed the situation with him. He remained in the city for the next two days, holding meetings and stressing the importance of holding Donbass.

On 19 February, Russian tanks reached Sinelnikovo station. Manstein recalled:

> Thus the enemy not only cut the main communication of the group 'Mitte' and on the left flank of our group, but was already 60km from our headquarters, where the Führer of the Third Reich was visiting. Not a single combat unit was between us and our enemy!

When the news of the approach of Soviet tanks came to the city's airfield, Hans Baur, the Führer's personal pilot, asked permission to fly to a safer airfield south of Zaporozhye, but Hitler said he would be leaving soon.

Urgent measures were taken to defend the airfield by forming a few battle groups, which included several gun spositioned around the perimeter. Patrols were also set up on the nearby road leading to the north-east. On the evening of 19 February, Hitler at the insistence of Manstein and the commander of Luftflotte 4, Generalfeldmarschall Wolfram von Richthofen, who was also in Zaporozhye, departed. According to the memoirs of Hitler's Luftwaffe adjutant Nicolaus von Below, during the take-off of the Condor artillery fire could be heard in the distance, but this does not mean that Hitler was almost captured. General Popov's tank group was no closer than 50 or 60km from Zaporozhye and, given the time of year, was at least two days' journey away. Recently, dramatic claims have circulated in literature and on the internet that Soviet tankers 'nearly captured Hitler' and 'saw his plane fly away', but these are strong exaggerations.

Hitler's visit had brought no results, with Manstein spending its duration trying to explain the military situation to the stubborn Führer. The situation at the front was still difficult. Every night, a pair of crews from KG 51 flew to the area north-east of Zaporozhye to follow the Russian tanks by their headlights and warn their comrades of their approach. On the night of 22 February, Hauptmann Häberlen was awakened by a pilot in his Gruppen, Feldwebel Schultheiss, shouting 'the Russians are coming!'

A group of twenty to twenty-five Russian tanks was approaching Zaporozhye. Häberlen ordered all serviceable Ju 88 As to be prepared for an urgent attack. The bombers were loaded with high-explosive bombs and fragmentation SD 2-Splitterbomben (nicknamed 'devil's eggs' because of their great killing power). Häberlen recalled:

> All the crews started at 06.00. During my first flight to the area where Schultheiss found the tanks, I saw several vehicles, despite their winter camouflage. I attacked them with a dive, dropping to 50 metres. Then I flew around for over an hour to see if there were any other Russian tanks in the area, and found several more enemy groups. After that, I flew with four 500kg bombs, then performed seven more sorties against enemy tanks before noon. By evening, most of them were out of action. Only after we had done that command woke up and gave us the order to attack the Russian tanks. But we've already done our job. Thus the 'dam' [holding back the element of the Russian offensive] was saved.

During one of the flights, Leutnant Karl-Heinz Geruschke was shot down and made an emergency landing near the Soviet tanks. Seeing this, the pilot of another Ju 88, Leutnant Eberhard Winkel, quickly landed in front of the astonished Red Army soldiers to pick up the crew. To the risk of being hit by gunfire was added the fact that there was no guarantee Winkel would be able to take off again in the deep snow. However, the evacuation was successful. While the navigator and the side gunner were firing at the enemy, other crew members were helping their comrades to get on board. Putting one pilot in the cockpit, and three directly into the bomb bay, Winkel dramatically increased speed and the plane rolled a few hundred metres before managing to get off the ground. Such bold actions were commonplace in the Luftwaffe, not only near the front line, but also in the deep rear of the enemy (similar examples are given in this book). Winkel first flew in the direction of the approaching tanks, then made a sharp turn and was eventually clear of the fire of light anti-aircraft guns that accompanied them.

'Military fate', an expression German pilots liked to use, was often cruel and unpredictable. It could save someone in an incredibly dangerous situation, and it could do it many times. And at the same time, it could finish him off at any moment soon after his miraculous salvation. On 3 March 1943, Ju 88 A-4 Wrk Nr 2266 '9K+DB' from St.I./KG 51, piloted by Geruschke, went missing with its crew in the Merefa area. However, military fate was more kind to Winkel; he lived almost to the end of the war. In September 1944, he changed seats from the Ju 88 to the Me 262 bomber and was assigned as commander 3.(Jabo)/KG 51. On 21 March 1945 he was shot down and killed during a dogfight in Me 262 A-1a Wrk Nr 111973 '9K+AL'.

After continuous air strikes, the Russian tank group was stopped and the surviving tanks turned back. This moment was the culmination of the Soviet winter offensive and Häberlen and his comrades soon had the opportunity to see at first-hand the results of their aerial attacks. Arriving on the Kubelwagen at the site of the bombing, they saw numerous traces of destruction: burned tanks and in the middle of the field numerous immobilised fuel trucks and vehicles of American production.

Soon after the Soviet tank column moving on Zaporozhye was defeated, Häberlen unexpectedly met with the commander of Luftflotte 4, Generalfeldmarschall von Richthofen. As Häberlen's Ju 88 was returning from a mission, its course intersected with a Ju 52 transporting von Richthofen, which was also coming in to land. A signal rocket was fired from the transport, which meant 'get out of the way'. However, Häberlen ignored this order and continued to fly on the same trajectory. After their arrival at the airport, the bomber was approached by Richthofen, who drove around in a luxury Mercedes-Benz SSK. Von Richthofen had decided to punish the commander of I./KG 51 for 'hooliganism', but what he saw made him relent. It turned out that Häberlen's Ju 88 A aircraft was loaded with 2,250kg of bombs. The pilot recalled:

> Struck by this, he said, 'I never heard that such a thing was possible!' I told him that I was the only one in the group to fly with such a load because I knew that on this extended runway a Ju 88 could take off with such a weight.'My respects, Hauptman,' he said and left.

Von Richthofen's surprise can be understood because such a load almost corresponded to that of the American strategic four-engine B-17, which usually carried 2.5 tons of bombs. As a result, the fanatic von Richthofen, obsessed with destruction, did not punish Häberlen for cutting him up on landing.[5]

Meanwhile, at the front of the Army Group South came a turning point. Gathering together his Panzer divisions, including the II SS Panzer Corps, the talented Manstein began an offensive. The tanks were supported by dive bombers from KG 51 and He 111s from KG 27. They attacked Soviet positions and roads, and bombed railway stations in the cities of Izyum, Kupyansk, and Balakleya.

Now it was the turn of the Russians to panic and run away from the German tanks. However, until quite recently the situation had been just the opposite. The commander of the 46th OKRAE, Captain Anatoly Samochkin, had on many occasions during January and early February observed from the air the evidence of the complete defeat of the Wehrmacht and its allies. At the airfields, Russian pilots saw hundreds of abandoned German planes, the personal belongings of pilots, and stocks of fuel, bombs, transport and maintenance equipment. The Russians, who received very poor supplies, were amazed by the Germans' abundance of oil, canned food, pasta, wine, tea with lemon, and cigarettes.

The Soviet aviation regiments had moved rapidly westward, following the advancing troops. On 18 February, the 46th OKRAE relocated to Osnova airfield, on the south-western outskirts of Kharkov. On 23 February, the pilots, together with inhabitants of the destroyed city, celebrated Red Army Day. There were numerous concerts, banquets and drinking binges at which toasts were raised to Stalin and the liberation of Ukraine. Samochkin recalled:

> We were in Kharkov for two more weeks. The city itself was a pile of ruins. Every big building was burned or blown up: the Department store, the hotels, the flying club, the house of Soviets, the house of the Red Army. Almost nothing remained of the station and the post office. Even the tobacco factory, working under the Germans, burned. However, by some miracle there was an absolutely untouched monument to Taras Shevchenko.

Samochkin's squadron flew the Su-2, a single-engine, two-seat high-speed bomber that was similar to the American Vultee V-11. Before the war, the Russians had high hopes for the Su-2, but it did not live up to expectations. In 1942, production was discontinued and the surviving aircraft were converted into spotters for the artillery. The Samochkin detachment was one of the last units to fight the Su-2 in 1943.

By the end of February, the Germans had reached the Seversky Donets River near Barvenkovo, captured Lozovaya, and on 6 March surrounded a large group of Soviet troops south of Kharkov. At the same time, SS tanks began an offensive on Kharkov and Belgorod. The Russian aviation detachments had to be hastily evacuated to the east. Samochkin recalled:

> In the morning I was ordered to be ready to relocate. I'm sitting by the phone, waiting for orders. Dinner has passed, evening is approaching – there is no indication. Everywhere there is shooting, the city is covered in fire. On the roads through Merefa to Kharkov, before our eyes, there are German tanks. To our relief, because of their poor intelligence, or because we well disguised, the Germans did not see us. People at the airport understood what 'smelled' and asked only one question, when would be the flight out? I couldn't make a decision myself, and I didn't know where to fly to. I waited by the phone and it didn't ring. The engineer and pilots were ordered to be ready for take-off, to be in the aircraft and wait for the signal. The direction of take-off was towards Merefa, and there were already enemy tanks there.
>
> 'Comrade commander, maybe the connection does not work, or maybe we have been betrayed?'
>
> 'No, the connection is working, wait!'
>
> Evening. It was getting dark. I was already very worried. Bad thoughts went through my head, although outwardly, I tried to be calm. If we didn't take off in half an hour, that would be it. And suddenly we got the long-awaited call. From headquarters came the order – take off urgently and land in Volchansk. I ran to my aircraft with engineer and co-driver Michael Chehljad and on the radio I gave the order:'Take off after me, at no intervals, one after the other.'
>
> As soon as the plane came off the ground, I retracted the landing gear and chassis covers and with a small turn to the left, I left the road where the tanks were travelling. All the aircraft followed me, but the Germans had already noticed us and opened fire with machine guns. But the armour protection of the aircraft below is impenetrable to machine-gun fire. The guys were focused by the situation itself, forcing them to be extremely attentive, without unnecessary fuss and chatter in the air. I saw the chief of staff had also taken off in a U-2. The airfield was completely deserted.

As a result of the hasty relocation, a lot of different types of Russian fighters, dive bombers, attack aircraft and U-2B night bombers were gathered at Volchansk airport. Due to a lack of space, the machines stood close to each other, representing an ideal target for bombing. Until recently, the entire armada had been intending to pursue the Germans crossing the Dnieper, now the Russians had to urgently prepare already abandoned air bases in the rear, behind the Seversky Donets. Volchansk airfield was soon attacked by Luftwaffe. During this Samochkin's 46th OKRAE lost half its aircraft and after that the use of the Su-2 came to an end.

The same style of operation of German bombers – in which they were used both as attack aircraft, and as short and long-range bombers – was employed on other sectors of the Eastern Front. In early 1943, II./KG 4, which from 30 January was headed by Major Reinhard Graubner, was based at Seshchinskaya airfield, north-west of Bryansk. When, as a consequence of the retreat of the 2nd Army, the entire southern flank of Army Group Centre was threatened, II./KG 4 attacked the Soviet troops advancing on Kursk, bombed railway stations, railway junctions and stages in the rear of the enemy. The summary of the 1st Luftdivision reported on 10 February:

> II./KG 4 10.2.1943 in bad weather and visibility attacked military targets in the space of Nikolskoye 1 and 2, as well as Ponyri 1 and 2. Attacks were made on infantry positions, columns and clusters of troops in villages, with good results, from low heights. After the bombardment, the remnants of the infantry and vehicles were shelled with onboard weapons, resulting in big bloody losses to the enemy. These attacks were so effective because of the high concentration of enemy troops. In the area of the targets during the subsequent raids, there were many corpses of Russians and horses, destroyed cars and guns, especially in Nikolskoe-2. The devastating impact of the airstrikes has been fully confirmed.[6]

Graubner then received numerous letters of thanks from the 2nd Panzer Army for his strong air support.

Hitler was pleased. His troops were advancing again, and the crisis had been overcome. On 10 March, the Führer flew back to Zaporozhye to personally thank Manstein for his success, and to present him with the Knight's Cross of the Iron Cross with Oak Leaves. On 26 March, the Germans again captured Kharkov and Belgorod. 'The key to Ukraine' was again in their hands. This moment coincided with the beginning of the spring thaw, and eventually the front line gradually stabilised.

In March, II./KG 4 mostly attacked Russian rail traffic. In fact, the group began to specialise in such missions. Starting on 12 March, the unit bombed the stations in Livny, Yelets and Uzlovaya, and trains on the Yelets–Kursk–Kastornoe and Kirov–Sukhinichi–Kaluga–Iznoski lines. As a result, traffic in these areas was almost paralysed. The Germans paid for this with the loss of several aircraft and their inexperienced crews (on 10, 20, 22 and 30 March). According to German army intelligence obtained during the interrogation of Russian prisoners, the most successful attacks were those on Livny station on 14, 15 and 16 March. As a result of these raids, the tracks, station building, ammunition depot and the city itself were destroyed. The water supply was out of order for a month, and train traffic was completely paralysed for seven days.

On the nights of 14 and 22 March, II./KG 4 carried out two raids on the Kursk-OST airfield. During the first, according to German data, five Yak-1 fighters were destroyed. The results of the second strike were much more effective. At the airport, thirty-five aircraft were damaged and destroyed at once, identified as Yak-1s, Hurricanes, P-39 Airacobras, Il-2s and U-2s. After that, Kursk became one of the main bombing targets for two and half months. The actions of Major Graubner's II./KG 4 were so highly viewed that the Luftflotte 6 commander, Generaloberst von Greim, granted special leave in April for the group's most distinguished crews.[7]

Meanwhile, the situation in the central sector of the front also stabilised. Although the Germans were soon forced to evacuate the Rzhev salient, which had threatened Moscow throughout 1942 and was the scene of fierce fighting, they nevertheless kept the important railway and aviation hubs of Orel and Bryansk in their hands to the south. They would play an important role in future events.

In mid-March, the Luftwaffe had a new important goal – the Bataysk railway junction and bridges over the Don River in the Rostov-on-Don area. This severely damaged sector had only recently been abandoned by German troops. The Russians had only managed to restart through railway traffic on the Armavir–Tikhoretsk–Bataysk–Rostov–Shakhty–Kupyansk–Millerovo–Kantemirovka–Voronezh line around the same time, using temporary crossings laid on the ice. At the same time, the restoration of the destroyed railway bridge across the Don began. This route, which was a connection between the fronts, as well as being used for the delivery of reinforcements and equipment from Moscow, the Volga Region and Siberia, was of major

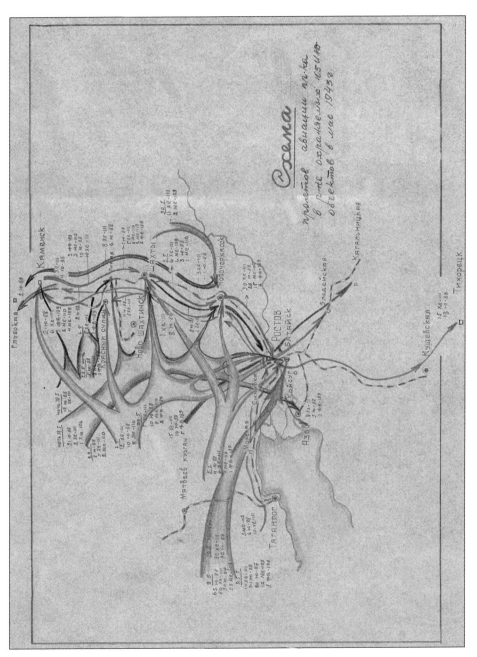

The frightening Russian scheme of Luftwaffe air attacks near Rostov in May 1943.

strategic importance. It also facilitated the main supply of troops to the North Caucasus front, which led the offensive against the 17th German Army in the Kuban.

The 105th IAD PVO was assigned to provide air defence for Rostov-on-don, Bataysk and the railway section from Tikhoretsk to the Shakhty. It consisted of fifty-nine fighters, which were a whole collection of different types: fifteen Yak-1s, twelve LaGG-3s, eleven I-16s, ten Hurricanes, four MiG-3s, four I-153s and three Yak-7Bs.

At 13.20 on 14 March, seven He 111s attacked Bataysk station, where there were many trains at the time. An alert was not given, and the bombing resulted in numerous fires and casualties. The Russian fighters only took off after the bombers had already left the area. At 16.01, a pair of LaGG-3s from the 234th IAP was scrambled to intercept a Ju 88 seen flying at a high altitude in the vicinity of Rostov (it was photographing the results of an air strike). The Russian pilots did not catch up with the Ju 88, but seven minutes later they saw new explosions at Bataysk station. Twelve Ju 87s accompanied by five Bf 109s had made a second attack on the target.

This was only the overture to the main performance. Between 10.35 and 11.30 on 20 March, the Luftwaffe carried out several raids on the Bataysk railway junction, in which, according to Soviet data, eighty-five Ju 88s and He 111s participated, accompanied by fighters. The raid was performed with horizontal and dive bomber attacks. Three hundred high-explosive and fragmentation bombs were dropped on the station, and in the resulting explosions and fires, eighteen cars, two locomotives and railway tracks were destroyed. The Russians scrambled ten fighters, including three Yak-1s, four Hurricanes, two LaGG-3s and a Yak-7B. The first to arrive above Bataysk were the four British fighters, which immediately tried to attack a group of fifteen Ju 88s of I./KG 51. Russian pilots reported five downed bombers but in fact, only one He 111 of 7./KG 4 was shot down during this attack. Another Ju 87 D-3 Wrk Nr 131067 of 4./StG 77, was damaged and crashed with 70 per cent damage during an emergency landing on its own territory. Interestingly, all the usual British weapons in the 182th IAP Hurricanes had been replaced with Russian ones; with 20mm ShVAK guns and 12.7mm BS machine guns.

Between 16.38 and 17.11 on 21 March the Luftwaffe carried out a major raid on Rostov-on-Don and ferries on the Don River. Ju 88 As from I./KG 51 were the first to attack, dropping bombs from 4,000m. They were followed by Ju 87s, which dropped their bombs from 700–800m following a dive. This time the Russian fighters could not intercept the bombers because the warning came too late.

The next attack took place between 14.05 and 14.32 on 22 March, with the main objectives the ferries on the Don River, railway facilities, and the Central and Nakhichevan airfields. According to Soviet data, the raid involved seventy-five aircraft comprised of He 111s, Ju 88s, Ju 87s and Do 215s, accompanied by thirty Bf 109s. Simultaneously, twin-engine bombers bombed horizontally through windows in the clouds, and Stukas suddenly fell out of the clouds and dived to a height of 700m before releasing their load. As a result, the raid caused a lot of damage, and the Central airfield was covered with small fragmentation bombs, which the Russians called 'frogs'.

At 13.05 four Hurricanes of the 182nd IAP had taken off on patrol flown by Senior Lieutenant Gromov, Lieutenants Zayets and Perepelitsa and Junior Lieutenant Monahov. At 13.50, after receiving a message from the air surveillance posts (VNOS) about the approach of bombers, a pair of Yak-1s flown by Junior Lieutenants Sannikov and Kharlamov took off from the Central airfield. Four minutes later five more fighters took off: Senior Lieutenants Vernikov and Fionin in Yak-1s, pilots Abramenko and Osokin in LaGG-3s and Senior Lieutenant Durakov in a Yak-7B. The four Hurricanes were the first to engage in the Ust-Koisug area. Attacking from the front and above, they engaged a large group of bombers, identified as Ju 88s and Do 215s, which were approaching in a long, stretched formation. The pilots fired a volley of unguided rockets, shooting down one and damaging three other aircraft. After that, the four went straight through the line of bombers, being fired on from all sides. Gromov's Hurricane was hit and he made an emergency landing. The remaining three were attacked by Bf 109s, with which they conducted a fruitless battle and then returned to their base (Hurricanes could be in the air for no more than an hour and a half, and the fuel was running out). The Russians reported two downed bombers and two fighters, but the Germans did not actually suffer any losses.

Between 15.15 and 16.05 on 25 March, the Luftwaffe carried out major air attacks on Bataysk, the Don crossing and the city of Azov, which involved 180 bombers and forty to fifty Bf 109s and Bf 110s. Zerstörer Bf 110s conducted an assault on Bataysk airfield, while direct hits destroyed the structure of the bridge being restored across the Don, smashing some of the construction equipment and killing dozens of workers and civilians involved in the reconstruction. The Bataysk railway junction received such severe damage that it was permanently deactivated. This time the Russians used a radar station for the first time and scrambled fourteen fighters to intercept the raiders. As a result, they managed to gain the necessary height before the approach of the bombers. The 105th IAD PVO claimed nine downed aircraft, including four Bf 110s. In fact, the Luftwaffe lost just one Zerstörer Bf 110 E Wrk Nr 5257 of I./ZG 1, which was shot down by a Russian fighter in the Bataysk area. The crew, pilot Leutnant S. Schmeling and radio operator Unteroffizier H. Theisen, were both killed. Between 15.37 and 15.50 (Moscow time) Zerstörers from I./ZG 1 shot down four LaGG-3s over Bataysk. Two victories were recorded by the group commander, Major J. Blehschmidt, with one each for Oberfeldwebel Brunnike and Feldwebel Dentzer.

The next combined air attack on Bataysk (involving the simultaneous use of horizontal and dive bombers) was carried out by the Germans on the afternoon of 27 March. The Russians tried to increase their efforts and prevent the destruction of a strategically important asset. Twenty-eight fighters from the 182nd, 234th, 266th and 738th IAP took off to intercept, and an air battle was fought over Rostov and Bataysk. The Soviets claimed thirteen downed aircraft, including nine Ju 87s and four Bf 109s. In fact, they had lost just Ju 87 D-3 Wrk Nr 110296 of 5./StG 77 along with its crew (pilot Oberfeldwebel F. Ganuschek, gunner-radio operator Obergefreiter W. Dromer). Russian losses were again higher. A pair of I-16s flown by Senior Sergeants Chupeyev and Gorbatov were shot down by fighters from JG 3 (victories were recorded by Oberleutnant Albrecht Walz of St./JG 3, Leutnant Hans Weik of St.I./JG 3, Leutnant Wolf-Udo Ettel of 4./JG 3 and Feldwebel E. Sibler of 9./JG 3). Gorbatov was able to leave his falling plane with a parachute, but Chupeyev died. Feldwebel L. Munster of 4./JG 3 shot down a Hurricane flown by Senior Lieutenant Nechushkin of the 266th IAP. Munster was unable to identify the type of plane he was shooting at and his victory was mistakenly recorded as an I-180. This was actually an experimental Soviet fighter, created in 1939–40 to replace the I-16, but not produced.

I./KG 51 Hauptmann Häberlen also participated in these powerful air attacks on Bataysk, as reported in the citation for the award to the pilot in the Knight's Cross of the Iron Cross on 30 April 1943:

> 20–27.03.43 during the massive raids on Bataysk and Svoboda, thanks to the clever tactical use of his unit, Häberlen was able to cause strong damage and destruction with a large number of explosions and fires with the strongest attacks of fighters and powerful air defence.

The next raids on Bataysk were conducted on 31 March and 1 April. On 12 April, the Germans decided to attack at night. He 111s from I./KG 27 took off from Sarabus (Crimea) at 16.40 Berlin time. Hans Reif from 3./KG 27 wrote in his diary:

> On the evening of April 12, we took off for a raid on Bataysk. There was a lot of cloud in the sky, so we could only see what was right below us. Steppe fires burned all over the Don. Or were they deliberate false fires? I had my doubts, but Hauptmann Zollweg did not hesitate to attack almost the first fire, which he considered to be the burning Bataysk. The final stretch of the route was already completely dark. I noticed for the first time that anti-aircraft guns were firing without searchlights. I had a question: did the Russians not have enough equipment or did they already use electronic guidance devices? At least some of the shells 'laid down' very accurately.

The attack was carried out horizontally from 2,000–3,000m. However the Luftwaffe suffered some losses. He 111 H-6 Wrk Nr 7587 '1G+LK' of II./KG 27 sustained engine damage and made an emergency landing on German territory. He 111 H-6 Wrk Nr 7193 from the same Staffel was mistakenly fired at and shot down by German anti-aircraft artillery around Kerch when returning from the mission. Pilot Unteroffizier Kittel immediately ordered the crew to take to the parachutes. The navigator and radio operator managed to leave the aircraft, but flight mechanic Unteroffizier Hans Teckelmann and flight gunner Unteroffizier Kurt Stal did not have time and were killed when their plane crashed into the Sea of Azov.

The culmination of the air attacks against Bataysk came on 9 May, with the first raid coming between 07.28 and 08.15 Moscow time. Soviet radar stations detected the approach of a large group of aircraft from the direction of Stalino. They flew in circles near Taganrog waiting for the approach of the fighter escort, and then they flew via Sinyavka and Azov to Bataysk. The bombardment was carried out horizontally from 3,000–4,000 min groups of two and three. Some 300 high-explosive bombs were dropped on the targets.

This time the 105th IAD PVO, recently replenished with new equipment, met the Germans fully armed. By the morning of 9 May, there were forty-five combat-ready fighters at air bases around Rostov (two Hurricanes, seven Yak-1s and one Yak-7B from the 182nd IAP; six Yak-1s and one LaGG-3 from the 234th IAP; five Hurricanes and six Yak-1s from the 266th IAP; and seventeen I-16s from the 961st IAP). All these aircraft were scrambled to intercept the attackers.

Crossings of the river Don in the city of Rostov-on-Don. May 1943.

At 07.45, with the help of radio guidance, nine different types of fighters from the 182nd Regiment were directed to the first group of bombers. Then came six Yak-1s from the 234th Aviation Regiment. However, both groups found themselves below the formation of Ju 88s and He 111s because incorrect information on the Germans' altitude was transmitted to the pilots. As a result, the first aircraft able to attack the bombers, with rockets, were nine I-16s of the 961st IAP, which arrived in the interception zone later than the others. Then the rest of the fighters took it upon themselves to climb to the correct height and join the fight.

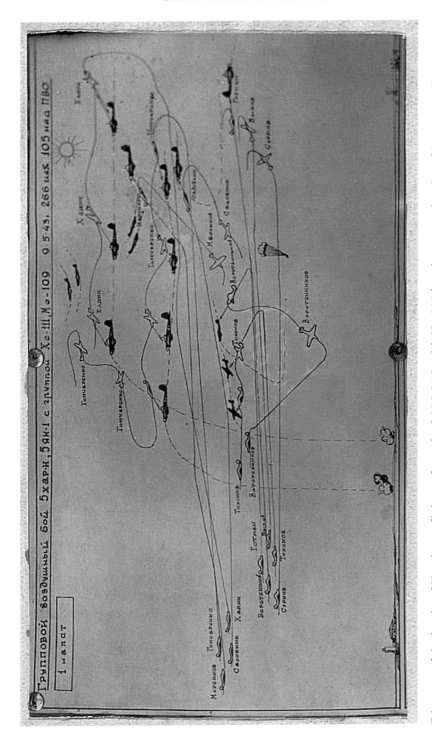

Diagram of the battle of Hurricane fighters from the 266th IAP with He 111 bombers over the city of Rostov-on-Don on may 9, 1943.

Between 10.55 and 11.09, the second major raid of the day on Bataysk took place, in which, according to Soviet data, 110 aircraft participated (thirty Ju 88s, thirty Ju 87s, twenty-five He 111s and twenty-five Bf 109s). Ju 88s and He 111s dropped their 'cargo' horizontally, while the Stukas, circling above the target, flipped their wings and dived on the town. Between 10.35 and 10.45, thirty-one Russian fighters were scrambled, including sixteen I-16s, eleven Yak-1s and four Hurricanes. The first group to be detected were the Ju 87s, which were attacked in the Kojsug area from the front and above. Russian pilots reported that they shot down two or three Stukas. At the same time, the formation of Soviet fighters collapsed, with some of them attacked and shot down by Bf 109s. As a result, the subsequent groups of bombers were attacked only by individual pairs and single aircraft. According to German data, between 12.08 and 12.34 Leutnant Broks and Oberleutnant Joachim Kirschner of 5./JG 3 shot down three Yak-1s over Bataysk.

The third raid followed between 13.50 and 14.01, which, according to Soviet data, involved forty twin-engine bombers accompanied by fifteen Bf 109s. Bombing was again carried out on the level at 2,000–3,000m and by diving. This time, the 105th IAD was able to scramble only twenty-four fighters, which took off between 13.14 and 13.20. The first attack was carried out by I-16s from the 961st IAP firing rockets, then the remaining fighters attacked the enemy from the front and above, and then from behind and above.

In total, about 800 high-explosive bombs of various sizes were dropped on Bataysk during three large air attacks. The main railway tracks to Tikhoretsk and Salsk were destroyed, as well as the locomotive depot, and more than 100 wagons and tanks were smashed and burned. The fires at the railway junction blazed until night, although by 18.00 it was possible to partially restore through train traffic. The Russians, as always, declared their air defence had been a great success. The 105th Air Defence IAD carried out 101 sorties, with the pilots reporting forty downed aircraft, including twenty-two Ju 87s, nine Ju 88s, five Bf 109s and four He 111s. Fifteen were claimed by the 961st IAP, eleven by 266th IAP, nine by 182nd IAP and five by 234th IAP. The Russians' own losses were also high. Six fighters were shot down (three Yak-1s and three I-16s), five pilots were killed (Lieutenant A.V. Kirichkov, Senior sergeant V.P. Bakhtin and Sergeant I.I. Elagin from the 961st IAP, commander of the 182nd IAP Major V.I. Kostomarov and Captain I.Z. Bedilo, squadron commander of the 234th IAP). Another eight fighters were damaged and made forced landings (five I-16s, two Yak-1s and one Hurricane). The 961st Aviation Regiment was the most severely affected, losing almost half of its aircraft. In general, the Russians lost a third of their fighters. According to German data, the only two I-16s shot down on this day by German fighters (at 10.03 and 10.06) were by Major Helmut Bennemann from St.I./JG 52, which were his eighty-seventh and eighty-eighth aerial victories. The rest of the Russian interceptors were destroyed by the bombers' gunners.

In fact, the Russians exaggerated their own successes many times over. For example, KG 27 'Boelcke', which participated in two attacks on Bataysk, did not suffer any losses. According to German data, during these strikes only one aircraft was shot down by fighters: Ju 87 D-3 Wrk Nr 100017 'S2+HT' from 9./StG 77. The crew, Unteroffizier H. Kanis and side gunner Feldwebel K. Weiss, went missing. In addition, Ju 88 A-4 Wrk Nr 88-8767 of 6./KG 3 'Blitz' was shot down by anti-aircraft fire. The entire crew including pilot Unteroffizier G. Lafler was killed. Another Ju 87 D-3, Wrk Nr 1429 of 8./StG 77, suffered 35 per cent damage but was able to fly back to base. A total of fourteen damaged and downed Russian fighters for one downed Ju 87 was a stunning result for the Germans. The air raids on Bataysk clearly demonstrated that the Luftwaffe still far outperformed the Russians in tactics, technology and the skill of its pilots.

'They were literally hanging over us'

In the south, the Russians also gave the Germans no peace. In January, the 17th Army began a retreat from the North Caucasus to the Kuban. Hitler ordered that a bridgehead be created there and that it should be held with fanaticism, preventing the Soviets approaching the Crimea. German and Romanian divisions were slowly retreating to the Taman Peninsula. Their main task was to hold off the Russian onslaught before the engineering units built a strong line of defence between Novorossiysk and Temryuk. In February, the Kuban saw a fierce battle, with the Russian fleet landing troops in the rear of the 17th Army in the area of Mount Myshako (south-west of Novorossiysk). However, despite a lack of forces, the Germans managed to block the Russians on a small bridgehead, localising this potential threat. The Soviets called this small section of the coast 'Malaya Zemlya'. On 12 February, the Germans evacuated Krasnodar, and two weeks later they withdrew over the Protoka River to the so-called 'Poseidon line', while to the south mountain riflemen and mountain rangers took up a defence on the well-fortified hills around the village of Krymskaya. It was turned into a powerful strong point, prepared for a long defence. By early spring, the 17th Army had retreated to a convenient 120km line, protected in the north by numerous marshes, in the centre by rivers and canals, and in the south by numerous heights. This line was defended by twelve German and four Romanian divisions.

The 17th Army was only supplied by air and by sea through the Kerch Strait. The Russians did not stop their fanatical attacks, throwing more and more infantry divisions and tanks into battle and attacking the German positions through the swamps and mud. Therefore, Luftwaffe support was vital for the Kuban bridgehead (Kubanbrückenkopf).

From 30 January the specialised III./KG 4 under Major Werner Klosinski was based in Crimea. One of the tasks of the bomber crews was to tow Go 242 cargo gliders with ammunition and food across the Kerch Strait. These landed at specially prepared airfields at Timoshevskaya and Slavyanskaya. On the way back, the unit's He 111s took out wounded soldiers. III./KG 4 was also involved in bombing missions, the main targets being Russian ports on the Black Sea, including railway stations and air bases. For example, on 20 February, air strikes were carried out on the port of Tuapse and the airfield at Gelendzhik, and on 25 February on railway stations in Armavir, Krasnodar and Kropotkin. Between 3 and 10 March there was a series of night raids on the airfields at Krasnodar and Adler, where Soviet bombers and attack aircraft were based that had been attacking German troops.

The airfield at Bagerovo, where III./KG 4 was based, proved too small for bombers to land at night. After five He 111s crashed, the unit was moved to Saki airfield. On 25 March, a successful raid on Gelendzhik was carried out, which was even mentioned in the Wehrmacht General Command report the next day. After the fall of Stalingrad, II./KG 55 also settled on Saki air base. The main objectives of the bombers were ferries on the Kuban River and advancing Soviet troops in the Armavir and Krasnodar areas. As the Russian attacks on the Kuban bridgehead intensified, the Luftwaffe moved more of its units to this sector.

Starting on 9 April, the Germans began to stage major air attacks on the Soviet troops. On that day, attacks by bombers and stormtroopers on the 56th Soviet Army left seventy-eight Russians killed and 248 wounded, with three tanks and seven cars destroyed. On the morning of 12 April, the Luftwaffe carried out a powerful air attack on railway facilities in Krasnodar, dropping 150 high-explosive bombs. Eighty-seven buildings and structures were destroyed, with nine railway cars and eight trucks smashed, 156 people killed, and 176 injured and concussed.

On the morning of 14 April, the Russians launched an offensive along the entire front, to which the Germans responded with brutal air attacks. The next day, 1,000 Luftwaffe sorties were carried out over the Kuban bridgehead. At 06.30, the first group of Ju 87s appeared over the 56th Army's positions and dropped their bombs to a howl of the Stukas' sirens. Groups of twenty to thirty bombers struck the same targets until dark, and from 16.00 they became continuous. General Andrey Grechko, commander of the 56th Army, reported: 'Enemy planes continuously hung over our positions. Such a massive air strike pinned our troops to the ground, and the artillery had to stop firing.' The 9th and 18th Russian Armies were also unable to attack because of the endless bomb attacks.

After repelling the Russian attacks, on the morning of 17 April the Germans themselves went on the offensive in the Myshako area. The goal of Operation *Neptune* was to eliminate the bridgehead south of Novorossiysk. At 07.00 the first Stukas appeared in the sky, and at 09.00 a large group of He 111 joined the fray. Then the 'Malaya Zemlya' bridgehead was subjected to brutal and continuous air attacks that lasted from morning until late at night. KG 27 crews took to the air four times that day, completing about 250 sorties. Hans Reif of 3/KG 27 wrote in his diary:

> From 17 to 21 April, Operation *Neptune* took place. We were supposed to help eliminate the Russian bridgehead South of Novorossiysk. To do this, we basically attacked flank artillery batteries that supported the Marines on the eastern shore of Tsemess Bay. Our first raid took place shortly after 6 o'clock in the morning.[8]

From 17 to 20 April, Ju 87s from StG 3 and II./StG 77 carried out 1,409 sorties against the bridgehead. However, despite the strong support of the Luftwaffe, the German shock group, consisting of the 4th Mountain Infantry Division and the 125th Infantry Division, was unable to throw out the Russians. The Germans deeply infiltrated into Russian positions in several areas but they did not have the strength to develop their success. On 23 April, Operation *Neptune* was terminated.

The Russian command was so frightened by the bombing that it began the urgent transfer of its fighter aviation reserves to the Kuban. By mid-March, there were eleven fighter aviation regiments in this sector, which had about 200 combat-ready aircraft. Another 100 fighters were with naval aviation (air force of the Black Sea fleet). In just three days (18–20 April)

Spitfire Mk.VB from the 57th Guards IAP. Spring 1943.

thirteen fighter regiments and almost 400 fighters were transferred to the Kuban. On 25 April, the 57th Guards IAP arrived in this sector, armed with thirty-two Spitfire Mk.VBs. The commander of the VVS Red Army, Marshal Alexander Novikov, arrived to personally command this huge force to ensure it would cover his troops reliably. This 'armada' was opposed by only one Luftwaffe unit, JG 52, which periodically helped one air group from JG 3.

On the morning of 29 April, the Soviets launched a powerful offensive aimed at the complete elimination of the Kuban bridgehead. The Red Army air force carried out 1,268 sorties, during which, according to their information, seventy-four German aircraft were shot down, including sixty-four Bf 109s. As usual, the Russians greatly exaggerated their success. In fact, in this air battle, the Luftwaffe lost only four aircraft (one He 111, one Bf 109 and two Ju 87 D-3s). In contrast, Soviet aviation losses were extremely heavy, with thirty-nine planes shot down, comprising twenty-eight fighters, six bombers and five attack planes. The next day, there was a similar picture: the Russians carried out 963 flights and claimed twenty-four downed aircraft. Soviet anti-aircraft batteries claimed another six aircraft. In fact, the Luftwaffe lost just two Bf 109s, one Fw 189 A and one Ju 87, while the Russians lost nineteen aircraft.

In total during April, the Germans lost ninety-five aircraft over the Kuban bridgehead, including eighteen He 111s, eighteen Ju 88s, twenty-nine Bf 109s, nineteen Ju 87s, five Hs 129s, three Fw 189s, one Ju 52 and two Bf 110s. The number of VVS Red Army aircraft shot down and missing amounted to 275.

In May, air battles broke out in this sector with renewed vigour. On 3 May, the Russians flew 1,130 missions and claimed thirty-one downed aircraft. In fact, the Germans lost four aircraft (one He 111, Hs 129, Ju 87 and Bf 109). The Soviets' own losses were twenty-six aircraft. On this day, Marshal Novikov addressed his pilots with a desperate appeal:

> Hero pilots! Today, our ground troops and tanks have successfully broken through the enemy's defences and are developing success. Your task is to ensure victory over the enemy with well-aimed strikes and reliable cover of the advancing troops from the air. You did well this morning. I am confident in your strength and victory. Remember, he who is bold in battle always wins.

At the same time, at the Dnepropetrovsk-Yuzhny air base, the commander of Fliegerkorps VIII, General Martin Fibig, made a similar appeal to the German pilots. He called on them in this 'decisive hour' to fight for the Führer, the people and the Fatherland.

On the night of 4/5 May, the 17th German Army evacuated the village of Krymskaya, retreating to a pre-prepared line of defence. The Russians took this as a turning point in the battle and intensified their attacks all along the front, but they were not successful again. As soon as a crisis situation developed in any area, German bombers appeared in the sky, then Hs 129, Fw 190 and Hs 123 attack planes, which targeted the Russian infantry and tanks without hindrance, literally mixing them with the ground. Soviet fighters made hundreds of sorties and reported many aerial victories, but were not able to achieve the main task: to protect their troops. The Russian tactic was to circle the positions of their troops and wait for the Luftwaffe. However, they never patrolled in German air space, which allowed the bombers to approach and attack the target without hindrance. Usually, 'Stalin's Falcons' attacked the He 111s, Ju 88s and Ju 87s at the time of their approach to and over the target, which was ineffective. There was too little time to intercept. The Russians did not pursue the returning damaged bombers over German territory, allowing them to safely return home. This had been the case since the beginning of the war – the Red fighters had flown a lot, but they had been of little use.

Meanwhile, the Luftwaffe continued to do their job. On 14 May, 800 German planes flew over the Soviet 56th Army's positions, dropping more than 2,000 high-explosive and fragmentation bombs. Some areas and strongholds were attacked fifteen times a day. German losses amounted to only one Ju 87 D-3 from 6./StG 2. On 23 May, the Germans carried out about 1,000 sorties over the Kuban bridgehead. Bomber crew member H. Falten, only recently transferred to 9./KG 27 from the training unit IV./KG 27, recalled:

> On 23.05.1943 took place my 1st combat flight over the Kuban bridgehead and the Krymskaya. When flying through the front line, my place was in the lower part of the cabin at the MG machine gun, designed to shoot backwards. The height of the attack was about 4,000 metres, and I saw the bombs being dropped. The leader of the group was the first to open the bomb bay doors, after which all the machines did it synchronously. Then the bombs fell. Between the flying bombs I saw the parachutes of the downed crew, who were shot down by Russian anti-aircraft fire. After dropping the bombs, we went back on our course, and I had to check the bomb bay to see if all the bombs had left it. Only after that could the pilot close the bomb bay doors. When flying over the Sea of Azov, we began to drop to a lower height. During such flights there should have been an escort of fighters over the Kerch Strait, but often it was not present. Either they took off too early and had to return early due to lack of fuel, or they were involved in aerial combat and thus could not perform escorts.

The crew Falten saw parachuting were Unteroffiziere Fritz Blindinger, Paul Frisenhan and Obergefreiter Kurt Jakob from He 111 H-16 Wrk Nr 160269 of 7./KG 4. This group bombed Soviet positions in front of III./KG 27. All three pilots landed on Soviet territory, which they had just bombed, and were taken prisoner.

At dawn on 26 May, with shouts of 'Hooray!', countless numbers of Russian soldiers again rose to the attack. Thanks to powerful artillery and major attacks by stormtroopers and bombers, at first they were successful. Soviet infantry broke through the first line of defence and occupied several villages. But at 10.00 a real hell began for the Soviets. Over the positions of the 37th and 56th Armies passed groups of He 111s and Ju 88s, which subjected them to carpet bombing. In the intervals between the two-engine bomber raids, small groups of Hs 129s and Ju 87s appeared, diving to strike at the frontline and the rear of the attacking units. Russian ground observers recorded 1,700 German planes in the sky, and about 3,000 high-explosive and fragmentation bombs of all calibres were dropped on the 56th Army positions. The 383rd Rifle Division's journal of combat operations recorded:

> During the period of 11.00–14.00 enemy bombers passed over our positions in a continuous stream, and the roar of bomb explosions did not stop for a minute. After 14.00, the division's positions were subjected to continuous attacks by enemy stormtroopers operating at low altitudes and hitting the soldiers with bombs, machine guns and cannon. Some planes made 10–15 calls, being over our lines for 20–25 minutes.

As a result, the 37th Army was forced to withdraw almost to its original positions and with difficulty held several occupied areas. The army's losses on the first day of the offensive were 567 killed and 1,135 wounded. Russian tank units lost 100 tanks and self-propelled guns out of 200 available. In response to the Luftwaffe's actions, the Russians flew 1,627 sorties that day, which was a record for the battle of Kuban. They claimed sixty-eight downed aircraft (including forty-five Bf 109s), with another twelve claimed by anti-aircraft artillery. The VVS Red Army's losses were twenty-five aircraft, including eleven fighters. This allowed the Soviets to declare a complete defeat of the enemy. The commander of the 4th Air Army, Major General Vershinin, sent a telephone message to all the aviation regiments: 'We not only filled their muzzle, but also broke their will! Stalin's Falcons, go all the way. Victory will be ours!' In fact, the Luftwaffe lost only seven aircraft that day: three He 111s, two Ju 87 D-3s, one Fw 190 A-5 and one Bf 109 G-2.

On 27 May came the climax of this fierce aerial battle. The Luftwaffe carried out a record number of sorties, some 2,500. Along the battle lines of the Soviet 56th Army alone were dropped 5,000 high-explosive and fragmentation bombs. The journal of combat operations of the North Caucasus front reported:

> 37th Army. Units of the army, having started the offensive, met continuous counterattacks of the enemy and were subjected to massive air attacks, suffered heavy losses. 55 Guards rifle division, as a result of persistent battle, captured height 121.4, suffering over 50 per cent of losses … 56th Army. Resuming the offensive, the army units, shackled by enemy fire and paralysed by continuous bombardment of enemy aircraft,

suffered heavy losses and had no progress … the aircraft continuously bombed the battle lines of the 37A and 56A. In some periods of the battle over the battlefield there was simultaneously up to 300 enemy aircraft.

The positions of the 145th and 159th Rifle Regiments defending the stronghold of Podgorny, which had been occupied a day earlier, were attacked by stormtroopers from 06.00. They were then twice attacked by German infantry and tanks and eventually dislodged. Some companies and regiments of the 37th and 56th Army were almost completely disabled in one day as a result of air strikes. The report of the headquarters of the 37th Army read:

> In one bombing attack of enemy aircraft made by 80–100 aircraft in the area of Gorishchny all the personnel of one rifle company of the 32nd Guards Rifle Division were killed. Parts of the 55th Guards Rifle Division suffered losses of more than 50 per cent.

The effectiveness of Luftwaffe actions on this day was also recognised by the commander of the 56th Army, Andrey Grechko, who recorded:

> Having more than one and a half times superiority in forces, the German aviation temporarily seized the initiative of actions in the air. The Nazis supported the counterattacks of their ground troops in groups of 50–100 aircraft. Maintaining air supremacy, during the day, Hitler's aircraft made 2,658 sorties. In the air and on the ground, we had a difficult situation. The advance and especially the manoeuvre of our troops on the battlefield in the daytime was hampered by the continuous attacks of enemy aircraft. Already on the first day of the offensive, shortcomings were revealed in the actions of our fighters to repel massive attacks by enemy aircraft. Often they got involved in a battle with the enemy's fighters and let his bombers into our rear.

After such unprecedented air support, on the second day the next Soviet 'decisive offensive' in the Kuban completely ground to a halt. The VVS Red Army carried out 1,363 sorties and claimed forty-eight downed aircraft. In fact, the Germans lost only seven aircraft: four He 111s, two Hs 129s and one Fw 190. Russian losses amounted to thirteen aircraft.

On 28 May, the Luftwaffe flew 2,000 sorties, again inflicting heavy damage on the Russians. Losses of troops of the North Caucasian front for this day totalled 4,500. In response, the Russians carried out 912 sorties and claimed fifty-four downed aircraft, including fifty Bf 109s. Another twelve were claimed by Russian anti-aircraft batteries. Their own losses amounted to twenty-six aircraft. In fact, the Germans lost nine aircraft, including three Bf 109s, two He 111s, one Ju 88A-4, one Ju 87, one Bf 110 and one Fw 189.

The last major operation of German bombers over the Kuban bridgehead was a massive air attack on Krasnodar on 30 May. The railway junction was seriously damaged, with almost 300m of track wrecked, and six passenger railway carriages, twenty-two carriages containing wounded, two carriages with ammunition, three ambulance carriages and sixty-two buildings were destroyed, including the city's water pump. Seventy-six people were killed and 148 injured. This was another mighty challenge to Stalin's Falcons. After flying 100km over Russian airspace, which should have been literally teeming with fighters, the bombers reached the target without interference, dropped their bombs and went home. The Soviets scrambled their interceptors with great delay, and only a few pilots managed to randomly attack the retreating planes. Although the Soviets boasted of ten downed bombers, only one He 111 H-16 Wrk Nr 160411 '1G+OK' of II./KG 27, was actually lost. This plane, according to German data, was shot down by a fighter over the railway crossing at Krasnodar-Krymskaya. The entire crew – the pilot Unteroffizier Hans Limpinsen, navigator Unteroffizier Fritz Fux, radio operator Unteroffizier Willi Schmidt, flight mechanic Unteroffizier Werner Heinemann – was listed as missing.

Hans Reif, of 3./KG 27, summed up his impressions of such a large battle for the Kuban bridgehead: 'Before that, we had experienced something similar only in the Voronezh region, but to a much lesser extent.'

In June, the Russians continued their attacks on the Kuban bridgehead, but by this time the 17th Army had created a perfect line of defence (*Gotenkopf*). This was an almost impregnable position that the infantry could defend without the help of Luftwaffe.

The total losses of German aircraft on the Kuban bridgehead from 1 March to 25 June 1943 amounted to 268 aircraft, including eighty-five Bf 109s, forty-one He 111s, forty Ju 87s, thirty-six Ju 88s (including bombers and scouts), twenty-two Hs 129s, eleven Fw 190s, ten Bf 110s, five Fw 189s, five Ju 52s, two Hs 123s (both destroyed on the ground), two Go 145s, and several other liaison aircraft and cargo gliders. Of this number, only 222 losses were due to combat and 175 'full', i.e. shot down and missing.

The VVS Red Army lost about 1,000 aircraft from 1 March to 25 June, including 581 fighters (168 LaGG-3s, 149 Yak-1/Yak-1Bs, eighty-two P-39 Airacobras, seventy-seven La-5s, fifty-four Yak-7Bs, twenty-eight I-16/I-153s, sixteen Spitfires and five P-40 Kittyhawks). A total of 220 Russian fighter pilots were killed and captured, and several aviation regiments were completely destroyed.

The combat losses of German fighters were far fewer. JG 3 and JG 52 lost fifty-two fighters (damage from 60 per cent to 100 per cent on the German scale), with thirty-two pilots killed and missing (nine of them captured).

The Soviets' strike aircraft also suffered heavy losses. The elite 230th Assault Aviation Division (230th SHAD) alone lost seventy-four Il-2s. The Kuban was a total victory for the Luftwaffe.

The Luftwaffe returns to the Volga

The Soviets were shocked by the rapid resurgence of the Luftwaffe after Stalingrad and the scale of air attacks in various sectors of the Eastern Front. Their own efforts to build a huge fleet of fighters had no effect. The command of the VVS Red Army was in a state of constant anxiety; it did not know where to expect the next attack.

In mid-April, long-range reconnaissance Luftwaffe aircraft began to appear frequently over the Volga, carrying out aerial photography of the ice situation. The command of the Volga military flotilla immediately suspected that the enemy was once again preparing to mine the river to hinder the movement of oil caravans from Baku. In 1942 the Russian river fleet on the Volga had suffered huge losses. As a result of air attacks, mines, artillery attacks and sabotage, 335 vessels had been destroyed, including seventy-four tugs, forty-four oil barges (with a tonnage of 279,460 GRT), 153 dry cargo barges (with a tonnage of 205,638 GRT), and forty-nine vessels of the technical fleet. At the bottom of the Volga still lay a lot of undetected mines, and the fairway was cluttered by the wrecks of sunken ships. Therefore, the opening of the river to navigation was held in suspense. On 24 April, in the Vladimirovka (now Akhtubinsk) area, the motor fishing boat *Kormilets* had been blown up by a mine and sank with the entire crew of four. Then the tugboat *Erivan* met a similar fate. Despite these incidents, the resumption of navigation was successful. In April, forty-nine convoys left Astrakhan and delivered 467,000 tons of oil products to the central regions of the USSR.[9]

Further events showed that the fears of the Volga rivermen about the Germans' aerial reconnaissance were not mistaken. On 27 April, Major Paul Claas of the specialised air group I./KG 100 'Viking' arrived at Stalino airfield from Germany after a rest in France. The commander of the 1st Staffel, 29-year-old Hans Bätcher, was by this time a recognised expert in bomber aviation. In 1942, he participated in all the Luftwaffe operations on the southern flank from the Crimea to the Caucasus and the Caspian Sea. In November to December 1942, Bätcher participated in the supply of the 6th Army in Stalingrad. By the time he returned to the Eastern Front, he had already completed 458 sorties, becoming one of the record holders. From 21 July1941, when Bätcher participated in the first major raid on Moscow, he had constantly sowed death and destruction.

Such personalities as Klaus Häberlen and Hans Bätcher can be compared to the Nazgûl – ghost kings from J.R.R Tolkien's cult trilogy *The Lord of the Rings*. Subject to the will of the evil Lord Sauron, these servants of darkness, riding on winged creatures, had incredible strength and were ready to destroy any enemy at the order of the master. They tirelessly sowed terror in the ranks of their enemies and left behind them ruins and corpses. Where the Führer's 'Nazgûl' appeared, high-explosive and incendiary bombs were rained down on the heads of Soviet soldiers, sailors, and civilians with amazing accuracy. It seemed that they were invulnerable and could not be killed by mortals.

This time I./KG 100 was ordered to mine the Volga in order to again paralyse the transportation of oil products from Baku. The distance from Stalino air base to this river was 550–600km. On the night of 29/30 April, the group carried out its first mission, dropping bottom mines of the type BM1000 in the Kamyshin-Stalingrad section. Two of them were dropped by Bätcher. According to the records in his Fliegerbuch (logbook), the He 111 commander of I./KG 100 took to the air at 19.05, dropped mines in square Qu.50 378, then returned at 01.10 after a five-hour flight.

These sorties required a great deal of skill from the pilots because the mines were dropped at a low altitude so that they would not be blown ashore by the wind. In addition, it was necessary to ensure the operation was carried out in secret, for which the following tactics were used. The planes went to the Volga Region at an extremely high altitude, then turned off their engines and descended. At the same time, the navigator of the bomber took into account the strength and direction of the wind to accurately determine the moment for dropping the mine. After disconnecting its 'cargo', the plane continued to glide for some time, and only after it had flown a certain distance did the pilot turn on the engines and pick up speed. During the first mission, I./KG 100 encountered anti-aircraft fire and night fighters.[10] Despite this, all the bombers returned safely to base.

The next night, the He 111s of I./KG 100 reappeared over the Volga, this time dropping mines south-east of Stalingrad. As a result, the river was again, as in the summer of 1942, mined along a stretch of 800km, from the farm at Zolotoy (80km below Saratov) to Zamyana (60km above Astrakhan). Soon the mines claimed their first victims. On 2 May, the steamer *Sergey Lazo* hit a mine near the village of Solodniki and its captain, Yakov Krasnov, was killed. At 18.37 on the same day, an He 111 commanded by Bätcher took off with two BM1000 mines, which were dropped into the Volga in square Qu.50 3733. This time the flight took place without opposition from air defences. On 10 May, river minesweeper *No. 26* from the Volga military river flotilla hit a mine in the Zamyana area, and the next day, river minesweeper *No. 21* was blown up in the shallows around Verkhne-Solodnovnikovsky.

Bätcher made his next flight to the Volga on the evening of 11 May. According to Fliegerbuch records, the He 111 took off at dusk, 19.10 Berlin time. The bomber dropped two BM1000s in square Qu.493 and returned to Stalino at 23.19. On the morning of the next day, river minesweeper *No. 119* was blown up in this area while trawling. On 13 May, in the Svetly Yar area, the steamship *Vanya-Kommunist* was lost on a mine. On the same day, I./KG 100 suffered its first loss when, during the flight to the Volga, He 111 H-11 Wrk Nr 8135, pilot Heinz Hepp went missing.

From mid-May, I./KG 100 began to carry out attacks on ships in addition to its mine-laying missions. 'Target: ships in the southern reaches of the Volga, square 6970. 7 SD250 + 4 SC50,' reported Bätcher Fliegerbuch on 15 May. Against river vessels, the Germans used mostly fragmentation bombs, as it was believed that even near misses caused them serious damage. On the evening of 17 May Bätcher again attacked vessels on the Volga, dropping seven 250kg fragmentation and four small high-explosive bombs. In both attacks his He 111 came under heavy anti-aircraft fire.[11]

On 17 May the command of the Volga military flotilla organised the convoy of oil barges and military transports by gunboats, armoured boats and patrol boats. In areas where there was a mine threat, ships were escorted after sweeping. Many minesweepers also had anti-aircraft weapons and fired at aircraft. Since the section of the Volga from Astrakhan to Saratov was about 600km long and there were not enough warships, several methods of convoy were developed at once: relay race, through (continuous),

He 111 bombers in the sky.

partial, combined and reinforced. However, the whole system did not work immediately, but only at the end of May and into June.

In a relay race convoy, the warships only covered the ships from the impact of enemy aircraft within their area, passing them on to 'neighbours'. In a through convoy, the guard ships escorted the transport vessels from the exit point to the destination port or throughout the dangerous area. The essence of the partial convoy was that the armoured boats and patrol boats covered the transports only within their mobile firing positions, then the vessels went on independently, on occasion shooting back at the bombers. In a combined convoy, the guard ships, usually gunboats, served simultaneously as tugs during the entire passage. A reinforced escort was carried out by the guard ships together with the ships located on mobile firing positions.[12]

In addition to the protection ships, the air defence of transport ships created permanent and manoeuvrable shielded points, which were protected by coastal and ship anti-aircraft guns and machine guns, as well as patrol ships and fighter aircraft.

So it can be seen that the activities of I./KG 100 'Viking' fairly frightened rivermen and sailors, forcing them to allocate a significant amount of forces and means to the air defence of shipping. A major battle between the armoured boats of the Volga military flotilla and the 'Vikings' occurred on 19 May at Stalingrad-Kamyshin. When planes were sighted over the river at midnight, the boat crews began a barrage of fire with all their weapons. At the same time, other ships were fighting in another sector at the Black Yar.

Meanwhile, the Volga military flotilla suffered serious losses. On 17 May in the vicinity of Stupinsky shallow, the gunboat *Red Dagestan* hit a mine and sank, and nine days later, in the Yara Nasonych area, the gunboat *Krasnogvardeets* exploded. Both ships lost thirty members of their crews.

Simultaneously with the convoying of ships, major initiatives were launched to neutralise German bottom mines. The State Defence Committee ordered a significant increase in the number of minesweepers, mainly through the conversion of low-value river vessels (mainly fishing). In connection with the mine threat, in mid-May the People's Commissar of the Soviet Navy, Nikolai Kuznetsov, and People's Commissar of the river fleet, Zosima Shashkov, arrived in Stalingrad. The meeting, which was held in the cabin of an armoured boat, was attended by the head of river traffic on the Volga River and its tributaries, V.P. Tsybin, and the new commander of the Volga military flotilla, Rear Admiral Yuri Panteleev. Additional measures were developed to strengthen the monitoring of the dropping of mines. In the most targeted areas observation posts of military sailors were set up and organisation of barriers was improved. Ships' passages were marked by high-sensitivity piloting (navigation facilities) and night lighting was masked.

But it was not easy to organise all this work, especially during a strong spring flood. The river depth increased in places to 25–30m, and it was difficult to keep bulky mine barriers at such a depth and against a strong current. Soon the entire Volga from Kamyshin to Cherny Yar was 'decorated' with the most incredible barriers. Some of them were made from the remains of the destroyed Stalingrad: old electrical cables, wire, in fact everything that could be used as a material for creating navigation aids that mark dangerous spaces. In May to June, the Russians converted 165 self-propelled and non-self-propelled transport vessels into minesweepers and trawl barges. They had a lot of work to do. In total, during May, according to the observation service, German bombers dropped 354 bottom mines in the Volga. Some of these were equipped with multi-pulse fuses, so to detonate such a mine the minesweeper had to pass over it fifteen times or more. Even more terrible were mines with acoustic fuses; the means of their operation was poorly studied by the Russians at that time and hence effective means to deal with them were practically absent.

Despite all the measures taken, the cargo turnover of ships left much to be desired. Due to the need to observe a strict order of convoying, the narrowness of the mine-safe channel and a shortage of ships, the movement of oil caravans on the Volga went much slower than desired. In the last ten days of April, 445,000 tons of oil products were transported along the Astrakhan–Saratov section, and 765,000 tons were shipped during the whole of May, which was 76.5 per cent of the planned total. A painful loss in May was the sinking of three large oil barges, *Tarlyk*, *Katun* and *Komsomolka*, by mines. Some 30,000 tons of crude oil poured into the river. This event aggravated the environmental disaster on the Volga. During 1942, 500,000 tons of oil entered the river, turning its banks and mouth into a solid black oil slick.

The Germans also brought new victims to the 'altar' of the river war. On 24 May He 111 H-11 Wrk Nr 110088, flown by pilot Unteroffizier Eugen Strophff, and its crew of four went missing.

I./KG 100 continued minelaying along the Volga in late May and early June. According to Helmut Abendvoth's Fliegerbuch, on 30 May, his He 111 '6N+OK' took off from Stalino at 19.37, dropped two BM1000 mines into the river, and then returned at 23.22. The next day he took off at 19.40 and landed at 23.45. The duration of the flight was 245 minutes. On 2 June at 19.37, Abendvoth took to the air again in the same aircraft with two BM1000 mines on board. Dropping them into the river in square Qu. 5148, he returned to base at 23.55. On 31 May, near the village of Nikolskoye, the steamship *Kharkov* was blown up.

In 1943, the Luftwaffe laid a total of 399 mines in the Volga (354 in May and another forty-five from 1 June to 10 July). In the same year, the USSR lost six warships and fourteen civilian vessels on the river. If you do not take into account the mine setting in 1942, I./KG 100 achieved one explosion per twenty exposed mines, which is a very high return for this type of weapon.

Chapter 2

New Goal

'It was tempting to move from Russia to France'

The main reason for the astonishing effectiveness of the German bomber force was its flexibility. The same units and crews, depending on the situation, could carry out tactical missions (attacks on the front edge of the defences, attacking troops, the near rear, places of concentration of troops, front-line communications) and strategic raids (attacks on railways, railway junction stations, supply bases in the rear of the enemy). If necessary, these same crews could carry out air raids on cities and objects in the deep rear at a distance of 1,000km. And at any moment they could turn their bombers into transports, providing supplies to troops and surrounded groups.

The backbone of the Kampfgeschwader were experienced aces who were able to achieve results through individual professional actions and at the same time lead inexperienced youth. Despite the most serious losses, veterans usually remained unharmed and were shot down only in rare cases. As a result, even severely battered aviation groups could constantly maintain the minimum required level of combat readiness.

In early 1943, the situation in the Third Reich changed significantly. The Luftwaffe could no longer hold most of their units on the Eastern Front. In Africa, Allied forces were rushing to the sea in Tunisia, and British and American bombers were increasingly bombing German cities. Luftwaffe management had increasingly to resort to the pernicious practice of 'patching holes'. Therefore, experienced units that had made thousands of sorties on the Eastern Front had to be sent to the West with increasing frequency.

According to the Luftwaffe's plans, KG 4 'General Wever' was to be re-equipped with new He 177 heavy bombers in early 1943. This Kampfgeschwader, which had specialised in strategic bombing and other special missions since 1940, was supposed to be the first to be fully equipped with these machines. Thus, KG 4 was to end a protracted 'mission' to the

Eastern Front, the end of which was initially optimistically planned for the autumn of 1941. The He 177 was primarily wanted for attacks against naval targets in the Atlantic and raids on British cities. These missions were to be retribution for the raids by British bombers on the territory of the Reich. However, the crisis at Stalingrad and subsequent events only allowed this plan to be partially implemented. On 9 February, only Major Wolf Wetterer's I./KG 4 departed for Lechfeld for rearmament on the new type. The other two groups continued to fight on in the good old He 111.

Sometimes only individual crews were sent to the Western Front. In March, II./KG 4 lost five experienced crews. Herbert Sunner was among them:

> I said goodbye to II./KG 4 in March 1943 at Seshchinskaya airfield.Without any prior notice, an order was received: five experienced crews should be immediately sent to Chartres in France under the order of the air command of the raids on England (Angriffsführer England).

This unit was formed by order of Hitler in early 1943. Its head was appointed Inspector (commander) of the Bomber Force Oberstleutnant Dietrich Peltz (formerly a pilot of the dive bomber Ju 88 A and commander of II./KG 77, which specialised in single raids and pinpoint strikes on strategic targets). Using the new Do 217 K, Me 410, Ju 188 and He 177 bombers, Peltz was to launch new attacks on Britain.

Many pilots, tired of the monotonous Russian landscapes, cold weather and endless attacks on the same targets, gladly accepted the transfer to the West, as Sunner recalled:

> First of all, it was tempting to move from Russia to France, but this was soon followed by disappointment … The redeployment was carried out in a great hurry, first in the Ju 52, then by train across Europe to a new location. After retraining in KG 2 on the Do 217 and later on the Ju 188 in the middle of the year, we started fighting against England. However, success could no longer be achieved at the expense of weak forces. Of the 20 crew members of the former KG 4, only 3 survived: Helmut Kramer, Herbert Sunner, and Heinz Niklas.[1]

At the end of April, I./KG 55 was also withdrawn to Barth airfield in Germany, where it became III./LG 1. The latter thus became a fully fledged

Kampfgeschwader, although it formally retained the status of training and combat. The 'new' I./KG 55 was formed on 1 May at Stalino airfield on the basis of a separate transport aviation group, KGrzbV5, which was also equipped with He 111 aircraft.[2]

For Hauptmann Häberlen and his I./KG 51, a bright fighting career on the Eastern Front also came to an end. On 6 May this bombardment group was transferred to Illesheim airfield in Germany. He wrote in his memoirs:

> We had to rearm with the newly developed heavy fighter type Me 410, and then attack the 'Flying Fortresses'. They got that name because of their huge defensive firepower. We had to use our special weapons against the American four-engine B-17 bombers, flying at this time already in large numbers. We were looking forward to the events that were ahead.[3]

For Häberlen there was also disappointment. The Me 410 was completely unsuitable for fighting 'Flying fortresses', so I./KG 51, which had temporarily become a fighter group, had to return to the usual work – air strikes on ground targets, only this time on England. The pilots very quickly realised the difference between the West and the East. In nine months, Häberlen's unit lost 138 pilots, despite the fact that the crew of the Me 410 consisted of only two.

The remaining groups, KG 4 and KG 51, unlike their former comrades, remained on the Eastern Front and continued to perform the usual tasks. Despite some weakening and sending some units to the West, the Luftwaffe bomber force in the East was still a serious force in the early summer of 1943. They had yet to show their power in long-range raids into the Russian rear.

The von Greim Plan

Back in April, the Oberkommando der Wehrmacht planned a new offensive in the Kursk region (Operation *Zitadelle*). However, the beginning was constantly postponed. Hitler wanted to concentrate a large number of new Tiger and Panther heavy tanks in the area of impact, so he constantly shifted the timing. In the planning of this offensive, all facets of Hitler's 'talent' as a commander were revealed. With the obstinacy of a madman, he had nullified all the advantages of a sudden offensive operation and allowed the Russians to organise a strong defence. Despite this, incompetent Soviet command had no precise information about the German plans. The Russians expected the Wehrmacht to attack not only in the Kursk sector, but also in other directions. They were seriously afraid of an air and sea landing on the Black Sea, an offensive in the Rostov region, as well as the use of chemical weapons. Fearing a repeat of last year's mistakes, Stalin forbade his military leaders from being the first to attack; he was waiting for Hitler to make the first move. As a result, in April and May, there was a lull on the entire Eastern Front except for in the Kuban bridgehead. The Soviet troops were exhausted after the winter fighting and needed to be replenished with personnel, equipment and supplies. The German army had a temporary respite and no longer needed massive air support. There was a unique situation when almost all Kampfgeschwader could be used for strategic missions.

There was a discussion about which target to choose for the bombers in June 1943. The chief of the Luftwaffe General staff, Generaloberst Hans Jeschonnek, who was impressed by the Allied air attacks on German cities, was a supporter of similar attacks on Soviet cities in groups of twenty to thirty bombers. He was the only one of the German top aviation commanders who had expected impressive results from the massive bombing of London in the summer and autumn of 1940.

However, the opinion of the Third Reich's Minister of Armaments, Albert Speer, reflected the views of the military–industrial circles. German industrialists, for whom a protracted and total war had long ago become clear, insisted on undertaking massive air strikes on Soviet industry of military importance, for example, power plants in Moscow, Rybinsk and Gorky areas. General Günther Korten, commander of Fliegerkorps I, strongly objected to this method of using bomber aircraft. He believed that it would be difficult to attack such pinpoint targets from the air at a great distance.

As a result of a comprehensive discussion of the situation, a compromise decision was made, proposed by the commander of Luftflotte 6, Generaloberst der Flieger Robert von Greim and his staff. According to him, the Kampfgeschwader should attack the Soviet centres for the production of weapons before the start of the summer campaign. Among von Greim's main arguments was the desire to paralyse the production of Russian tanks and other military equipment, military materials and ammunition for a long time. According to Greim, such a Luftwaffe air attack would have done more good for the ground forces than the continuous and tedious destruction

General der Flieger Robert Ritter von Greim and commander KG 27 Oberstleutnant Hans-Henning von Beust. Air base Olsufevo, June 1943. (Photo from Boelcke Archiv)

on and near the front line. The struggle with the huge masses of Soviet armoured vehicles, which German troops faced on all fronts, took a lot of effort. In addition to the Panzerwaffe, anti-tank divisions with self-propelled guns, field artillery, and German infantry equipped with armour-piercing weapons, the Luftwaffe's anti-aircraft units had increasingly been called upon to repel tank attacks. As a result, their 88mm guns were constantly distracted from their main tasks. The units themselves were transformed from formally anti-aircraft to actual anti-tank units. Greim believed that even one successful air attack against an archaic Russian tank factory could stop production for several weeks.[4]

The commander of Fliegerkorps IV, General der Flieger Kurt Pflugbeil, proposed two targets for massive raids – the cities of Gorky and Saratov.

The decision to conduct a major strategic air operation was finally made in May. If successful, the Luftwaffe command expected 'if not to completely stop the supply of weapons and ammunition to the Russian front, then at least to noticeably break them'. First of all, the Germans hoped to disrupt the supply of Russian tank troops with equipment and fuel. Some optimists in the Luftwaffe General Staff saw more attractive prospects. It was hoped that, due to lack of equipment, the Russians would be forced to abandon the upcoming autumn–winter offensive, which could lead to the transfer of activity by the Western Allies to the East to help their coalition partner. And this, according to some Oberkommando der Luftwaffe generals, could eventually lead to the postponement of a large-scale Allied invasion of France.[5]

The city of Gorky, located at the confluence of the Oka and Volga Rivers 400km east of Moscow, was chosen as the main target. The city was home to many important military facilities, the largest of which was the Gorky automobile plant, 'Molotov' (GAZ), which was built with the participation of the US Ford company in 1930–32. It was located in the south-western part of the city on the banks of the Oka River. At the same time, German intelligence provided the Luftwaffe command with 'crucial data' that alleged that weekly production of this enterprise amounted to 800 T-34 tanks. Based on that figure, it appeared that almost all the tanks of this model came from the GAZ production line. Where this fantastic number came from is not entirely clear; we can only assume that this supposedly reliable information came from the Abwehr. The fact is that the quality of German intelligence left much to be desired and it is no secret that intelligence data, including that for the Eastern Front, was simply fabricated by the Abwehr. Nevertheless, this information was

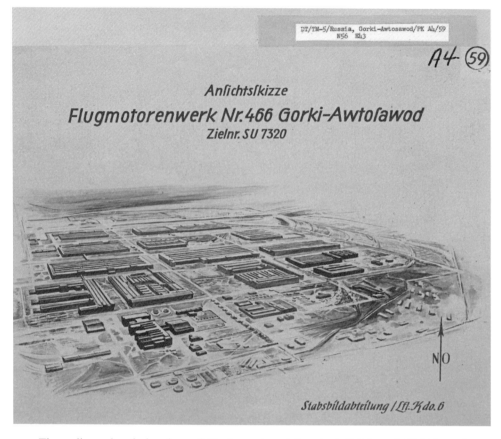

DT/TM-5/Russia, Gorki-Awtosawod/PK A4/59
N56 E43

A4 59

Anfichtsfkizze
Flugmotorenwerk Nr.466 Gorki-Awtofawod
Zielnr. SU 7320

N|O

Stabsbildabteilung / Lfl.Kdo.6

Three-dimensional drawing of Gorky automobile plant 'Molotov' (GAZ) and aircraft engine plant № 466.

taken as fact, and the common terms 'tank factory in Gorky' and 'head factory of Red tank products' were used. In fact, the Molotov automobile plant did not produce any T-34 tanks.

However, the wheel shop did use its unique American equipment to make type ZIS and GAZ wheels for all the automobile and artillery factories in the country. To imagine the scale of production, the plan for 1943 was almost one million wheels of all types.The workshops also made chassis details for tanks and aircraft. Dozens of components were supplied by GAZ to other enterprises, including tank factories in the Urals.

In addition, other areas of the plant assembled American Studebaker, Ford, Dodge and Chevrolet trucks, and every month about 1,500 were sent to the front. In the Avtozavodsky district, repair base No. 97 was engaged

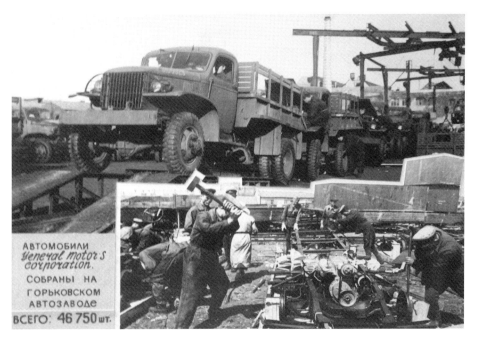

Assembly of Chevrolet trucks at the Gorky automobile plant 'Molotov'. 1943.

Women work on the production line for the manufacture of tyres.

in the preparation of tanks and armoured vehicles supplied to the USSR by the Allies under the Lend-Lease programme. The repair of broken and damaged imported equipment (tanks and armoured vehicles) was also carried out here. In Gorky tank units were equipped with Shermans, Churchills, Valentines and others.

Because of all these operations, the city was a huge military production cluster, a real tank centre for the Soviets. Given this, and the fact that the production cycle at many aircraft, tank and artillery factories depended on the smooth operation of the Molotov automobile plant, the choice of it as the main target by the Luftwaffe was correct.

The second target was the city of Saratov, also located on the Volga. According to German intelligence, there was a 'developed cartridge industry', making cases for small arms, and a large oil refinery cracking plant. However, as in the case of Gorky, information about the nomenclature of military products in Saratov was inaccurate. In fact, there were no cartridge factories in Saratov; the largest enterprise of this profile was located to the north in Ulyanovsk. In addition, aircraft factory No. 292, which produced Yak-1 fighters, was for some reason not considered as the main goal. However, the Kirov oil cracking plant was an important strategic object. It was the main supplier of fuel and lubricants for the central sector of the Eastern Front. In the spring of 1943, rail tank vehicles from Saratov

Saratov oil cracking plant 'Kirov'.

went directly to the Steppe, Voronezh and Bryansk fronts, so the smooth operation of the enterprise was extremely important for the Soviets.

Subsequently, the city of Yaroslavl, located 250km north-east of Moscow, was added to the list of priority goals. There, according to German intelligence, were factories for the manufacture of rubber products and a motor factory. In this case, the information was accurate. In 1943, the chemical plants of Yaroslavl produced more than 40 per cent of the country's rubber, and the Yaroslavl plant No. 736 most of its tyres. Hence, this factory was the main supplier of tyres for cars, aircraft and artillery, rubber rings for tanks and other military equipment. Also in Yaroslavl was the largest paint factory in the USSR.

However, the German scouts wasted their time finding out the details of military production in Gorky, Saratov and Yaroslavl. In fact, any Russian rear city, especially a medium or large one, was a centre of military industry. In the 1930s, Stalin, obsessed with 'world revolution', considered any newly opened industrial enterprise to be directly or indirectly producing military products. In addition, any branch of the Soviet military industry was represented by many similar enterprises, dispersed in different cities and parts of the vast country. Thus, the attack on several cities and the destruction of several military factories was comparable to attacking the mythical Hydra, when in place of one severed head, two new ones grew. However, as we have already noted above, there were weaknesses in the Stalinist military industry, but the Germans only planned attacks on

Yaroslavl tyre plant.

really strategic objects (such as power plants with German generators, the destruction of which would completely stop the work of industry) at the end of the war.

'Fascist bloodsuckers are preparing a new monstrous crime'

While the Luftflotte 6 headquarters in Smolensk and the Luftwaffe Main Command in Berlin were discussing plans for upcoming operations, the people of Gorky had recent memories of air attacks as the city had been raided repeatedly by the Luftwaffe. The first occurred in November 1941 during Operation *Typhoon* and during 1942, German bombers appeared many times over the city. But these attacks were carried out only by single planes or groups of two and three and did not cause major damage to the numerous military enterprises. After the battle of Stalingrad, Soviet propaganda instilled in its citizens that the enemy was defeated, its air force was weakened and that Stalin's Falcons were firmly in control of the air space. Therefore, people were no longer afraid of air attacks by the Nazis.

In the spring of 1943, Gorky lived a difficult but still peaceful life as a rear city. For almost two years, the people had become accustomed to the state of war and it had become an everyday reality. Hungry citizens enjoyed the news from the front along with successful purchases of scarce products. On 9 February Professor of the Pedagogical Institute, Nikolai Dobrotvor, wrote in his diary: 'We took Kursk. Hurray! Hurray! Hurray! I brought 1 pound of white flour and 2 kilograms of oil, 1 kilogram of meat.' He wrote a week later: 'Millions of times Hooray! I bought 2 kilograms of green onions in the store.'[6]

In the first six months of the war everyone lived in a state of constant anxiety and feared the arrival of the Germans. Now, in 1943, everything was going on as usual. People changed jobs, got married, had children, got divorced, attended university, went to dances, visited movies and theatres. Everything was almost as it was in peacetime. Only the anti-aircraft guns and balloons, barricades in squares and vacant lots, and the marching through the streets of military units and equipment reminded people about the war.

However, Party chiefs urged the population not to relax and not to lose vigilance. They said the threat was still there. On 26 March, at a meeting of the Gorky city office of the Bolshevik party, one of the Party bosses shouted:

Gorky automobile plant (GAZ) on the left bank of the Oka river (modern view).

> In their bestial rage and malice, the fascist fiends and bloodsuckers are preparing a new monstrous crime. As established by the captured materials, the fascist bandits are preparing to use toxic substances against our cities in the rear of the battle!

The city still lacked bomb shelters, fire reservoirs, self-defence groups or fire trucks, and did not observe blackout. The majority of the population did not believe in the threat of air attacks. On 1 June, the chief of staff of the local rescue service (MPVO), Lieutenant Colonel Antropov, wrote in his report to the city office of the Bolshevik Party:

> The city of Gorky is the largest industrial centre of the country, which plays an extremely important role in supplying the Red Army with all types of weapons. The fascist aviation will seek to disrupt the normal operation of the factories and factories of our city at the first opportunity.

As further events showed, these warnings were prophetic!

The air defence of Gorky and neighbouring cities was carried out by the Gorky Corps District PVO under the command of Major General of

Artillery Alexey Osipov. The five anti-aircraft artillery regiments (ZenAP) and several separate artillery divisions had 515 anti-aircraft guns, including 433 large-calibre guns (76mm and 85mm) and eighty-two small-calibre guns (25mm and 37mm). The command of anti-aircraft artillery was carried out by Colonel P.A. Dolgopolov. Gorky's air defence density was one and a half to two anti-aircraft guns per square kilometre.

For comparison, the air defence of London in 1940 had a density of 0.5–0.8 anti-aircraft guns per sq km, the air defence of Moscow in July 1941, 3.1–5.8 guns per sq km, and the air defence of Berlin in 1944, 0.4–0.6 guns per sq km. Gorky air defence units were armed with thirteen gun-pointing stations (SON-2), and two RUS-2S Pegmatit radar stations, located in the village of Pravdinsk and near Sejma station. In addition, 107 barrage balloons and 231 anti-aircraft searchlights were in service.[7]

Large-calibre anti-aircraft artillery battle positions were located around the city in three sectors. Anti-aircraft artillery regiments built their battle lines in several lines of batteries. However, their depth was small: the forward line of the batteries was only 5–7km from the borders of the defended objects. Many batteries were actually located directly near the objects and even on their sites. The greatest density of anti-aircraft artillery fire was created over the targets, and not on the approaches to them, which would be more reasonable. To repel night air attacks, the main method of firing large-calibre anti-aircraft guns was a barrage, associated with a large expenditure of ammunition. The explanation for such primitive tactics was simple.

First, there were not enough anti-aircraft searchlights, and the size of the light zone created by them did not provide the necessary anticipation for firing anti-aircraft artillery.

Second, shooting at an unobserved target according to tracking stations had been poorly mastered. The Russians sought to create the greatest density of fire over the target of the bomb attack to disrupt the formation of bombers. They never aimed at a particular plane.

The 142nd Fighter Aviation Division (142nd IAD PVO), under the command of Colonel Viktor Ivanov, had significant forces. By June 1943, its units were fully supplied with ammunition, fuel, and communications equipment. Organisationally, the division consisted of four air defence aviation regiments (423rd, 632nd, 722nd and 786th IAP PVO) and three airfield service battalions (BAO). The fighters were based at five airfields – Strigino, Pravdinsk-Istomino, Dzerzhinsk, Kazan and Kovrov. The division had eighty-seven interceptors, of which seventy-two were serviceable, and 159 pilots.

Aircraft in the 142nd IAP PVO at the beginning of June 1943[8]

Type of aircraft	Total	Including serviceable
La-5	19	17
LaGG-3	23	17
MiG-3	33	26
Yak-1	2	2
Yak-7b	3	3
I-15bis	1	1
I-153	2	1
I-16	4	2
Total:	87	72

In addition, the division was soon to receive another ten La-5s and thirty-three Hurricanes. However, the standard of the division's pilots was extremely low. A check conducted in May by the Military Department of the Bureau of the Gorky regional office of the Bolshevik Party showed that the division, despite having a large number of aircraft and personnel, was not prepared to repel massive air attacks. There was no combat training or the practising of joint actions in the air. Pilots could operate only as part of a link (three fighters) or singly. During the first half of 1943 Division Commander Colonel Ivanov never organised classes with regimental commanders. Training in air-to-air combat was extremely poor. For example, Squadron Commander Yarygin only shot at a target in flight once in five months. Theoretical shooting classes were held only once a month, and then formally. As a result, most pilots of the 722nd IAP PVO, equipped with high-altitude MiG-3 interceptors, did not know how to aim correctly. Pilots who were expected to fly at night and at high altitudes were not prepared for this.

The Russians used communications inefficiently. Long conversations and monologues were conducted over the radio instead of clear commands. Reports, for example, 'Patrolling over Balakhna', were transmitted in plain text, without a cipher. The units lacked proper order and discipline. The duty section of the 423rd IAP was not ready for departure during a training air raid and this did not take place. The commander of the regiment, Elizarov, arrived at his plane without a parachute, while the chief of staff mixed up the flares. The duty pair of fighters of the same regiment, which was in readiness state number 2, was not combat ready when the test alarm was sounded because the pilots had gone to lunch. The 786th IAP PVO's aircraft were at readiness state number 1; that is, the pilots should have been in the cockpit and waiting for the signal to start. However, instead of the required thirty to sixty seconds, they took off in six minutes. During a training alert on 2 June, the regiments at Strigino and Dzerzhinsk did not respond to the signal at all. Instead of training and education, the commanders mercilessly punished the pilots with arrests for the slightest misdeeds. In the first half of 1943, the 142nd IAD PVO did not conduct any training in combat and tactical training.

The reasons for this collapse of combat training stemmed from the very essence of the Soviet regime. The state of workers and peasants created by Lenin was based not on intelligence and competence, but on blind loyalty to the regime, based on illiteracy and ignorance. Lenin's successor, Stalin, essentially pushed the situation to the limit. His executioners destroyed almost the entire intellectual elite of civil and military management. The Bolshevik leaders, being themselves models of stupidity and ignorance, seriously believed that revolutionary enthusiasm could easily replace education and intelligence. In addition, the general managerial incompetence was often compounded by various vices inherent in a wide range of Soviet officials. For example, the commander of the Gorky corps area of air defence, General Alexey Osipov, and the commander of the aviation division, Colonel Viktor Ivanov, were alcoholics.

The Air Surveillance and Communication Service (VNOS) of the Gorky region was carried out by two battalions and about thirty freelance observer posts. Most of these posts were located along the banks of the Volga and Oka Rivers, along roads and railways, which were the main landmarks for enemy aircraft flights. The main type of communication was via a wired telephone. Radio communication was considered only as a duplicate channel for transmitting messages. And this after two years of war!

Despite the large human resources, by 1943 the USSR began to feel the effects of the colossal loss of the male population at the front. Almost from the very beginning of the war, the incompetent and ruthless Soviet leadership began to call women into the army. The Bolsheviks understood the problem of gender equality as the right to use their citizens, regardless of gender, in the most difficult and dangerous jobs.

In May 1943, there was another replenishment of air defence units by drafting in young girls. Among the recruits was a native of the Lukoyanovsky district of the Gorky region, Pelageya Parshina, aged 22. On 15 May she was sent a summons from the military enlistment office, and she and a friend were forced to go on a long journey to the regional centre in Gorky, riding on the buffers between the cars of a crowded train. After Parshina arrived at the Military Commissariat, she was sent to her place of service – the 741st ZenAP, whose positions on the eastern bank of the Volga, in the Batalovo area. Parshina served as the fourth member of the personnel of an 85mm anti-aircraft gun, and was responsible for the elevation of the weapon. From that moment on, the young woman fell into a different reality. Although they were in the rear, they lived and served as if they were at the front. At first, the battery positions did not have any living space so they had to sleep on the ground, on canvas covers from the guns. Then they dug dugouts, but it was not very convenient to live in them either: they had an earthen bed, and instead of a mattress just ordinary hay. At first, there were not even separate facilities for women. They were taken to have a bath in small groups every ten days.

Parshina recalled:

> Violations of the military regulations were punished to the full extent of wartime. For being late for a check-up or showing up for an alarm without a headdress, the girls could be put in a pit that served as a prison as a punishment. Sometimes, during an alarm, we would grab our boots and cap in our hands, run to our anti-aircraft gun, and then get dressed.

However, Parshina was not destined to become a Russian 'Éowyn', that is, to kill one of the Führer's Nazgûl. Russian girls were brave and desperate, but they could not become a fully fledged replacement for men.

Thus, in so many ways it was obvious that the Russian air defences were totally unprepared for the coming raids of the Germans.

Chapter 3

Two Deaths Carmen

'It smelled like a new offensive'

At the end of May, Luftwaffe bombers conducted a series of continuous raids on railway junctions and train stations in front-line areas. These raids were carried out with the aim of paralysing Russian railway transport in preparation for the attack on Kursk. The apotheosis of this action was Operation *Carmen*, a massive air strike on the railway junction in Kursk. The name was not chosen by chance. In Georges Bizet's opera of the same name, which the public first saw in 1875, a dramatic love story is played out in four acts, ending in tragedy. The main character, Jose, kills his beloved. Operation *Carmen* was planned as a series of four combined massive raids involving dive bombers, conventional bombers, attack planes and fighter-bombers. The result of the 'drama' was to be the complete destruction of a major transport hub.

The first raid was carried out at dawn on 2 June, for which dive bombers from II./KG 51 took off from Bryansk air base. Among them was Hans Grotter's Ju 88 A-4 '9K+JN'. According to its Fliegerbuch, the plane took off at 02.50 Berlin time and returned at 04.45 after 115 minutes.[1]

The second attack, which took place at 07.20 Berlin time, involved fifty-five aircraft, including twenty Bf 110s from I./ZG 1, eleven Ju 88 As from III./KG 1 'Hindenburg', twenty-four He 111s of II./KG 4 'General Wever' and several 'Jabo' Fw 190 As from JG 51. The latter were not used as fighters and dropped bombs.

Aerial photography taken shortly after the bombing by a Ju 88 D reconnaissance aircraft from 4.(F)/11 showed that the entire area of the railway junction was covered by fire, and several trains were burning on the rails. This was followed by another strike, and then on the night of 3 June, a major night air attack. This was one of the largest operations of this kind since the beginning of the war, during which the Kursk railway junction was virtually wiped out.[2]

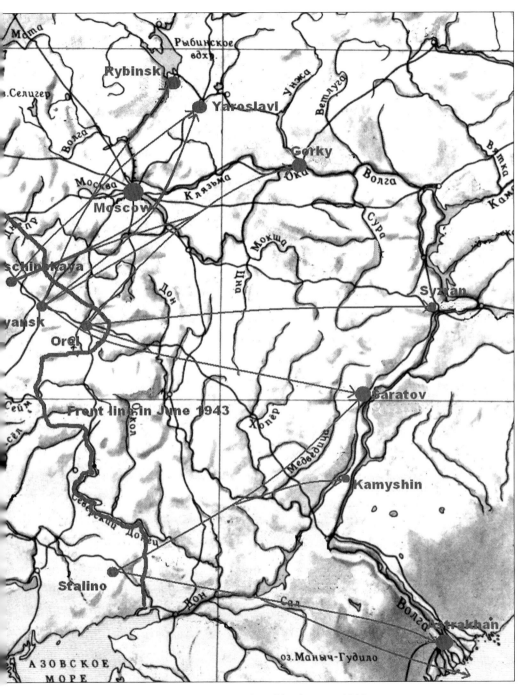

Luftwaffe air attack scheme against Russian cities in June 1943.

The Russians, as usual, greatly overestimated the success of their air defence. They claimed to have shot down 145 German planes! In fact, the Luftwaffe lost only ten aircraft confirmed, while another five were severely damaged (50–70 per cent):

- He 111 H-6 Wrk Nr 7441 from 5./KG 4, Unteroffizier Arnold Eckenberg, was hit by anti-aircraft fire and mostly destroyed (90 per cent) during an emergency landing on German-held territory. All five members of its crew were injured;
- He 111 H-6 Wrk Nr 7315, Unteroffizier Schrey, from 6./KG 4 was hit by anti-aircraft artillery. His crew (including the wounded Unteroffizier Alfons Schiebel) managed to reach the front line and jump out with parachutes;
- He 111 H-6 Wrk Nr 7456 of 6./KG 4 was damaged by anti-aircraft fire over Kursk but reached Seshchinskaya air base (damage 30 per cent);
- He 111 H-6 Wrk Nr 7052, Unteroffizier W. Kretchmer of 3./KG 27, was hit by a Soviet La-5 fighter (from the 40th GIAP or 41st GIAP) and made an emergency landing on Russian territory. Kretchmer himself managed to cross the front line and enter German territory, but flight engineer Obergefreiter H. Gruss drowned while crossing the river and the rest of the crew were missing;
- Ju 88 A-4 Wrk Nr 4442 from 7./KG 1 shot down by anti-aircraft fire, crew missing:
- Ju 88 A-4 Wrk Nr 4441 of 8./KG 1 was shot down by P-39 Airacobra fighters from the 30th GIAP, the crew was missing;
- Ju 88 A-4 Wrk Nr 2623 8./KG 1 was hit by Airacobras in the same battle, flew to its air base, but crashed during landing. The entire crew was killed;
- Ju 88 A-4 Wrk Nr 4435 of III./KG 1 was shot down by anti-aircraft artillery, the crew was missing;
- Ju 88 A-4 Wrk Nr 4431 from III./KG 1 was hit by anti-aircraft fire and seriously damaged (50 per cent) after an emergency landing on its territory;
- He 111 H-11 Wrk Nr 110074 of 9./KG 55 was shot down by a La-5 fighter of Captain V.N. Kravtsov from the 40th GIAP, the crew was missing;
- Bf 109 G-4 Wrk Nr 19356, Unteroffizier Werner Maisch from 6./JG 3, was shot down by a fighter; the pilot was missing;
- Fw 190 A-5 Wrk Nr 7165 of 3./JG 26 was shot down by anti-aircraft fire over Kursk, the pilot was missing;

- Bf 110 F-2 Wrk Nr 5133 of I./ZG 1 (crew Oberleutnant G. Schmidt and Unteroffizier K.-H. Koelzow, both injured) and Bf 110 G-2 Wrk Nr 6127 3./ZG 1 (the crew of Unteroffizier J. Lonzek and H.-H. Kelch, both killed) were both shot down in combat with Soviet fighters. It has been reliably established that they were fighting with the Yak-9s of the 910th IAP PVO. Two victories were won by Captain Sergey Koblov and one each by Senior Lieutenant N.A. Chasnyk, I.D. Vlasov and Lieutenant A.A. Eldyshev. Russian pilots identified their opponents as 'Do 217s';
- Two more Zerstorers, Bf 110 F-2 Wrk Nr 2701 of I./ZG 1 and Bf 110 G-2 Wrk Nr 5212 of 3./ZG 1, were damaged in this battle, but despite heavy damage (50 per cent and 70 per cent) were able to return to their airfield at Lednya.

The Soviets were again shocked by the power of the German air attacks. Unlike the planned Wehrmacht Operation *Citadel*, whose goals were obvious to the Russians, they knew nothing about the Luftwaffe's future plans. In May, Soviet intelligence received information that the Germans were allegedly preparing a massive air attack on Moscow. Even the approximate date was called – 5–6 June. In early June, there were frequent flights of German reconnaissance aircraft in the Moscow area.

On the morning of 1 June, a MiG-3 of Junior Lieutenant Gennady Syreyshchikov from the 565th IAP intercepted and by ramming managed to down a Ju 88 D Wrk Nr 1069 '5F+PM' of Oberleutnant Josef Felten of 4.(F)/14. The German crew was killed, so no information about the flight goals could be obtained by the Russians. On 2 June at 07.33 near Vyazma the flight of the next reconnaissance plane, which followed the route Gzhatsk–Mozhaisk–Zvenigorod, was recorded. Soon the plane was 12,500–13,000m over Moscow. During the previous appearance of this mysterious aircraft (26 March 1943), the Russians misidentified it as a 'Messerschmitt Jaguar'. That referred to the high-speed bomber called the Bf 162 'Jaguar', which was developed in 1935 by order of the RLM. The Russians knew about this project, but had no information about its development (in fact, the Bf 162 was not mass produced). They assumed incorrectly that the Germans had turned the 'Jaguar' into a secret high-altitude reconnaissance plane.

The ghost of the 'Bf 162' slowly flew over the Soviet capital, having stayed in the zone of the city's anti-aircraft artillery for fifty-six minutes. However, the artillery did not fire and thus did not interfere with the flight. Neither could the interceptors, some of which could barely climb to an altitude of

Kursk railway junction after the air attack on June 2 (Operation *Carmen*).

11,600m. Different types of fighters were scrambled to intercept, among them was the high-altitude Yak-9PD No. 01–29 of the inspector for piloting techniques of the 6th IAK PVO, Lieutenant Colonel A. Sholokhov. As he climbed his water temperature reached 105°C, and the oil temperature was 95°C. Sholokhov soon reached a height of 8,500m and a message came on his radio: 'the German plane has passed Vnukovo', which meant that the enemy was somewhere nearby. Looking around, Sholokhov saw the 'ghost' …

A thick vapour trail was clearly visible in the clear sky, at the end of which was a small black dot approaching the southern outskirts of Moscow.

The Yak-9PD immediately turned in the direction of the city. After a fifteen-minute pursuit with a simultaneous climb, the fighter caught up with the enemy. The altimeter showed 11,650m! Then Sholokhov looked up and saw right above him at a distance of 1.5km the silhouette of a twin-engine aircraft. The lieutenant colonel could clearly make out the yellow engines on the wings and the indistinct outlines of the crosses. At that moment, he realised that he was seeing the mysterious 'Jaguar' he had heard so much about earlier. However, he did not have time to look at it for long. Soon the fuel pressure dropped to almost zero, and Sholokhov had to drop almost a kilometre. After that, he made a second attempt to climb and again reached 11,400m. But then the pilot saw steam come out from under his engine cowling, and the cockpit glass began to cover with ice. It was clear that it would not be possible to get to the enemy, and as a result Sholokhov was forced to end his pursuit and land. The other fighters were also unable to intercept the enemy.

Sholokhov could not attack the target, but he saw it close enough to identify it correctly. He assumed that he had seen a Ju 86 (he was correct, it was actually Ju 86 R-1 Wrk Nr 0285 'T5+WB' of 1.(F)/100). The pilot said that it looked like a Bf 162, but only from below at the rear. It was distinguished from the 'Jaguar' by its thick, cigar-shaped fuselage. The fact that a high-altitude reconnaissance plane had appeared over Moscow served as a confirmation for the Soviets that the Nazis were preparing for a raid on the city.

While the Soviets were wondering where the Germans would strike next, the Luftwaffe command set the final start time for the operation – the evening of 4 June. In view of the success of the just completed air attack against the Kursk railway junction, it was decided to assign the code name Carmen II. The initial plan of operation also provided for four consecutive massive raids, which should result in the destruction of the main target – the tank factory in Gorky. If the situation at the front allowed, similar air attacks on Saratov, Yaroslavl and other targets in the vast Volga Region were to follow in the future.

The high level of training of bomber crews, only partially crewed by young people with little front-line experience, gave a high chance of success of this first large-scale strategic operation against the Soviet military industry. During the two years of the war, long-range reconnaissance aircraft had taken a huge number of aerial photographs of all Russian cities and important sites up to the Urals. The location of the targets was precisely defined and the development of the mission was not a difficult task. Many pilots already had experience of raids on Gorky and other cities, conducted in 1941–42.

The main object of the first attack – the Molotov (GAZ) automobile plant in Gorky – was on the left bank of the Oka River in the south-western outskirts of the city. The enterprise covered an area of 4sq km, but around it over a huge area were all sorts of auxiliary and transport facilities. The main vulnerable point of the large industrial complex was a single water abstraction pump, which supplied the industrial shops and residential areas. The data received from intelligence made it possible to develop a detailed plan for the first strike. First, the He 111s of the specialised aviation group I./KG 100 'Viking' were to appear over Gorky, which were to serve as pathfinders. After marking the target with photoflash bombs, the second wave of bombers was to destroy the water abstraction intake station and the main water supply nodes in the GAZ area. Then followed the attack bombing of incendiary and high-explosive bombs directly on the production buildings. Most of the aircraft had a new high-altitude sight, Lotfe 7D, which allowed for targeted bombing from high altitudes, including at night.

In anticipation of the first raid a large quantity of all kinds of ordnance was delivered to the airfields at Olsufevo, Seshchinskaya, Bryansk, Orel-West and Karachev. These comprised heavy incendiary bombs, BM1000 mines, high-explosive bombs weighing from 50 to 2,000kg, 70kg fragmentation bombs and conventional cassette boxes, and these represented to the ground staff 'a very impressive collection'[3] of deadly devices. Extra fuel supplies were also prepared.

In order to maintain secrecy, the transfer of bomber aviation groups to the airfields of the Orel salient began immediately before the attack. 'We were based in hot Melitopol and accordingly had light summer clothes,' recalled P. Mobius of 9./KG 27. 'Then the order arrived for departure with luggage for two or three days, in fact only with a toothbrush. We flew alone to a front-line airfield, Olsufevo. For deception, it was ordered to fly there at an altitude of 100m and fly around areas where the guerrillas were active. It smelled like a new offensive, and we were intrigued.'[4]

On the morning of 4 June, bombers from II and III./KG 55 also flew from Stalino (in the Donbass) to the air bases at Karachev and Seshchinskaya. I./KG 100, which was to perform the role of pathfinders, relocated from Stalino to Bryansk. According to the Fliegerbuch of Feldwebel Helmut Abendvoth, his He 111 '6N+EK', took off at 06.57 and after 160 minutes of flight landed at the new air base at 09.32.[5]

In total, nine bomber aviation groups from seven Kampfgeschwader were concentrated at air bases in the Bryansk and Orel regions. Generalleutnant Alfred Bulowius, Commander Fliegerdivision 1, took overall control of their operations.[6] It was decided to use all available combat-ready aircraft

He 111 H-16 '1G+LN' from 2./KG 27 at Olsufievo airfield. June 1943. (Photo from Boelcke Archiv)

Suspension of the SC250 bomb in the bomb bay of the He 111 aircraft. (Photo from Boelcke Archiv)

in the first attack in order to use the surprise effect to inflict maximum damage to the Molotov plant. In order to record the results of the raids on Gorky, 1.(F)/100[7] of Hauptmann Marqardt, equipped with reconnaissance Ju 88 Ds, Do217 Es, Ar 240s and Ju 86 Rs, was specially allocated. Weather reconnaissance over the target was conducted by a front-line unit,Wetterflugstelle 'Schatalowka'. It was located at Schatalowka-Ost airfield (Russian name Shatalovo) near Smolensk and was equipped with Ju 88 A/Ds.

The Fiery Falling Leaves

On the afternoon of 4 June, work was in full swing at German airfields, with commanders studying maps of Gorky and target diagrams, and developing flight routes and bombing tactics.

Navigator J. Wolfersberger from 5./KG 27, who joined this Kampfgeschwader at the end of 1942, recalled:

> In the early morning of June 4, we were woken up and given maps of the entire course of the Volga and the area up to Leningrad, it seems that something big had to happen in the air. They said that it would be a raid on Moscow, and that there were already schemes of goals, but, about 16 hours before, the purpose of the raid it was finally announced: Gorky, the centre of military industry on the Volga… With the onset of summer, we were rarely seen on the street in the afternoon, it was hot and we often spent the time until noon lying in. Often our conversations concerned the possibility of making an emergency landing deep in Russian territory or the need to jump out on a parachute, and what we had to do in this case. Just in case, it would be good, it would be nice, to keep a map in your head, and therefore the direction of rivers, railways, and the like.

The pilots were aware of the importance of the upcoming operation. The fact that Luftwaffe were once again preparing to perform offensive tasks immediately raised the morale of the crew members. Intensive aviation training on the basis of accumulated combat experience had already guaranteed half the operation's success. All that remained was to get right into the area of the target and hit it. Meanwhile, in the evening a weather

The crew of the bombers from KG 27. Far left is J. Wolfersberger. (Photo from Boelcke Archiv)

scout Ju 88 D from WeFlugSt 'Schatalowka' returned and the crew reported cloudless skies in the Gorky area with wind blowing north-east at a speed of 2.7m per second.[8] Wolfersberger continued:

> At about 17 o'clock, a preliminary order came, defining the crews and aircraft, it gave confidence that everything was already decided. If nothing special happens, I will participate in the flight one way or another. The preflight briefing was scheduled for 19.00, and before that we still had time for dinner, writing letters. There were hardly any military ranks to be distinguished now, everyone was dressed in flight suits, and the friends were greeting each other with handshakes.

Shortly before 20.00 one of the officers called a briefing and immediately the chief[9] appeared in the doorway.

> 'Hello pilots!'– he greeted us, and immediately commanded.
> 'At ease, pilots and navigators to me!'

With paper and pencils in our hands, we crowded around a large table on which a map lay before us.

'So, the raid with all available aircraft on the military plant in Gorky on the Volga. Start time from 20.00 to 20.10 in the following sequence: "Anton", "Caesar", "Paula", "Emil", "Fritz", "Berta", "Sigfrid", "Otto", "Mari", "North pole" and the last "Kurfurst".[10]

'Bomb attack in the area of 22.40–22.45, ahead of us will be a aircraft from II./KG 4, so the target may already be on fire, and, in addition, lit by lighting bombs. The latter will help facilitate bombing. Approach the target from north to south, then turn to the right. The height is arbitrary, but, nevertheless, not less than 2,000m. The wind blows from the course of 30° at a speed of 10km/h, over the goal, cloudless. Are there any questions? Check your watches!'[11]

At the same time, He 111s from KG 55 'Greif' took off one by one from Seshchinskaya airfield. At 20.00 Berlin time, the first wave departed. He 111 H '6N+EK' Helmut Abendvoth from I./KG 100 took off from Bryansk airfield at 20.13.[12] Shortly before that, bombers from II./KG 51 'Edelweiss' had also taken to the air from the same base. According to Hans Grotter's Fliegerbuch, his Ju 88 A-4 '9K+PN' from the 5th Staffel, took off at 19.45. Curiously, the military motor factory in Gorky ('Kraftmotorenwerk in Gorky'[13]) was designated as a target. Perhaps it was the aircraft motor factory No. 466, located on the territory of GAZ but allocated to a separate enterprise. The Germans were well aware of this fact, the pilots even had three-dimensional drawings of it.

Pilots later recalled that each Kampfgeschwader was given an individual route to its target, but the bright night allowed them to fly in a sparse formation of the units. A route was chosen that skirted Moscow from the south. The bombers crossed the front line, marked by the glow of skirmishes, in a linked formation. At the same time, pilots from KG 27 recorded a few searchlights and individual shots from anti-aircraft guns, but these did not cause any harm to the aircraft.

Wolfersberger continued:

We are slowly climbing higher and the horizon line in the east is getting lighter. The flares from the engine exhaust pipes are fading, but there are enough of them to see the circles of rotating propellers. Somewhere ahead, enemy anti-aircraft guns are firing, the beams of two or three searchlights are groping around in the air like the fingers of a dead man. Aha, perhaps these are our 'friends'. We slightly change the engine speed, which misleads the observation posts of anti-aircraft gunners, and we overcome the first line of defence without the slightest damage.

In total, 168 bombers participated in the first major raid on Gorky, including He 111s from II./KG 4 'General Wever', Major Reinhard Graubner; KG 27 'Boelcke', Oberstleutnant Hans-Henning von Beust; II and III./KG 55 'Greif', Majors Heinz Hover and Wilhelm Antrup; and I./KG 100 'Viking', Major Paul Claas; with Ju 88 As of III./KG 1 'Hindenburg', Hauptmann Werner Kanter; II./KG 3 'Blitz', Major Jurgen de Lalande; and II./KG 51 'Edelweiss', Major Herbert Voss.

The aircraft flew at an altitude of 4,000–5,000m in small groups at intervals of ten to fifteen minutes. For navigation on the first leg of the flight, the crews used a powerful radio transmitter of the Moscow radio station Comintern, which it was not difficult to find on a certain wave, and with its help they correctly determined the direction. In addition, the Russian patriotic songs and hymns the station broadcast brought variety to the long and tedious flight. After a while, the glittering ribbon of the Oka River appeared, which served as a perfect guide for the final run to the target...

The Russian air defence command received the first reports of the appearance of German aircraft at 21.42 (Moscow time). VNOS outposts reported that a group of ten aircraft had crossed the front line in the Sukhinichi area and were moving in the direction of Kaluga. Another group of twenty-two aircraft crossed the front line north-east of the city of Orel, passed over Gorbachevo and moved to the north-east. To the south, several more He 111 and Ju 88 groups crossed the front line. The headquarters of the Moscow air defence (PVO) front immediately suggested that this was a massive raid on Moscow, which was then reported by Soviet intelligence! At 22.05 'Readiness No. 1' was entered in all divisions.

Meanwhile, VNOS posts and radar stations continued to monitor the movement of targets. The first group of bombers arrived over Serpukhov and continued heading north-east. The second group was in the Tula region and was approaching Kashira. Anti-aircraft artillery regiments in

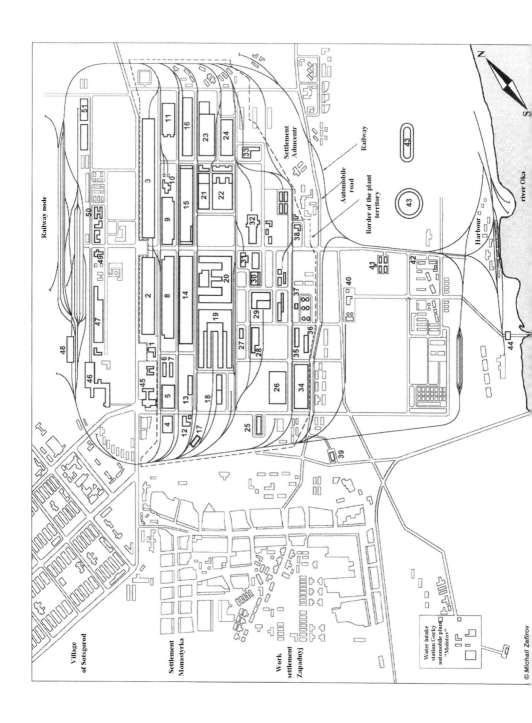

Opposite: Scheme of Gorky automobile plant 'Molotov'. (Author Mikhail Zefirov)
The captions to the diagram of the plant:

1. The main administrative building
2. Instrumental-stamping shop
3. Mechanical Assembly (tank) shop № 5 Body shop (tank shop № 5)
4. Warehouse rubber
5. Mechanical repair workshop
6. Blacksmith shop for repairs
7. Model shop
8. Press workshop
9. Wheel workshop
10. Etching shop and warehouse
11. Engine shop № 1 (aircraft engine plant № 466)
12. Garage truck tractors
13. Logistics warehouse related parts
14. Main assembly conveyor
15. Engine shop № 6
16. Armature-radiator shop
17. Warehouse rubber
18. A workshop for the manufacture of wire
19. Forging shop № 1
20. Foundry shop malleable iron № 1
21. Shop fettling of casting
22. Foundry shop grey cast iron № 2
23. Non-ferrous metal casting shop (aircraft engine plant № 466)
24. Repair-foundry shop (aircraft engine plant № 466)
25. Assembly shop
26. Workshop for the production of truck frames
27. Shop for the production of electrical components
28. Overpass thermal and power station
29. Thermal and power station № 1
30. Thermal and power station № 2
31. Central distribution substation № 1
32. Woodworking workshop
33. Engine oil warehouse
34. Shop of mechanical processing of details № 2
35. Warehouse
36. Shop of forging dies
37. Oil storage
38. Gas generating station
39. Warehouse gasoline
40. Pumping plant
41. Acetylene station
42. Oxygen station
43. Oil storage
44. Water intake station
45. Garage № 2
46. Tank repair plant
47. Department receiving of primary documentation
48. Coal storage
49. Fire station
50. Dormitory for plant security guards
51. Shop of mechanical processing of details № 4

these areas began barrage fire. Soon photoflash bombs were dropped by pathfinders in the Diaghilev and Kolomna areas to mark the route. At 22.44 in Moscow, for the first time after a long break, the 'air alarm' signal was given. The batteries of the 1203rd, 1201st and 82nd ZenAP, which were defending the distant approaches to the capital from the south, began a barrage on the course of the bombers, which were already just 100km from the city.[14] At the same time, thirty-four night fighters were scrambled from the airfields at Lyubertsy, Vnukovo, Chkalovskaya, Dubrovitsa, Lipitsa, Ramenskoye, Kashira, Monino and Inyutino. In the sky over Moscow 430 barrage balloons (including 153 of the tandem type) rose rapidly to 3,300 to 5,000m. Thousands of the capital's residents fled to shelters and basements, and many wore gas masks as there were rumours of an impending chemical air attack.

But at 23.00 the Russians realised that the target of the attack was not Moscow. All the bombers had passed south of the city and were heading east. Where are they going?…

In the city of Gorky, the warm evening of 4 June did not portend any important events. At the factories the night shift began and the tired day shift workers returned to their ragged barracks to prepare to go back to 'forge a victory' after a short sleep. The few residents who were free from work walked the streets late at night, enjoying the summer warmth. Young couples strolling along the walls of the ancient Kremlin, which rose on a high slope just above the confluence of the Oka and Volga rivers, were the last to watch as the friendly June sun set behind the smoking chimneys of the vehicle plant in the west. No one would have thought that their home city was in danger.

At 22.30, the headquarters of the Gorky corps air defence district suddenly received an alarming message from the central post of VNOS in Moscow that a large group of enemy bombers was moving in a north-eastern direction. After that, the RUS-2s radar stations were put into operation, the operators of which soon confirmed that enemy aircraft were approaching from the Vladimir and Ryazan regions. At 23.56 local time, on the order of the commander of the corps area PVO, General Alexey Osipov, the 'air alarm' signal was given. This signal was received by the city's districts for one to three minutes and duplicated by electric sirens and factory horns for eight minutes.[15]

At 00.10, VNOS posts near the villages of Vyazniki and Kulebaki began to report that large groups of bombers were flying over them to

Receiving system based on the GAZ-AAA truck, was one of the three components of the Radar station RUS-2.

85-mm anti-aircraft gun firing.

the east in gradually converging courses. Now there was no doubt that the planes were heading for Gorky. Anti-aircraft gunner I.A. Levitsky recalled:

> The battery of the gun-aiming station (SON) was switched on. Soon it was reported that a group target was approaching from the west, the range to the target is more than 50km. A 'Readiness No.1' was declared. The anti-aircraft gunners were ready for battle. The commander of battery SON reported that the targets were moving in small groups at intervals of 10 to 15km at an altitude of 5,000 to 6,000m.

Soon there were reports that the first planes were approaching the city, and General Osipov ordered the anti-aircraft artillery regiments to start a barrage. The first began to shoot anti-aircraft guns and 742th ZenAP Lieutenant Colonel M.F. Yevgenov then opened artillery fire in all sectors. Nine-kilogram shells buzzed upward, and the sky above the city lit up with coloured bursts of explosions. The roar of hundreds of guns shook the streets and neighbourhoods. Lev Mardariev, who lived in the Sormovsky district, recalled: 'A hundred metres from our house there was an anti-aircraft battery. The roar of the shooting was such that the whole house shook like an earthquake.'

Anna Mitina, an anti-aircraft gunner who served in the city of Gorky air defence.

Then shrapnel rained down on the roofs of houses and barracks. Anti-aircraft gunner Pelageya Parshina remembered:

> The first shot of the gun stunned me, but it was necessary, at all costs, to continue shooting. When the gun was fired, it literally jumped up and down, raining down on us a hail of fragments of exploded shells. The shards were sharp and red hot. Many were later injured, some even had their hands torn off.

The first Luftwaffe aircraft over Gorky were pathfinders from I./KG 100, which carried MK.250 containers with white photoflash bombs. To hide the main objective of the attack, the Germans dropped them simultaneously over several areas of the city and over the bridge across the Oka River. Descending smoothly on parachutes, the flaming rockets lit up the area like chandeliers suspended in the sky. Anatoly Korovin, a worker at artillery factory No. 92, recalled: 'These chandeliers shone so brightly that it was as bright as day everywhere in the city.' At the same time, the bombers dropped a huge number of 'incendiary leaves'– pieces of thick foil, smeared with phosphorus. Like fallen leaves burning in the night, they slowly descended on the city, creating a terrifying representation of light.

The first group of Ju 88 A dive bombers attacked the water abstraction intake station and the main nodes of the water supply network of the Avtozavodsky district in Gorky. The first powerful explosions thundered, throwing bright flames into the sky. As a result, the main water conduit with a diameter of 600mm was destroyed in six places, moreover, the explosions tore craters up to 25m long. A direct hit of a heavy high-explosive bomb at the intersection of Molotov Avenue (now Oktyabrskaya Avenue) and Oktyabrskaya Street destroyed the water supply and heating control unit. Hits on the Avtozavodsky thermal power plant, which was on the site of the Molotov automobile plant, put out the boilers, which led to an immediate stop of the plant's turbo generators. At the same time, the substation that supplied power from the city's power grid failed. Thus, the Molotov plant had no power or water.[16]

Meanwhile, new groups of Ju 88 and He 111 were approaching the city, which in addition to high-explosive and fragmentation bombs, carried heavy incendiary bombs filled with a mixture of petrol, rubber and phosphorus. The KG 55 'Greif' pilots later recalled that the target was well lit by signal rockets. Additional lighting created multicoloured fireworks from the fire of anti-aircraft artillery of all calibres and a dense grid of searchlights. When approaching the city the first attacking waves of aircraft found the target was clearly recognisable. While above the target, the squadron commanders gave the necessary instructions to ensure the success of the attack all their crews.[17] Sectors of the Molotov plant were divided between the Staffel, each navigator holding a photograph of the object to be destroyed. Seeing the brightly lit 'chandeliers'of the production shops, the bombers began to strike their targets. The main blow was inflicted on the blacksmith, foundry and mechanical assembly buildings. The massive explosions rattled the floors, sent production equipment flying into the air and brought down multi-ton cranes. The combustible mixture set fire to the roofs and spread over the walls, melting metal beams and igniting everything in its path.

J. Wolfersberger from 5./KG 27 reported:

> We are still 50km from the target, anti-aircraft guns are already active, as well as there are enough searchlights. In the air hung one lighting bomb, then another, and the first bursts of bomb bursts below. The anti-aircraft gunners are nervous, they still don't know which factory we're attacking. Bombs fall at short intervals, followed by several strong explosions followed by fires. So, our goal is before us. Ahead a wide ribbon of the Volga clearly stands out... Now 22.38. One of the aircraft already reports: 'To everyone, the radio operators, lighting bombs hanging south of the plant, in the middle of the target fire.' The radio operator of the next plane reports the approach to the target and again below the flash. Anti-aircraft guns send us a lot of unpleasant greetings.[18]

After hitting a large number of high-explosive and incendiary bombs, a terrible fire engulfed the mechanical assembly building No. 1, which contained the main assembly line, engine shop No. 2, thermal shop and chassis shop. The housing was a seven-span building with an area of 66,500sqm, in two spans of which were mounted overhead cranes. The structure was made in the form of a metal Fachwerk[19] with cinder-concrete stones filling the walls and with metal trusses.The frames of the outer walls and light apertures were also made of iron. The roof consisted of precast concrete roof slabs with slag insulation, covered with roofing material. Because of the extreme temperature, the upper girders of the trusses and the bases of the light apertures began to melt, the compressed elements lost their

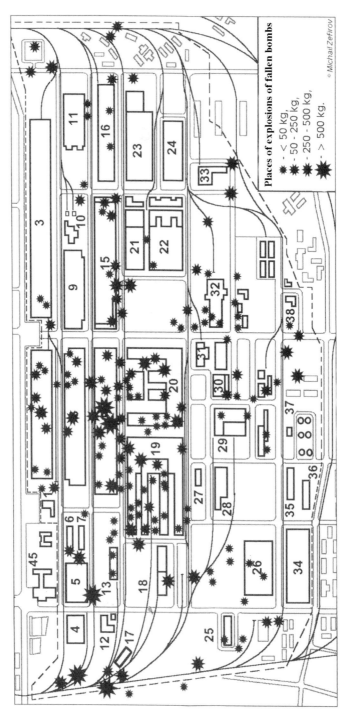

Scheme of registered bomb hits in the Gorky automobile plant 'Molotov' on the night of June 4 to 5. (Author Mikhail Zefirov).

stability, and as a result, a number of sections of the building completely collapsed. The burning oil-soaked floor and reserves of technological oil heated the lower part of the columns to the point where they lost stability and settled, dragging down the metal roof structures. In areas where the temperature from the fire was less, parts of the upper column lost stability without collapsing, but with significant deformation and subsidence.[20] The workers trapped in this hell had no chance of survival.

In the nearby foundry building No.1, blast furnaces exploded as a result of direct bomb hits, and a huge, almost kilometre-high column of fire rose into the sky. Wolfersberger saw this terrifying sight from the cockpit of his bomber: 'Explosions are visible below, the bombs lay down very well, and now – what was it? A powerful explosion raises a huge column of fire over the plant. Meanwhile, other bombers are coming up and also dropping their cargo.'

A few seconds later, his plane passed over the plant and sent eight 250kg incendiary bombs rushing down with a howl: 'Now the gaps follow one after another, and these bombs also fall exactly on target. Tomorrow, the long-range scout will determine exactly what we destroyed.'

The ghost of the 'Condor'

Meanwhile, the Russians were desperately trying to counteract the raid. However, their efforts were ineffective because of the chronic problems mentioned in the previous chapter. In addition, when trying to repel the raid, other serious shortcomings of the Russian air defence were revealed. The anti-aircraft artillery regiments defending the city lacked operational fire control. The commander of the 742nd ZenAP, Lieutenant Colonel Yevgenov; the commander of the 784th ZenAP, Lieutenant Colonel Biryukov; and the commander of the 1291th ZenAP, Major Zuger, were not at their command posts, but on observation towers. They saw only what was happening above their heads, and did not have time to respond to the rapid change in the situation. Besides, their teams came to the batteries late and were no longer in touch with the true situation. Communication with the gun batteries was conducted by telephone, while radio communication was practically unused. In the course of the bombardment, the wires in many places were cut off, and then communication ceased altogether.[21] There was no interaction of the anti-aircraft artillery with searchlights. The latter barely lit twelve aircraft, but none of them were fired at by artillery. Therefore, the anti-aircraft gunners conducted only a chaotic barrage on the intended course and altitude of the bombers, and not over the target where the bombers were more concentrated.

The available gun-aiming stations (SON) were used inefficiently, due to the lack of practical skills in such shooting. Anti-aircraft gunner Pelageya Parshina recalled: 'The Command constantly taught us that it is not necessary to shoot down a bomber going over the city, it is necessary to drive it away, don't let him drop the bombs.' Thus, ordinary gunners were taught that barrage fire was the most effective means of air defence. It was also discovered that the work of the radar station RUS-2s in the Sejm was 'interfered' with by the high right bank of the Oka River.[22]

The Russian night fighters were also doing badly. The commander of the 142nd Aviation Division, Colonel Ivanov, was heavily drunk during the air attack, as usual, and his deputy, Colonel Kovrigin, had to take command. Only twelve night fighters were scrambled and distributed in their 'patrol zones'.

At 23.40, Captain Shilov's La-5 also took off. According to the pilot, patrolling west of Gorky at an altitude of 2,700m, he noticed in the bright part of the sky the silhouette of a bomber, going to the target, which was identified as an Fw 200 Condor! Shilov closed with the enemy and on a counter-course opened fire from a distance of 200m. The 'Condor' ghost turned to the left and began to move away. Shilov described further events in his report:

> Once behind the tail of the bomber, I made a second attack on the left, below, giving a long burst from a distance of 30–50m. At this time, the gunner-radio operator of the bomber opened chaotic fire. After the second attack on the enemy bomber there was engine smoke and flames appeared. He began to leave at high speed.

Continuing the pursuit, Shilov, according to him, made four more attacks. On the sixth attempt his La-5's guns jammed, and the pilot decided to ram his adversary, but he was obviously unlucky that night. As he approached the bomber near the village of Volodary his fighter was caught by searchlights and, blinded by them, Shilov lost visual contact with his quarry.

Meanwhile, the last groups of German bombers were approaching Gorky. Their crews had already seen dozens of kilometres of extended fires on the left bank of the Oka, indicating the location of the target. According to the recollections of the pilots, a huge flaming cloud rose above the ground after the explosions. The smoke from these major fires obscured the view of the last planes involved in the raid, thus they no longer had the opportunity to identify their individual targets.[23] Therefore, these planes dropped bombs on the residential sector of the Avtozavodsky district and adjacent facilities. As a result, houses No. 1 and 3 on Molotov Avenue (hospital No.1), three houses each on Zhdanov Street and Komsomolskaya Street, and four houses in Motor Lane were destroyed.[24] An SC250 bomb hit bathhouse No.1 on Molotov Avenue, broke through the roof and exploded in the basement. As a result, the walls collapsed and deformed the foundations, causing the failure of concrete floors and columns. In the interior many beams had been broken, and the remaining floors and walls had cracked in many places.

In the American settlement[25] the industrial ventilation unit was partially destroyed, and the repair base of the regional military commissariat burned down. In the area of a dairy farm, bomb blasts destroyed tram lines, severed wires, knocked down two poles, and destroyed the local barracks No.7. In Novo-Zapadny settlement, eight residential barracks completely or partially collapsed. In the village of Strigino three houses burned down. However, the worst affected village was Gnilitsy, 7km south-west of the Molotov plant. Whole blocks of small individual houses were destroyed there. In total, in the vicinity of the plant, German bombers destroyed fifty-seven houses and barracks. Given the high population density, this meant that hundreds of workers were left homeless.

In the Molotov complex, workshops 3-A, 3-C and 22 at the aircraft engine plant number No. 466 were damaged by high-explosive bombs dropped by Ju 88 A-4s of 5./KG 51. Twenty-four high-explosive and four heavy incendiary bombs, as well as one BM1000 mine, were dropped on Leninsky district (near Gorky's Avtozavodsky district). By a lucky chance, no production facilities were damaged. Several incendiary bombs fell on the factory of aviation radiators, No. 469 'Gromov',[26] but fires occurred only outside the workshops and were extinguished.

A total of 224 tons of bombs of all calibres were dropped on Gorky and surrounding areas on the night of 4/5 June. At the same time, the Russian rescue service (MPVO) recorded the fall of 433 high-explosive and 306 heavy incendiary bombs, including about 500 hits on the Molotov plant and its residential settlements. In addition, the Germans dropped twenty-five high-explosive bombs weighing from 50 to 500kg at the Kudma station of the Kazan railway, located to the south of the city.[27]

But the Luftwaffe did not have everything exactly according to plan, in particular, not all the crews were able to reach the target. During the long flight, nineteen bombers lost their way for various reasons and were forced to drop their deadly cargo wherever there was an opportunity. As a result, only 149 planes directly bombed Gorky. At the same time, some of the bombers attacked the secondary target. For example, He 111 H '1G+ML' from I./KG 27, which took off at 20.15 from Orel, raided the city of Stalinogorsk (now Novomoskovsk).

After their successful attack, the German crews had a long flight home. Since it soon became very cold when flying at 4,000m, most of the aircraft, after leaving the zone of anti-aircraft fire, dropped to 3,000m or lower. The pilots took off their oxygen masks and could relax. It was not long after midnight when the sky in the east began to lighten. Now the crew members who were free from tasks could read a newspaper or smoke a cigarette, relieving the tension.

This relaxation was associated with a serious risk as some planes flew through floodlit fields in the Moscow region. Four bombers were illuminated by searchlights, and one was unsuccessfully attacked by a night fighter. Anti-aircraft artillery, located south-east and south of Moscow, again led a powerful barrage. That night, the air defence of the capital expended more than 6,000 shells, while another 4,500 pieces were shot by anti-aircraft artillery divisions located south of Moscow. However, all this activity was completely useless: the Luftwaffe did not suffer any losses on this night.

Between 00.30 and 02.00, Berlin time, German bombers landed one by one at their air bases. For example, He 111 H '1G+FS' of 8./KG 27 landed at Orel at 01.00, having spent 283 minutes in the air. The crew reported bombing from a height of 4,000m, and that over the target were 'marked anti-aircraft fire, searchlights, night fighters'. He 111 H '1G+EL' of 3./KG 27 landed at Orel at 01.50; the duration of the flight was 360 minutes, exactly six hours. He 111 H '1G+DP' of 6./KG 27 landed at 00.45 at Domnino airfield after four hours and forty-five minutes of flight, covering a total distance of 1,550km.[28]

He 111 '6N+EK' of Feldwebel Helmut Abendvoth of I./KG 100, which completed its 357th combat flight, landed at Bryansk airfield at 01.25 after 312 minutes of flight.[29] Bombers from II./KG 51 also returned to the same base. Ju 88 A-4 '9K+PN' of Hans Grotter landed at 00.50. The duration of the flight was 305 minutes.[30]

The He 111 H '1G+NN' in which Wolfersberger was flying was also returning to its base:

> After crossing the front line, the flight mechanic and the radio operator leave their firing points and resume their normal duties. The mechanic has checked that everything is in order in the bomb bay, and monitors the amount of fuel and oil. From time to time, other planes are seen with navigation lights on, which also tend to return to their home airfield. We also turned on the navigation lights and reported that we would land in 12 minutes. The landing lights are already glowing ahead, and we are approaching the airfield at a low altitude. The landing gear is released, and after flying over the edge of the airfield, we land near the first lights indicating the runway. That's it, we're back on earth. Perhaps that's what everyone thinks, while their plane is taxiing to its parking lot and stops.
>
> There's a senior technician waiting for us, who gets the aircraft back at his disposal point. It's a good thing he didn't get any damage from anti-aircraft fire. We get out of the plane and tell our fellow ground personnel about the raid and the results achieved. In our success, their share is significant, if the machine is well prepared. Then we walk slowly to the flight control tower, where cars are waiting for us, where we meet other crews, and a lively exchange of opinions begins about the raid and its success, as well as what everyone saw during the departure.
>
> After landing the last plane, we go to the command post, where we present combat reports to the duty officer. The reports are brief and accurate, reflecting the situation in the war zone. Then food and sleep. At the same time, everyone thanks God for having survived another flight and secretly feels sorry for those who were injured in the raid.
>
> What a cruel thing, if you think about it, a war that often causes internal conflict: the plane soars peacefully in the moonlight under the eye of Almighty God, and how cruelly and inexorably death reaps its harvest when the doors of its bomb bay open and the bombs hit the targets. But we must sleep, tomorrow there will be another raid on Gorky.[31]

Stalin's interrupted sleep

While the German pilots shared their fresh impressions of the raid and lay down to rest, 700km to the north-east the fires they created raged in Gorky. When the city headquarters of MPVO realised the scale of what had happened at the Molotov plant, everything that was at hand was sent there. Forty-four fire trucks, five fire trains and four firefighting task forces arrived to extinguish the fires, an operation led personally by the deputy head of the fire department of the Gorky region, Captain Grachev.

Tackling the fires was hampered by damage to the water supply. The auto-pumps worked from three reservoirs, stretching long sleeve lines, which suffered weak water pressure. At 03.00, due to the heroic efforts of the repairers, the water supply in most areas was partially restored, and three hours later water was supplied to fight all the fires.

Above and below: The destroyed Assembly building (main conveyor).

It took until 07.30 for most of the fires to be contained, but they were still burning in the main mechanical assembly and foundry buildings. Smoke rose in huge columns, and all the residents of the city and the surrounding area knew that something terrible was happening at the plant. Only at 13.00, twelve hours after the air attack, was it possible to localise fires in these areas. Three fire department personnel were seriously injured and three others less seriously.[32]

Finally, the plant's management was able to assess the extent of the damage. The housing mechanical assembly building stood out against the smoking ruins. In the huge building, 80 per cent of the production area was destroyed and burned out. There was solid rubble on an area of 11,400 sqm. It was a mess of collapsed concrete slabs, columns, metal structures deformed by fire, pipelines, remnants of technological equipment and machine parts. Direct hits caused significant damage and destruction to the foundations of building structures, foundations under equipment and underground facilities of workshops. During the fires, the internal storm water sewerage of the workshops, industrial wiring, ventilation, power and lighting wiring, and motors of technical equipment were completely disabled.[33]

Charred rags and fragments of human bodies lay everywhere, and torn arms and legs hung from the remaining equipment. Almost nothing was left of the many workers who had been in their places at the time of the bombing.

The foundry building was also severely damaged. In the grey cast iron factory explosions and fires destroyed the moulding workshop, conveyor number 6, a warehouse of materials for moulding and homes. The malleable iron workshop was completely destroyed. The press-body, armature-radiator, spring and blacksmith workshops suffered badly from fire and explosions. At the GAZ thermal power plant, the fire destroyed the peat supply gallery, the bunker gallery, the ash room, the spare peat supply warehouse, the roof and the distribution devices. By some miracle, the turbine generators and boilers survived, and the station was back in use in a relatively short period of time.

In a nearby carbon dioxide shop, a gas cylinder warehouse was completely destroyed. In the thermal shop No. 2, the fire partially destroyed the roof, equipment and household buildings. In the mechanical assembly shop No. 2, the 6th Department and the conveyor were severely damaged, the roof burned down and collapsed. In mechanical assembly shop No.3, as a result of powerful explosions and fire, twenty machine tools and a water supply were destroyed, while the corner of the building had collapsed.

In places the metal bindings of the walls and light apertures were badly deformed by the burning of the wooden blackout covering.[34]

The chief of staff of the MPVO for Gorky, Major Antropov, summing up the bomb attack, wrote bitterly: 'The raid badly damaged a number of the main shops of the plant GAZ and plant No. 466, which will be reflected in general in the work of Gorky automobile plant 'Molotov'. It will take a long time to restore the destroyed workshops.' Although the director of GAZ, Livshits, in his order for the plant, declared 5 June a 'normal working day', it was clear to everyone that the largest enterprise in the Volga Region had been completely put out of action.

Destroyed chassis workshop.

A locomotive overturned by an explosion wave.

Approximate data received from the MPVO precinct units indicated there were 271 victims of the attack, including sixty-one killed and 210 injured and concussed. Seventeen corpses were not identified. The plant's administration reported 110 victims.[35] However, this total was significantly underestimated for the following reasons:

First, the exact number of people working the night shift remained unknown, and numerous blockages, especially on the main conveyor, did not allow full inspection of the shops.

Secondly, there was almost nothing left of people who had been caught in the epicentre of the explosions, with only fragments of bodies found.

Third, the heads of workshops and sites accounted for the dead irresponsibly, reporting contradictory and hastily compiled data. The Russians had always been more concerned with equipment damage than with human casualties. Therefore, it is no longer possible to determine the exact number of those killed, but the authors estimate the death toll was 200 to 250. Among the dead were the head of the forging machine workshop, Kitaev, the head of the press workshop, Lyshkov, and the deputy head of the stamping workshop No.1, G. Maslennikov.

At dawn on 5 June, the headquarters of the Gorky corps district PVO hastily made a report, which indicated that 'on the night of June 4–5, 1943, from 22.50 to 1.43, the enemy in small groups (2–3 aircraft) and single aircraft in the number of 35–40 bombers of the type He 111, Ju 88 and FockeWulf 'Courier' raided the point of PVO Gorky.'

Chief of staff MPVO Major Antropov prepared his operational summary, in which he wrote that allegedly 'all in, the raid involved up to 45 enemy aircraft such as "Heinkel 111", Ju 88 and FW 200 'Courier', of which about 20 aircraft broke through to the city'.[36] All this 'information' was completely false. The number of bombers was wrongly determined, and the statement about the 'breakthrough' of twenty of them was a typical Soviet attempt to disguise their own helplessness and show the 'effectiveness' of their air defence.

During the repulse of the air attack, the anti-aircraft artillery expended more than 22,000 shells, including 20,115 large-calibre shells and 1,940 small-calibre ones. But the total density of the fire was small. It also turned out that there was intensive fire from batteries around the cities of Kovrov, Dzerzhinsk and Balakhna, although no bombers appeared there. The barrage balloons were also ineffective (the Germans did not even mention them in their reports). Of the twenty-five balloons raised, seven were destroyed, and only five were hanging over the target by the end of the air attack. Air defence units also suffered losses. In the 784th ZenAP, two men were killed and four wounded, while one anti-aircraft artillery fire control device (PUAZO-3) and one 76mm gun of a 1914 model were disabled.[37]

The supposedly powerful air defences of Gorky suffered a complete collapse. Some citizens had decided to take the initiative and make their own arrangements for air defence. The director of machine-tool plant No.113 organised two groups of seven soldiers with rifles from the 1st Security Detachment guarding the enterprise 'for shooting at dropped photoflash bombs'. But it is unlikely that such measures could significantly change the situation.

On the morning of 5 June, Joseph Stalin was still asleep. The Red dictator, who was fond of night feasts with alcohol, usually slept until lunchtime. And no one dared disturb the chief's sleep, except in the most extraordinary cases. That morning such an emergency occurred! Stalin was awakened by the guards, who informed him of a sudden Luftwaffe air attack on Gorky and the destruction of the main Molotov factory. The sleep-deprived dictator was shocked. After that, he personally (a rare case!) wrote the resolution of the State Defence Committee No.3524. Enraged, Stalin immediately ordered the formation of a commission to investigate the causes of the poor performance of the Gorky corps district PVO. The commission consisted of the NKVD chief, General Commissioner of state security (Stalin's chief executioner) Lavrentiy Beria, NKGB chief Vladimir Merkulov, Secretary of the Central Committee of the Bolshevik Party (Central Committee of the CPSU (b)) Alexander Shcherbakov, Chairman

Avtozavodsky Street district of the city of Gorky after the bombing. (Drawing of the artist I. I. Permowski).

of the Moscow Council V.P. Pronin and commander of the air defence of the USSR General Mikhail Gromadin.

Deputy People's Commissar of Construction K.M. Sokolov (Deputy Minister), by order of Stalin, on 5 June flew to Gorky to personally lead the development of measures necessary for the restoration of the plant. Arriving at GAZ, Sokolov was amazed to see a picture of large-scale destruction. The mechanical assembly shop and foundry building No.1 were almost destroyed. It was clear that all this could not be restored in a short time.

Chapter 4

Missions on Schedule

'Exceptional hit accuracy'

On the evening of 5 June, the residents of Gorky were again frightened by air alarms. At 18.40 (16.40 Berlin time), two Ju 88 D reconnaissance planes appeared over the city and these recorded the destruction caused during the previous day's raid, at the same time scouting the weather over the target. The appearance of German aircraft was completely unexpected by the air defences, and no fighter was scrambled to intercept. In addition to Gorky, aerial photography was conducted of the nearby city of Dzerzhinsk from a height of 6,000m. Scouts photographed Chernorechensk chemical plant (in the German classification goal number 6226) and Igumnovskaya heat and power plant.

Two hours later, the scouts returned to their bases. After developing the film, photos were quickly printed, and the Luftwaffe commanders were able to see the results of their attack. The images showed that the entire central part of the GAZ was severely damaged.

Taking this data into account, in the second air attack it was decided to strike at the western sector of the area, in which there were various auxiliary workshops and constructions. Weather data showed clear, cloudless skies over Gorky, and the conditions for a second raid were ideal. Shortly before 20.00 (Berlin time) the bombers' engines again roared at Orel, Bryansk and Seshchinskaya air bases, and the heavily loaded aircraft began to taxi one after another to take off. He 111 H '1G+EL' of 3./KG 27 took off from Orel airfield at 19.50, He 111 H '1G+DP' of 6./KG 27 at 20.00, He 111 H '1G+FS' of 8./KG 27 at 20.13 and so on. He 111 H '6N+EK' flown by Helmuth Abendvoth of I./KG 100 took off from Bryansk at 20.30.[1]

A total of 150 aircraft took part in the second massive air attack on Gorky, although twenty-two of them attacked other important targets. For example, He 111 H '1G+ML' of 3./KG 27, taking off at 19.50 from Orel, carried out a second raid on Stalinogorsk. There were also attacks on Tula, Ryazan and Chern.

The main armada of 128 bombers flew further east. Some of them again followed the course close to Moscow on the route Kaluga–Serpukhov–Kashira–Kolomna–Shatura and then along the Oka. P. Mobius of KG 27 'Boelcke' recalled:

> The nights were bright and cloudless, and there was also the Northern lights. Sometimes, too, the lights of St Elmo danced on the wings. Therefore, navigation was not difficult, especially given the long flights over enemy territory and the expected strong air defence.[2]

Groups of three or five bombers flew at an altitude of 4,000–6,000m. The main formation flew over Kulebaki and Pavlovo, the rest going via Arzamas, using as reference points the Oka River and the railway. When approaching the object of their attack, the planes descended without breaking the formation.

By nightfall in Gorky it was cold again, up to 13°c. The wind stopped and there was complete calm. After 22.00 local time the central post of VNOS in Moscow again received a message about the approach of a large group of enemy bombers. The 'air alert' signal was given at 23.36. For eight minutes the hooters of factories and factories filled the air with the tense expectation of a new raid. At 23.40, an air alert was announced at GAZ.

About midnight, about 200 photoflash bombs flashed in the sky above the city, and the whole vast industrial area was again as visible as in daytime. After that, anti-aircraft batteries opened fire, adding to the fireworks of multicoloured bursts of shells. The main blow was again to the Molotov plant. Thousands of small incendiary bombs and incendiary pieces of foil fell down in a fiery rain, followed by heavy FLAM C250 bombs, filled with a mixture of oil and petrol. When this fell, a charge of TNT was detonated and the flammable liquid sprayed out, setting fire to everything around within a radius of 50m.

Director Livshits sent all seven serviceable auto pumps that were available at the plant to fight the fires, but the flames soon engulfed many objects and flared up more and more. The tongues of fire rising high in the sky illuminated the factory grounds for kilometres around. Meanwhile, new waves of bombers were approaching from the south-west.

Vladislav Guryev (during the war he was a teenager, his father worked at the Avtozavodskoj heat and power plant), watched what was happening from the high right bank of the Oka. He later recalled:

> We clearly saw German bombers flying over the Oka River. They went in groups of twenty planes, four in a row. It seemed that, using as a reference point the water tower located directly opposite the plant, they sharply turned 90 degrees and calmly, as if on exercises, bombed shops. And it was clear that each plane was heading for a specific building of the plant. Some bombers descended heavily, dived, and even turned on their headlights. All this was accompanied by a loud whistle, which rang in the ears. It was clearly visible how the bombs were separated from the planes. After the bombing, the planes abruptly gained altitude and disappeared into the darkness, and only at this moment the anti-aircraft guns began to shoot.

After the first attack of the dive bomber Ju 88 As, the water supply system was again damaged by direct hits in several places, and there was nothing to extinguish the fires again. Again, the main power line was put out of operation, forty-five insulators of an open substation were broken, and the back-up electric line through the Krasnaya Etna plant was cut off.

While the phone service was running, Livshits kept calling MPVO's city headquarters and demanding that fire trucks be sent. The chief of the fire service in the city of Vsevolod Vozyakov promised twenty-five fire cars and five fire trains, but for some reason these were slow to reach the scene, and the fire continued to spread.

The largest fire occurred in the main logistics warehouse. It was a five-span four-storey building with an area of 2,600sqm with a mushroom-shaped roof. The main structure was made of reinforced concrete, the walls of cinder-concrete stones. The vulnerable point was the roof, covered with bitumen, and windows with wooden frames. As a result of a direct hit by heavy incendiary bombs, there was a strong fire on the top floors. The warehouses were filled of a large number of combustible materials (rubber, cables, motors, batteries, etc.), and after these caught fire the reinforced concrete structures on the third and fourth floors were destroyed and severely deformed. On the lower floors these were cracked and splintered. The crossbars of the crane span, crane tracks and consoles, 152 reinforced concrete columns and the first and second floors were completely destroyed.

The roof and internal partitions were completely burned down. The heating system, internal air duct, power grid, fecal and storm water sewerage were put into disrepair.[3]

In addition, the assembly workshop, garage truck tractors, woodwork workshop, canteen, warehouse, blacksmith shop No. 2, locomotive depot, blacksmith and mechanical workshops, a woodworking plant, and all the warehouses of materials of the Strogaz No. 2 construction company were incinerated. The malleable iron foundry, blacksmith shop, model shop, repair and mechanical shop, mechanical assembly (tank) shop No. 5 and other objects were severely damaged. On the main conveyor, as a result of the second bombing, all the previously surviving equipment was burned down. It was possible to extinguish fires in a timely manner only in the tool-stamping unit and in the dilapidated spring workshop. GAZ's auxiliary facilities were also severely damaged by high-explosive bombs and fires: the hospital No. 7 was burned down, the yeast shop and flour warehouse were destroyed in the bakery, along with the factory kitchen, dining room and confectionery shop. The roof of boiler room No. 3 was burned and equipment was damaged.[4]

The last group of bombers could not aim accurately because of the vast columns of smoke and flames and dropped their bombs on the residential sector. As a result, house No. 37 Komsomolskaya Street burned down near the earth bomb shelter in which the residents were hiding. In Deputatsky Lane house No.11 was destroyed by fire. In the village of Gnilitsy fire completely destroyed house No.16 in Poljarnaja Street. In the Novo-Zapadny settlement, barracks No. 26 was burned down, while barracks No. 27 and No. 28 were destroyed by high-explosive bombs. Three more barracks burned down in the neighbouring Staro-Zapadnyj village. Nearby, at the intersection of the Entuziastov highway, the railway track was destroyed. Near barracks No. 6, a high-explosive SC500 bomb went straight into the earth bomb shelter where the residents were hiding. The powerful explosion tore people to pieces, scattering the remains over a radius of 100m. In total, thirty-five people died here. Nearby on Molotov Avenue, near house No. 7, another earth bomb shelter was filled up. The people hiding there were left shocked but alive. Neighbouring house No. 3 partially collapsed. In addition, three barracks of the Stroygaz No.2 construction company burned down.

The village of Monastyrka, south-west of the Molotov plant, was particularly heavily bombed. Powerful explosions brought down houses, shattered fences and sheds, and sent logs and burning planks flying through the air. A shower of incendiary bombs caused numerous fires that quickly engulfed entire streets. The inhabitants were terrified, holed up in the earth

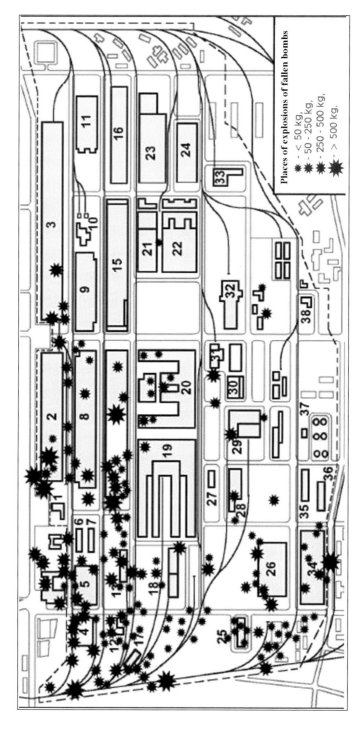

Scheme of registered bomb hits in the Gorky automobile plant 'Molotov' on the night of June 5 to 6. (Author Mikhail Zefirov)

bomb shelter and cellars, and prayed endlessly that another bomb would not fall on them. Even after the raid was over, most people did not dare to go outside, and many were completely numb. It was only at daybreak that the men began to creep out of their hiding places, and then a terrible sight met their eyes. The whole village was a pile of smoking ruins, the ground everywhere was pitted with craters and scattered with burned skeletons of trees. Incinerated corpses lay in terrible poses, some crouched. In total, seventy houses and barracks were destroyed, and the surviving buildings were severely damaged. The old stone church was almost buried by an explosion.

The Russian rescue service MPVO recorded the fall of about 200 high-explosive bombs on the Avtozavodsky district, including ten of 1,000kg, forty of 500kg, 100 of 250kg and about forty of 50–70kg.

Other parts of Gorky were also bombed, including thirty-two high-explosive bombs dropped on Leninsky district. Powerful explosions thundered in the villages of Karpovka and Instrumental'nyi, and at the bath No. 2, near the Krasnyj Kozhevennik plant. The stable of the machine-tool factory was partially destroyed, with a groom and two horses injured and one horse killed. The blast blew out windows at the plant and in the residential sector. One plane, possibly due to an error by the navigator, dropped bombs on the Kirov district, far from the industrial zone. One SC500 bomb exploded near the tram stop of the 2nd tool factory, while nine SC50s fell in a forest near the village of Gvozdilny. A heavy incendiary bomb fell on Igarskaya Street but there were no fires.

In an attempt to repel an air attack, anti-aircraft artillery fired an intense barrage for two hours, expending 28,000 rounds. Searchlights were able to illuminate five aircraft and keep them in their beams from thirty seconds to three minutes. At the same time, the gunners claimed one downed bomber. The Soviets night fighters were active, making thirty-one sorties. Pilots of the 142nd IAD reported four meetings with the enemy and two air battles. Lieutenant Lyunkov of the 632nd IAP, on his return to the airfield, said he shot down a He 111 near the village of Sosnovka, Vyksunsky district.[5]

According to German data, during the second massive air attack on the 'tank factory' in Gorky, one plane went missing: He 111 H-16 '1G+AH' of 3./KG 27 with crew: pilot Feldwebel Werner Bukan, navigator Unteroffizier Fridrich Tuhscherer, radio operator Feldwebel Johannes Neumann, flight mechanic Feldwebel Karl Bendert and side gunner Gefreiter Walter Elsner.

This time the Soviets said that out of eighty aircraft sent to attack the city, they allegedly 'broke twenty to twenty-five', while the rest 'were not allowed' by anti-aircraft artillery fire. All this, as usual, was not true. The air defence units of Gorky also suffered losses, with four people killed and seven injured, including two officers. The headquarters building and the garage of the 8th Barrage Balloon Division were burned down.

Meanwhile, at dawn on 6 June, the German bombers returned one by one to their airfields. On the way back, some planes again flew near Moscow, with one Ju 88 A flying near Noginsk, Reutov, almost being over the capital, but it then turned towards Lublino-Semyonovsk and followed the Kiev highway to the south-west. Moscow anti-aircraft artillery regiments conducted a frenzied barrage, expending 5,704 shells. Some 421 balloons were raised over Moscow.

He 111 H '1G+FS' of 8./KG 27 landed at Orel at 01.00, Berlin time, having spent 287 minutes in the air. He 111 H '1G+EL' of 3./KG 27 landed at 00.50 at Optuha after 300 minutes. He 111 H '1G+DP' of 6./KG 27 landed at 00.55 at Domnino, having spent four hours and fifty-five minutes in the air and covering 1,570km.[6] Feldwebel Helmut Abendvoth in He 111 H '6N+EK' had been a pathfinder and landed at Bryansk at 01.10. According to his Fliegerbuch, the duration of the flight was 280 minutes, and his time over the target was marked by heavy anti-aircraft fire.[7]

In total, 179 tons of bombs of all calibres were dropped on Gorky within an hour and a half. The Russian MPVO service recorded the fall of about 230 high-explosive[8] and several thousand different incendiary bombs on the city. According to official data, about 100 people were killed and the same number were injured. Clinics and hospitals received thirty-three seriously injured people, thirty-four with moderate injuries and twenty-six lightly wounded. The bodies of thirty-two dead workers were found at the Molotov plant in the morning. The bodies of many others were not found and they became 'missing'.[9]

Various local air defence units were involved in the aftermath of the bombing. A medical platoon of thirty-three people worked at various sites until 9am, providing assistance to thirty-one wounded and removing thirty-six corpses. Three ambulance squads and two medical sanitary squads worked in the Avtozavodsky district. An emergency recovery platoon of twenty-nine people participated in the excavation and extraction of victims from the blocked earth bomb shelters, and then transferred to dismantling the rubble, which continued all the next day. Military units reconnoitered the hotbeds of destruction and established the places where unexploded

BA-64 armoured car hulls in the destroyed shop.

Logistics warehouse related parts. In the foreground, a burned-out Ford truck.

bombs fell. In addition, the soldiers helped to remove the corpses from the earth bomb shelter of barracks No. 7 in Severnyj village. Two thousand soldiers from various rear units also took part in the clean-up operation.

At 02.00, due to a cable breakage, the connection between the Stalinist and Sotsgorodsky automatic telephone stations (ATS) was broken. To repair the damage, a team was sent out, which was able to partially repair the damage within an hour by making a temporary direct link of the city's command post with the Avtozavodsky MPVO command post. Communication between the ATS was restored only by 16.00. Emergency recovery teams of utility workers (plumbers and auxiliary workers) repaired the water mains.[10]

In the morning, the GAZ director, Alexey Livshits, wrote a report to the chairman of the city defence committee (the chief of the local office of the Bolshevik Party – the head of the region) Mikhail Rodionov, in which he outlined the terrible details of the raid:

> I inform you of the second enemy raid on the automobile plant 'Molotov' on the night of June 5 to 6…
>
> 1. The bombing lasted up to 2 hours (1.30) with exceptional accuracy. Planes were approaching the object, descending, diving and dropping bombs.

2. As a result of high-explosive, incendiary and combined bombs hitting several workshops, there were pockets of fires that spread and completely destroyed several auxiliary and production facilities.

3. Water in the water supply network of the plant was constant, but due to the fact that the route of the water supply network was damaged by direct hits in several places, the pressure in the network was lowered. There were only 7 auto pumps at the factory before the arrival of a large number from Gorky,

4. At the beginning of the alarm, 25 fire trucks and 5 fire trains were promised to the plant. These machines did not arrive at the plant during the bombing and the occurrence of fires, despite repeated requests and demands of the plant. The vehicles did not begin to arrive until after the end of the bombing, when the fires reached a very large force and a significant part of the buildings was already burning.

5. As a result of bombing and fires at the plant the following burned down: a workshop for the manufacture of engines, logistics warehouse related parts, rubber warehouse, tractor garage, canteen number 4, the main conveyor, locomotive depot, chassis shop, experimental workshop. The fire in 6 production rooms was promptly extinguished.

According to preliminary data, 60 bombs were dropped directly into the buildings of the workshops, and 100 bombs were dropped on the territory of the plant, not including the territory of adjacent residential settlements.

I consider it necessary to note the extremely weak air defence of the plant.[11]

'The hand of the clock was approaching midnight…'

At 18.36 (16.36 Berlin time) on 6 June air raid sirens again howled in Gorky. The eyes of the anti-aircraft gunners and the inhabitants of the city were fixed on the sky. Soon, the headquarters of the corps district PVO received a report from observers that three aircraft identified as Heinkel He 111s had appeared over the city at an altitude of 4,000m. Anti-aircraft artillery batteries opened a barrage, residents ran to shelters (the earth bomb shelters and basements), but there was no attack. In fact, over Gorky at an altitude of 7,000m flew three Ju 88 D (two of 1.(F)/100 and one of WeFlugSt 'Schatalowka'). Similar group reconnaissance aircraft missions were sometimes undertaken by the Luftwaffe during important operations over the deep rear. The crews could support each other in the event of a critical situation or an attack by Russian interceptors, and duplication allowed them to guarantee the successful completion of the mission. The Ju 88s flew directly over GAZ, took aerial photos and recorded weather conditions over the target, and then departed in a south-westerly direction.

The Russians raised the alarm by scrambling eighteen fighters from the 142nd Air Division PVO, but after returning to base the pilots said that they had no contact with the target. The scouts seemed to disappear into the vast

Aerial view of the target, taken on the evening of June 6.

blue sky … Note that reconnaissance flights over the target were always conducted at the same time and on a standard route, but the Soviets could not do anything about them. However, the appearance of reconnaissance aircraft showed that it was necessary to prepare for a new attack.

In the evening, work intensified on the German air bases. Technicians were completing the preparation of the aircraft for a long flight, while the pilots studied the photos of the target delivered by long-range scouts. According to the plan, it was now necessary to attack the northern sector of the Molotov plant and the large production buildings located there. Given the extremely weak resistance of the Russian air defence, the tactics, flight route, and even the start time did not change. As per the established schedule, the heavily loaded aircraft began to taxi one after another to the start. After 20.00 (Berlin time), the bombers from KG 27 began to take off. He 111 H '1G+EL' from the 3rd Staffel took off from Orel at 20.08, He 111 H '1G+FS' from the 8th Staffel at 20.17, and He 111 H '1G+DP' from 6./KG 27 at 20.20.[12] He 111 H '6N+EK' of Helmut Abendvoth from I./KG 100 started from Bryansk at 20.30.[13]

In total, 154 bombers from Kampfgeschwader 'Hindenburg', 'Blitz', 'General Wever', 'Boelcke', 'Edelweiss', 'Greif' and 'Wicking' participated in the third massive air attack on Gorky. At the same time, some of the crews again went to bomb secondary targets. For example, planes from 3./KG 27 made the third consecutive raid on Stalinogorsk.

The bombers flew to the target along two main routes: one group via Ryazhsk–Sasovo–Murom–Pavlovo, the second along the railway from Moscow to Gorky at an altitude of 2,000–3,000m. A few bombers flew through Arzamas to give them access to the target from a southern direction. As a result of difficult weather conditions on the entire route, pathfinders dumped signal rockets and in an area east of Yegoryevsk (south-east of Moscow) stragglers and stray planes were collected into groups. Russian air observers recorded these actions and tracked the course of the bombers. Anti-aircraft artillery in the area of Moscow, Serpukhov, Kashira, Kolomna and Shatura fired 1,553 large-calibre projectiles. However, again it was only blind barrage shooting, with no effect.

In the area of the target, the weather again favoured the raid: it was completely calm, and the temperature had dropped to 13° Celsius by night. At 23.55 local time (21.55 Berlin time), General Alexey Osipov ordered an air alert. The signal was received by all districts of the city and duplicated by means of notification within eight minutes. There was tension in the headquarters of PVO, with VNOS posts reporting large numbers of aircraft approaching. Summing up this data, the Russians realised that at least 150 bombers were approaching Gorky. Osipov and his staff prepared for the worst…

After midnight in the sky over the Molotov plant the photo flash bombs 'chandeliers' flashed again. It was clear that the main target of the attack would again be GAZ. The planes were coming at the target from three directions: the north, west, and south. The first to strike were the diving Ju 88 A bombers, then the He 111s joined them to drop their deadly cargo horizontally.

P. Mobius of 9./KG 27 recalled:

> We carried out these strategic raids in loose combat order as long as it seemed appropriate. Of course, the crews were forbidden to talk to each other. The minimum height when crossing the front line was set at 5,000 metres. Immediately after crossing the front line, we descended and continued to fly at 3,000 metres. We kept this height even during the bombing, because we were terribly cold even at this height due to insufficient heating. The target was Gorky, easy to spot thanks to the bright flashes of exploding bombs and fires. Clouds of anti-aircraft shell bursts appeared all around, and you could often see tracer bursts from the aircrafts' onboard weapons. We also felt the turbulence that could come from our other planes or night fighters.[14]

This time, as planned the main blow was dealt to the mechanical, press and tool workshops located in the northern part of GAZ. There was heavy bombing of workshops where tools were produced and parts were stamped. Inside the building, twelve high-explosive bombs exploded, including one of large calibre. Three more bombs hit the floor but did not detonate. In the cutting shop and the central test station, equipment was severely damaged, and 100 sq m of roof collapsed. In stamp workshops No. 2 and No. 3, a whole span of the roof collapsed. On the south side of the building, a transformer box was destroyed by a direct hit. Ten more heavy high-explosive bombs, including three large-calibre ones, fell on the street near the tool-stamping building. The explosion of several tons of amatol and TNT shifted the foundations, removed masonry and in places collapsed entire sections of the walls. Many load-bearing structures were severely deformed. Ten people were killed, two were seriously injured and three were slightly hurt.

Above: Fire crews of the city of Gorky. Demonstration of combat readiness.

Right: Chief of the fire service of the city of Gorky in 1943 Colonel Vsevolod Vozyakov.

**КОМСОМОЛЬЦЫ!
СОВЕТСКАЯ МОЛОДЕЖЬ!**

Следите за исправностью
противопожарного инвентаря,
ЗА ЕГО
ПОСТОЯННОЙ БОЕВОЙ ГОТОВНОСТЬЮ !

МЦ13390. Типография Автозавода, з. 2005, т. 5000

A leaflet encouraging young people to monitor fire-fighting equipment. (History Museum of Russian car-producer GAZ)

Severe damage was caused to the car bodies pressing workshop, with one of the walls collapsing and the roof and wooden partitions burning. Five high-explosive bombs, including two large-calibre ones, were dropped on assembly shop No. 5, where T-70 tanks were being assembled. Powerful explosions completely destroyed sections of the workshop and household buildings, but by some miracle part of the main equipment survived. Five heavy high-explosive and ten incendiary bombs fell on the shop that produced tank hulls and the building partially collapsed and the roof, household premises and part of the equipment was burned. Five people were injured here and one burned alive. In the central assembly building, the roof of the silencer assembly section was destroyed and four machine tools were damaged. In the spare parts workshop, the main warehouse and part of the household premises were destroyed. Around the Novokuzovnoj building thundered a series of powerful explosions, which deformed the walls, caused part of the ceiling to collapse and broke all the windows. Explosions and fires partially destroyed a repair and mechanical workshop. In motor workshops No. 2 and 3 there was a strong fire in the department for heat-treating metal that partially destroying the roof and equipment.

Several heavy high-explosive bombs hit the railway workshop, razing the entire building to the ground. At the same time, two fire trucks were destroyed and the entire combat crew of one of the fire engines was killed.

The most terrible fate befell the wheel workshop, also located in the northern sector of the huge plant. The building was a five-span building with an area of over 23,000sqm. The columns and crane beams were reinforced concrete, and the walls were made of cinder-block stones. The vulnerable point of the shop was the roof rafters, which were made of wooden trusses, and the roof covering made of bitumen. In addition, the outer walls and light openings were covered with wooden boards.

During the raid, for the first time the Germans used flammable liquid poured out of special devices installed on the Ju 88 bombers. Several planes at low altitude flew over the northern sector of the plant and dropped this liquid. Even residents of the Sormovsky district, who were 13–15km from GAZ, saw how huge fire jets cut through the night sky and fell on the factory buildings. Most of this 'napalm' hit the wheel workshop building. As a result, almost the entire roof burst into flames at the same time. Then the following groups of German planes dropped high-explosive and heavy incendiary bombs on the wheel workshop. There were several dozen fires that could not be extinguished. First the fire engulfed the wooden structures, then the whole building became ablaze. Due to the enormous temperature, reinforced concrete structures, columns, crane beams and crane tracks began to crack and crumble, metal cranes melted and bent, and even machine tools burned. Molten roofing material flowed down the walls and pipes, filling the storm drain.[15]

The strongest fires engulfed other machinery. Engine workshop No. 1 was doused with a combustible mixture, then the building was hit by an SC500 bomb and several incendiary bombs. As a result, a large fire broke out, destroying part of the roof and all the wooden structures of the mezzanine floors. A powerful explosion occurred in the hall of the design and experimental Department (KEO), which partially collapsed the walls and burned some of the drawings.

Some objects were saved. Three incendiary bombs hit the central factory laboratory, but the fire was tackled by groups of MPVO. There was a successful fight against the fire in the garage, where only household premises were destroyed. A fire in the personnel department building was eliminated by Red Army units. In the model shop there were three powerful explosions, then there was a fire, but the soldiers of the MPVO units managed to stop it spreading. Later, two unexploded high-explosive bombs were found in the ground near the workshop. The fire that engulfed the woodworking shop was also quickly extinguished.

However, attempts to fight the fire proved to be less successful elsewhere. The workshop that made fasteners for cars was burnt down, as was the Gazsnab canteen, cutting tool workshop, new entrance hall, warehouse of MPVO property, factory telephone exchange (ATS No. 2), engine workshop No. 2, press workshop, and the workshop for malleable and grey cast iron.

In total, according to the MPVO service, 170 high-explosive bombs weighing from 50 to 2,000kg were dropped on the Molotov plant, with German pilots achieving about ninety direct hits on the factory buildings. Aircraft engine plant No. 466, located on GAZ territory, received minor damage. Five SC250 high-explosive bombs fell and did not explode near the foundry building, and only one 50kg bomb hit shop No. 24. The explosion partially destroyed the building and caused a fire, which was eliminated by MPVO fighters.

The residential sector was also heavily bombed. In the village of Sotsgorod, direct bomb hits destroyed the buildings of the ATS, the district polyclinic, and the district Executive Committee (municipality). On Molotov Avenue, leading from the plant to the western part of the residential area, a large number of high-explosive and incendiary bombs fell. These partially destroyed house No. 28, partially burned house No. 1 on October Street, burnt down the garage of the regional office of the Bolshevik Party and destroyed the central club and district substation. Houses No. 1 and No. 3 on Kirov Street were almost totally destroyed by direct hits from several high-explosive bombs.

Two 50kg high-explosive bombs fell near the four-storey house No. 16 on Molotov Avenue, which had four entrances. One exploded near the corner next to entrance No. 1, the second in front of entrance No. 3 from the eastern facade. The blast wave completely demolished the roof of the house. The walls were deformed in many places, with cracks and deviations, and there was damaged masonry everywhere. The staircase of the third entrance collapsed completely, while that of the first entrance partially fell down. In most of the house, the floors were deformed, the frames and doors were blown out, all the windows were broken, and half the plaster crumbled.[16]

Nadezhda Nadezhkina, who worked during the war as head of the technical sector of the experimental section of the tool-stamping workshop, recalled:

> At that time I was lying at home with a cast on my leg – I had a fracture. I was not taken to hospital, they were full of wounded. The entire population of Sotsgorod went to the field outside

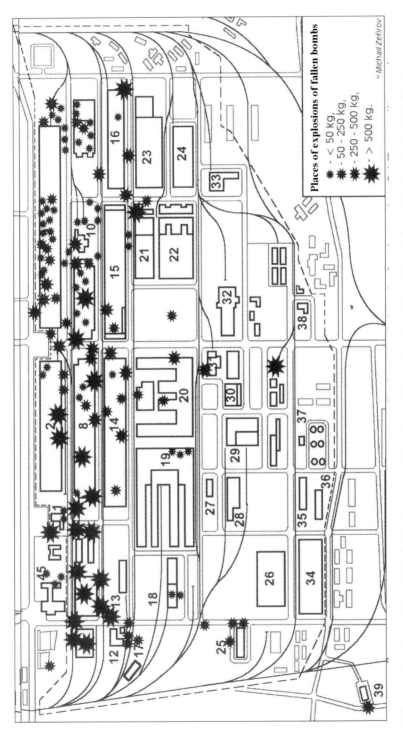

Places of explosions of fallen bombs
- < 50 kg,
- 50 - 250 kg,
- 250 - 500 kg,
- > 500 kg.

©Michail Zefirov

Scheme of registered bomb hits in Gorky automobile plant 'Molotov' on the night of 6 to 7 June. (Author Mikhail Zefirov) the city to avoid death. I was alone on the bed. No one around. The hand of the clock was approaching midnight. There was a nervous tremor and an agonising wait. To calm down, I took a guitar and played. I played and sang as best I could. I chose to sing songs that sounded like internal resistance and protest. If only not to lose heart, not to break down, not to crumble. Exactly at 12 o'clock the raid began. The density of the bombing was incredible. I later calculated that eight bombs had exploded near my house. They left deep craters. Fortunately, not a single bomb hit my house. The closest bomb exploded near one of the walls of the house. The house reeled from the blow, doors and windows flew out, and all the plaster fell off. I clung to the bed and hid my hands under me – better death than being crippled. Exactly at 2 o'clock the bombing ended. Wooden structures and sheds where firewood was stored by residents burned. There was a huge piece of bomb stuck in the wall above my bed, and I was covered in the debris of the destroyed house. The student briefcase with identification papers, which had been prepared just in case on the table, was cut in several places by the window glass, which had been shattered by the blast wave. The next morning my friends took me out of the rubble.[17]

In an American village, four houses were completely or partially destroyed in the bombing. Novo-Severnyj village was also badly hit, with No. 5 Rabochaya Street partially damaged and two barracks in Kommunal'naya Street burned down. Barrack No. 2 was almost smashed to pieces by a direct hit from a high-explosive bomb, and the militia's station building located nearby was half destroyed. In the village of Monastyrka, located south-west of GAZ, thirteen private one-storey houses along with their outbuildings burned down.

Some of the bombs fell on the positions of the 784th ZenAP artillery batteries. On the 13th battery, located at one of the main entrances of the plant, two guns were smashed and two gunner girls serving the gun were killed. Thirty bombs of different calibres fell in the area of the 14th battery. The surrounding area was peatland and high-explosive bombs either did not explode at all when dropped, or they exploded at great depth without causing much damage. The position of the guns of the 15th battery, which was in Avtozavodsky Park, was covered with high-explosive and incendiary bombs. The blast badly damaged the device to control the artillery anti-aircraft fire (PUAZO). Pieces of bombs killed the division's instrument technician, Lieutenant Simonov, and several other soldiers, including the battery's sanitary instructor, Anna Sorokina, were injured. However, the brave girl refused to be hospitalised and remained at the battle post. Close by, a battery of small-calibre anti-aircraft guns was almost destroyed. More than half the personnel were killed, many were injured and burned, and all eight 20 mm guns were disabled. Only one anti-aircraft gunner, Rosa Ionova, was not injured.

Hot and razor-sharp shards from their own shells rained down on the positions of the anti-aircraft guns. For this reason, the gunners had to wear helmets and jackets to avoid being wounded. Gunner Pelageya Parshina recalled: 'Fragments of shells rained down on us. Once my gun was hit by a heavy shard that shattered all devices for aiming the anti-aircraft guns. The question arose as to how to continue firing, to which the commander replied: 'Aim at random!'

Fellow anti-aircraft gunner Isaac Levitsky said: 'Three days of heavy fighting and the elimination of their consequences exhausted the forces of all personnel. It was especially hard for the girls, but they tried to keep up with the men in overcoming the hardships of fighting the enemy.'

After the long barrage of anti-aircraft fire, there was a shortage of ammunition. Commander of anti-aircraft artillery Dolgopolov later recalled: 'It also happened that by the end of the raid one shell remained for each gun.'

During the bombardment, spent shell casings were transported in cars to workshops located near the city. Thanks to the heroic labour of the workers, the casings were filled and the gunners received the shells back to enable them to continue their anti-aircraft fire, albeit ineffective and produced with 'disorganisation and lack of skill'. Often the cars delivered shells to the firing positions of the batteries during the bombing under the bursts of bombs. In this case, the drivers were doing their duty, risking their lives. There were cases when fragments of exploding bombs fell into boxes with shells, which led to the explosion of the latter and the death of the drivers.

At 02:30 local time, just as dawn was beginning to break, the long-awaited 'all clear' signal finally sounded. A total of 242 tons of bombs of all calibres were dropped on Gorky during the third major attack. The MPVO service of the Avtozavodsky district counted 402 high-explosive bombs weighing from 50kg to 2,000kg, of which 132 did not explode. In addition, about sixty heavy incendiary bombs were recorded falling. In addition to the large destruction on the GAZ site and in the adjacent residential sector, the spare Kanavinsky water pipeline was destroyed and the entire area was completely left without a water supply.

According to calculations made the next morning, as a result of the bomb attack in the Avtozavodsky district, 232 people were injured, including seventy-three killed.[18] Of the seriously injured people admitted to hospitals, eight died soon after. Fifty-six people were admitted to hospitals from GAZ, sixty-five from various military units, nineteen from the civilian population and nine from the fire department.

At 02.00, Major General Alexey Osipov signed a report No. 004 drawn up urgently for the commander of the air defence of the Soviet Union, Lieutenant General Mikhail Gromadin, which stated:

> On the night of June 6–7, 1943 from 23.04 until 01.37 the enemy made a group bombing raid on Gorky. The raid was carried out from the south-west and west direction.
>
> Routes:
> Ryazhsk–Sasovo–Arzamas–Gorky
> Ryazan–Murom–Pavlovo–Gorky
> Height 4–6,000m.
>
> In total, about 160 Ju 88 and He 111 aircraft were recorded. The bombing was carried out from a horizontal flight.
>   Main areas: Gorky automobile plant 'Molotov', Sotsgorod and Myza airfield. A large number of high-explosive, incendiary and lighting bombs were dropped.
>   Data is being refined. Communication with GAZ is interrupted. The main part of the bombs dropped on the approaches to the automobile plant 'Molotov', the area of Sotsgorod and its outskirts.

Anti-aircraft artillery fired 25,110 rounds and claimed to have downed four aircraft, three of which fell on the city! Even places where the aircraft fell were named: the Red October plant in Leninsky district, the village of Strigino and the territory of GAZ itself. Another bomber reportedly fell near the village of Derenevo. The searchlights managed to illuminate only two aircraft, one of which was shot down by anti-aircraft guns of the 784th ZenAP. Twenty-seven balloons were deployed to a height of 3,500m and two were lost.

According to German data, that night anti-aircraft artillery fire damaged Ju 88 A-14 Wrk Nr 144440 'V4+9R' of 8./KG 1 'Hindenburg' but it was able to make it to Orel-West airfield and crashed on landing. The bomber's crew was not injured. He 111 H of Feldwebel Hermann of II./KG 4 'General Wever' was hit by an anti-aircraft shell in the right engine over Gorky. As a result, the propeller began to spin spontaneously, greatly complicating the control of the aircraft. The pilots had to open the cockpit window and destroy the propeller blades with a machine gun! After that, the crew threw everything overboard to make the bomber as light as possible. Hermann managed not only to safely reach the frontline, but also to make a normal landing at Orel-West.[19]

Fighters of the 142nd IAD carried out thirty-six sorties and the pilots claimed four air battles and two downed aircraft near the villages of Spasskoye and Kstovo.[20] Captain Malakin in a LaGG-3 fighter patrolled in his zone at an altitude of 4,500m. Then said in his report:

> At 23.09 I saw a series of photoflash bombs being dropped by enemy aircraft over objects. I sent my plane into this zone, trying to get closer to the enemy. I found the silhouette of the Fw 200 'Courier'[Soviet name for Condor] against the background created by the light of the photoflash bombs. Approaching it up to 100 metres, I made the first attack from the front, from the side, opening fire from all types of weapons. Then I made a second attack from below and behind from a distance of 50–30m.

After that, according to Malakin, the 'Fw 200' caught fire and fell towards the ground. But he did not see the plane crash as the fighter was thrown violently to the side at that moment, and for a while it became uncontrollable.[21]Returning to the airfield, the pilot proudly announced his victory. However, the next day, the search for the 'downed Fw 200' did not yield any results.

The Germans later confirmed that they had actually been attacked by night fighters, but all of these were unsuccessful. H. Nowak of 8./KG 27 recalled that his bomber was attacked by a Russian plane in the Gorky area, but the crew noticed the pursuer in time and fired a signal round at him, which forced the fighter to turn away.

In fact, during the third raid, the Luftwaffe lost only one bomber. And neither fighters, nor anti-aircraft guns, apparently, had anything to do with it. One of the pilots 7./KG 27 'Boelcke' recalled: 'During the bombing of the tank factory in Gorky, we saw our plane, who did not observe the prescribed height. Thus, he was hit by a series of bombs dropped from aircraft flying above him and fell down.' It may have been Ju 88 A-14 Wrk Nr 144438 'V4+9R' flown by Leutnant K. Prinz of 7./KG 1 'Hindenburg', which went missing that night.

Meanwhile, the groups of bombers returned to their bases on the already familiar route. The planes were flying at an altitude of about 3,000m, meeting the June dawn. Once again, no one was following them, so the crews could relax after the tense minutes spent over the target. They took off their oxygen masks and stretched out in their seats. Some were reading a newspaper, some were smoking, while others turned the radio knob to catch some songs and music. But not every transmission turned out to be pleasant. One of the pilots of 7./KG 27 recalled: 'When we were looking for some music on the radio on the way back, we found a radio station that reported that KG 27 had killed thousands of innocent people and at the same time ave the name of our commander. It was a delicate matter for us!'

Around 01.00, Berlin time, when the fires were still raging in Gorky, the bombers came in to land. According to Fliegerbuchs, He 111 H '1G+EL' landed at 00.55 at Optuha, having spent 287 minutes in the air. He 111 H '1G+DP' landed at 00.55 at Domnino after flying for four hours thirty-five minutes and covering 1,470 km. He 111 H '1G+FS' landed at 01.06 at Orel 289 minutes after launch.[22] The He 111 of Helmut Abendvoth from I./KG 100 landed in Bryansk at 01.25, having spent 295 minutes in the air, which was five minutes longer than the day before. Heavy anti-aircraft fire was again observed over the target.[23] In fact, the planes flew to Gorky and back on schedule, like passenger liners!

On the night of 7 June, Soviet U-2 light night bombers dropped leaflets on the air base in Orel. They read 'Killers Gorky! We will destroy you!' With these threats, the Soviets warned of a response that followed a few days later.

'We were horrified when we realised who was in front of us'

On the morning of 7 June, the director of GAZ, Alexey Livshits, went to the wheel workshop. He was very worried because it was the only shop in the country that produced car wheels! When his car pulled up to the building, making its way between smoking piles of debris and huge craters, Livshits was so shocked by what he saw that he could not even get out. The beautiful building, built in the form of large arches, was a charred skeleton. The roof had completely collapsed, and inside, through gaping holes, the blackened remains of unique equipment were visible. The fire had completely disabled the industrial wiring, supply and exhaust ventilation pipelines, power and lighting wiring and the engines of the technical equipment workshop.The surviving roof structures were severely deformed and could no longer be repaired. The underground storm sewer was completely filled with bitumen. All the household premises of the workshop had also been burned to the ground. As it turned out, only seventeen of the 323 pieces of equipment survived. Recovering from this spectacle with difficulty, Livshits went to the still surviving head office to call Stalin.

Aerial view of the target, taken on the evening of June 7. The number '4' indicates the destroyed wheel workshop.

Damaged roof of the Novokuzovnoj building.

Destruction inside the Novokuzovnoj building.

During the three raids the Molotov plant had been almost completely destroyed, and the Germans managed to disable almost all the major facilities of the enterprise. The paranoid Stalin and his pathological entourage, of course, did not entertain the idea that it would be futile to restore a completely destroyed enterprise. They were ready for any sacrifice of the people under their control to restore the ashes of the Molotov plant – one of the pillars of the bloody Stalinist regime. It was clear that this rebuilding would require many months of continuous work.

On the morning of 7 June, a commission from Moscow headed by the chief Stalinist executioner, Lavrentiy Beria, arrived at the Moskovskij train station in Gorky in armoured wagons. Its mission was to understand the situation in the city after the attacks. Beria wanted to establish whether there had been treason or sabotage, and determine the measure of personal culpability of all the people responsible for protecting such an important industrial centre from attack.

Beria was not only the chief Stalinist executioner and chief of NKVD, the main punitive service of the Soviets. He was a member of the State Defence Committee (the highest body for governing the country during the war) and was responsible for monitoring the implementation of the decisions of this Committee regarding the production of aircraft, engines, weapons and mortars. Beria controlled the work of the Red Army air force (the formation of aviation regiments, their transfer to the front, etc), and the work of the coal industry and communications (railways, river transport, highways). This sinister bald Georgian in pince-nez, who usually wore a civilian suit, terrified all the citizens of the Soviet Union. The psychopath Beria was very active, energetic and at the same time cruel and prone to debauchery. He often caught young girls on the streets and forced them to become his mistresses. Beria's work was not controlled by anyone, and he could kill any 'enemy of the people' with impunity. The name of Beria was as terrifying to all Russians as that of Stalin!

Soon after his arrival, Beria visited the Gorky regional office of the Bolshevik party and the headquarters of the corps air defence district. According to eyewitnesses, he behaved quite 'democratically': he walked down the corridor and shook hands with everyone he met. Then Beria went to the Molotov plant. Struck by the picture of the large-scale destruction he saw, he called to himself the commander of the air defence, Major General Alexey Osipov, and spat in his face. This action reflected the typical treatment of Beria of his subordinates, but for Osipov, who expected immediate execution, such a 'punishment' was most lenient in this situation!

Late in the afternoon, Stalin's malicious envoy decided to inspect the 784th Anti-aircraft Artillery Regiment, one of the batteries of which was located in Avtozavodsky Park. Former anti-aircraft gunner Anna Sorokina later recalled:

> The personnel of the battery was lined up in a row. We were horrified when we realised who was in front of us! Beria turned to us and said, 'What are you doing?? The automobile plant is the most important industrial object of the country, your regiment is assigned to protect it, but you do not cope with the task. As a result, the automobile plant has already been put out of operation and continues to receive great destruction.'

After that the NKVD chief began to threaten the soldiers with a tribunal and subsequent execution.

But then the unexpected happened. At 18.36 local time, airraid sirens started blaring everywhere, and one of the officers reported that German planes were about to appear over the city. In the distance, the sharp firing of guns was heard. The 'meeting' immediately stopped, and all the attention of those present was focused on the sky. Soon two Ju 88s appeared at an altitude of about 4,000m. Their task was to record the results of the last air attack on GAZ. According to Sorokina's memoirs, on seeing the planes, Beria belligerently pulled out a gun, and his example was followed by the guards, who also took out a weapon. Then, however, the chief's formidable messenger and his retinue hastened to leave the 'field of battle'. Beria and the guards got into the cars and left.

Meanwhile, the command of the 142nd Fighter Air Division scrambled eighteen fighters. The pilots were ordered to intercept and shoot down reconnaissance planes at all costs, so as not to allow them to deliver aerial photos of the target to their bases. The pilots were determined to complete the task, and flew at maximum speed in a south-westerly direction. Some of them were lucky. About 19.00 south of the city of Vladimir (halfway between Gorky and Moscow), several fighters managed to overtake the enemy. According to Russian information, a fierce air battle ensued. Pilot Pavlov opened heavy fire at a Ju 88's cabin, aiming at the rear gunner, then fired several bursts at the fuselage. As a result, the bomber caught fire, but the scout pilot used a standard technique, diving sharply. He managed to put out the flames and at the same time get away from his pursuers. The second reconnaissance plane was also able to break away from the interceptors.

Two La-5s were shot down by German side gunners, and the pilot of one of them, Lieutenant Pavlenko of the 786th IAP PVO, was killed.[24] According to German reports, at 19.11 Ju 88 D-1 Wrk Nr 430861 'T5+GH' of 1.(F)/100 repulsed the attack south of Vladimir and shot down one LaGG-3.

'I saw a German plane… What to do?'

After the third successful raid on Gorky, the Luftwaffe command decided to give some of the crews a well-deserved rest. In addition, the air bases needed to replenish their supplies of bombs and fuel. As a result, only twenty He 111s from II./KG 4 'General Wever' and I./KG 100 'Viking' carried out the next attack on the Molotov plant on 7 June. One group flew through Ryazan-Murom with an exit to the target from the south-west, the second went through Arzamas with an exit from the south. As usual the bombers flew at an altitude of 3,500–4,000m.

This time, information on the approach of German aircraft came from the VNOS service half an hour earlier than on previous days. At 23.03 in the darkened city of Gorky airraid sirens were already howling and, freed from work, residents began to hide in shelters, anti-aircraft gunners gathered near the guns and firefighters near their vehicle pumps. The headquarters of the 142nd Air Division scrambled thirty-two night fighters, each of which went to its own patrol zone. Twenty-one balloons rose smoothly into the sky, and a grid of searchlight beams flashed. Everyone listened nervously to the summer silence.

Twenty minutes later, a distant hum of aircraft engines came from the south-west. The first to open fire at 23.29 were the 85mm guns of the 1291th ZenAP, and a minute later twenty-two flares flashed over the car factory. Then, high in the sky, one of the searchlights caught the silhouette of a twin-engine plane, and anti-aircraft guns began firing furiously. Soon, after a short pause, the sound of falling bombs was heard, and a short series of explosions occurred on the GAZ territory.

This time, German planes dropped 39 tons of bombs on Gorky. According to Russian reports, nine high-explosive and seven heavy incendiary bombs fell on the Molotov plant. Explosions and fires in the grey iron foundry workshop disabled the casting and molding conveyor, the section for manufacturing piston rings and other important equipment. The crane-beam and its tracks collapsed, trusses collapsed over the piston ring section and the moulding department, and the wall between the metal-working workshops collapsed.

г. Горький, Автозаводский райо...

Учетная карточка

очага поражения № „14"

Поселок **Соцгород**

Улица **пр Молотова**

Дом № **14**

Ф А Б

Калибр				
Тип	фаб.			
Разрыв				
Высота метания				
Дата	6/ХІ			
Время				

Тип. Автозавода, зак. № 2386, т. 500

Account card of the consequences of the bomb fall. (History Museum of Russian car-producer GAZ)

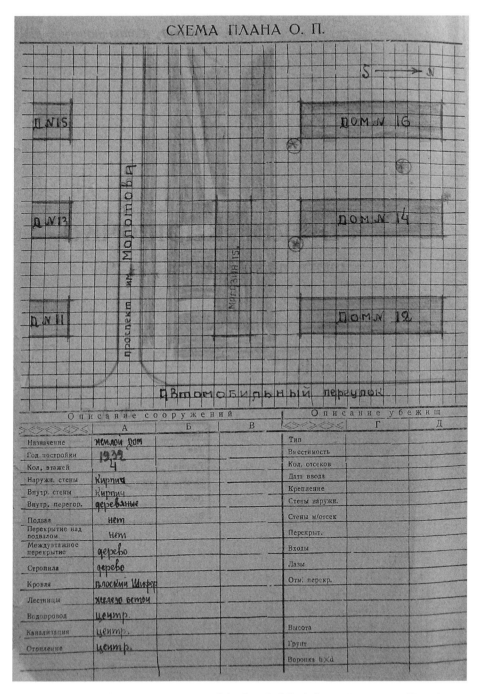

Account card of the consequences of the bomb fall. (History Museum of Russian car-producer GAZ)

Two more high-explosive bombs exploded at the north-west corner of the tool-stamping building. Aircraft engine plant No. 466 was seriously damaged. Direct hits of high-explosive bombs disabled the central factory laboratory and the chemical laboratory, and partially destroyed workshop No. 16. In the main building of the plant, the explosions destroyed household premises, part of the roof and metal structures in workshops No. 16, 24, 4, 3A, 3B and 13, household premises between main entrance No.1 and 2 and the dining room.

Several bombs fell in the historical part of the city of Gorky near Krasnoflotskaya Street (now Ilyinskaya). At the same time, one high-explosive bomb exploded just 100m from the bunker of the air defence command post. There at the time was the commander of the air defence of the USSR, Lieutenant General Mikhail Gromadin. At 00.23 there was a booming explosion, glasses shivered on the tables and plaster crumbled. In the vicinity of the headquarters, two residential buildings were destroyed, twenty-two houses were damaged by the blast wave of glass and window frames, and outbuildings in the courtyards were burned.

Although there were many night fighters in the sky around Gorky during the raid, only one of them was lucky enough to find the enemy. At 23.20 local time, the squadron commander of the 722nd IAP air defence, Senior Lieutenant Boris Tabarchuk, in a MiG-3 interceptor began patrolling the approaches to the city. Watching the bursts of anti-aircraft artillery shells, the pilot saw at an altitude of about 4,000m the barely distinguishable silhouette of a bomber heading for GAZ, and immediately went after it. It was He 111 H '5J+KN' of 5./KG 4 'General Wever'. Its crew consisted of pilot Unteroffizier Heinz Festner, the crew commander; navigator Leutnant Haeger; flight operator Unteroffizier Schafer, and two flight gunners, Obergefreiters Brockmann and Laibl. Major Cranz, the navigator on board, was supposed to control the bombing of the entire group.

The bomber dropped the 'cargo' on the target and the German pilots were unaware of the danger hanging over them. Tabarchuk approached the He 111 from the tail on the right side from underneath, but his plane was thrown back by the air current and he ended up higher than the bomber. It was at this point that the radio operator Schafer noticed him and immediately informed the pilot. But it was too late. Tabarchuk recalled later:

> I see the long black body of the Heinkel 111. Lower the altitude.
> I decided to attack from the ground. Approach. A burst of fire
> from the lower machine guns at me. The Germans noticed

me. I increased height a little and got into the turbulent flow created by the propellers of the German bomber. My MiG was thrown up. I again decline, and once again go on the attack.

As soon as the fighter's propeller was above the stabiliser, the MiG-3 rammed the tail assembly of the German aircraft. Festner recalled:

> According to the flight documentation, the altitude was approximately 3,600 metres. Immediately after dropping the bombs on the tank factory, the radio operator gave the signal: 'Fighter!' Immediately, the impact shook our entire plane. The aircraft swerved sharply to the right. When I tried to steer the plane back to a straight course with the rudders and altitude, it turned out that the He 111 was not coming out of the right turn. Only by using all my strength, resting both feet on the left rudder pedal and simultaneously squeezing the maximum left aileron (the steering column stood almost at right angles), and adjusting the speed of the engines, I managed to send the plane on a straight course. At the same time, the left engine had to be throttled, and the right engine was switched to increased speed.

The fighter was also severely damaged on impact; one of the propeller blades broke off and only half of the second was left, so Tabarchuk could not observe the fate of his victim. All he saw was the bomber swerving sharply to the right and disappearing into the darkness. After that, the Soviet pilot turned his machine, which was losing speed, to the south-west and decided to land at the nearest airfield, Strigino. The plane was poorly controlled, so Boris did not dare lower his undercarriage and landed on the fuselage. The MiG-3 ploughed through 75m of airfield, then stopped.

Meanwhile, the crew of He 111 made desperate efforts keep on the return course. The six crew members were in a very

Junior lieutenant Boris Tabachuk.

unpleasant situation at the time. The front line was more than 500km away, and the hostile Russian plains stretched below; they didn't want to land on them. Festner did everything possible to maintain control of the aircraft. As soon as he relaxed his efforts a little, the bomber immediately turned to the right. Leutnant Haeger said: 'If we fly this way and further, we will find ourselves in Moscow!' But, in the end, the pilot managed to bring the plane onto a south-west heading.

To lighten the plane, the crew threw overboard all the machine gun ammunition and the armour plates, however, the bomber still flew almost 100km/h slower than on the way to the target. As a result, the crew approached the front line in the morning. Fortunately for the Germans, the Soviet air defence did not take any measures to intercept the returning Luftwaffe aircraft. The radio operator contacted Orel-West air base and reported that they were returning with heavy damage. Firefighters and ambulances were immediately dispatched to the runway, while the airfield team continuously corrected the course of the damaged He 111 by radio and directed it to its home airfield. Seeing the familiar contours of the airfield, the pilot released the landing gear, which dropped safely and stood on the locks. After that, the plane successfully performed a smooth turn and landed normally.

Unteroffizier Festner continued:

> It was only after leaving the plane that we saw the extent of the destruction. The tail was almost completely destroyed. In addition, the plane of the rudder had bent in the impact so just the remaining part was left to turn the plane to the right. However, the left horizontal stabiliser remained intact, so it was possible to maintain altitude, avoid going into a dive and not crash.[25]

Subsequently, all the crew members were awarded the Iron Cross First Class. Leutnant Haeger, who had made a report to Luftflotte 6 headquarters, brought all five of them an autographed photograph of Generaloberst von Greim. The pilots also received wallets and lighters from the management of the Heinkel company after it learned about the incident. This episode was one of many examples of how German pilots managed to miraculously avoid death and escape from the Russian executioners.

In Gorky, meanwhile, there was a summing up of the latest Luftwaffe raid. The headquarters of the corps area of air defence made report 005, which indicated that allegedly '55 aircraft of the type He 111 and Ju 88 participated in the raid, of which 3–4 aircraft broke through to the city'. The head of the NKVD Department of the Gorky region, Colonel Zverev, simultaneously prepared his report, according to which the raid 'involved only 3 bombers at an altitude of 3,000 metres – one He 111 and two Ju 88s'. The anti-aircraft artillery spent 19,000 rounds within an hour and a half. At the same time, the batteries of the 784th and 1291 ZenAP declared six downed aircraft, even indicating the exact areas where they came down: two in the area of the village of Vyazovka, the rest in the area of the villages of Komarovo, Shitki, Kudma and Kusakovka. The report said: 'Found two aircraft, the rest are wanted.' Fighter aircraft carried out thirty-two sorties and Senior Lieutenant Boris Tabarchuk rammed the He 111, which crashed near the village of Shcherbinka. Searchlights illuminated three aircraft at an altitude of 5,000m.[26] In total, the Soviets claimed seven downed bombers.

In fact, all the bombers from II./KG 4 and I./KG 100 returned safely to their bases. It is unclear what aircraft were 'found' by the Russians at the time of compiling the report, and it is quite mysterious how the victim of a ram, the surviving He 111 H '5J+KN' had 'fallen' in the vicinity of Shcherbinka.

He 111 H '5J+KN' of 5./KG 4. Damage after ramming over the city of Gorky.

Then this aerial victory was miraculously 'confirmed'. According to the documents of the corps area of air defence, the He 111 was found near Kudma station. The military Department of the regional office of the Bolshevik Party later claimed that the plane was found 'in the area of the station Myza'. For some reason Tabarchuk never visited the downed bomber.[27] On 8 June, General Mikhail Gromadin, commander of the air defence of the USSR, arrived at the airfield of the 722nd IAP and presented Tabarchuk with the Order of the Red Banner in the presence of all the pilots.[28] On the same day, the newspaper *Izvestia* published a small report about Tabarchuk's 'kill'.

On 9 June, an article about the fourth raid on Gorky was published by the newspaper *Gorkovskaya Kommuna*. It said:

> On the night of June 8, a group of German planes tried to raid Gorky. On the approaches to the city, the enemy planes were scattered by our fighter aircraft and anti-aircraft artillery. Two German planes were able to break into the area of the city and dropped several bombs on residential buildings. There was one fire, which was quickly eliminated. 7 German bombers were shot down while repelling the raid.

Residents of the city who read this Bolshevik lie spat, knowing full well about the real destruction caused by the German aircraft.

Tabarchuk himself soon gave an interview to a correspondent of *Izvestia* in which he told about his feat with great imagination, significantly distorting many facts:

> I was flying at an altitude of about 4,000 metres, when I saw a German plane very close. He was flying toward the target with a full load of bombs and kept at a considerable height. He didn't see me in the sparsely cloudy night sky. Taking advantage of this, I settled down under the tail of the German plane and flew at the same speed as it. So we flew for several minutes. What to do? Shoot? What if the plane is armoured and my bullets don't do anything to it? The German suddenly turned away and noticed me. The situation was dangerous. I told the commander on the radio that I was going to ram, gave full throttle, caught up with the fascist and slashed his tail with a screw. The German plane

immediately began to fall. I began to descend to trace the crash site of the German plane. After a short period of time, I saw the flames of the explosion rise up on the ground – one less bandit.

This article shows how the totalitarian state's press covered aviation. The wording describing the 'feat' of the Stalin Falcon was extremely formulaic and primitive. Soviet pilots always had to shoot down an enemy plane that had not yet managed to drop its bombs, so the feat looked more significant than a bomber that had already delivered its 'cargo' and was flying home.

An indicator of the highest degree of emotional shock that arose due to the unpunished flights of the Luftwaffe as a result of the collapse of the Soviet air defence is an amusing but revealing case that occurred with the grandfather of one of the authors of this book. At that time, he worked as a trackman on the railway and lived in the village of Efimievo, near the routes of the German bombers. Outraged by the brazen flights, the author's grandfather, during the next appearance of the Germans, grabbed a primitive gun and fired in the direction of the German bombers.

On the evening of 8 June, at 18.45 local time, a reconnaissance plane from 1.(F)/100 appeared in the area of Gorky on the already established 'schedule'. The Ju 88 D flew over the city at 7,000m and photographed the Molotov plant. At dusk, the plane returned safely to its base. Soon, the films were developed and the Luftwaffe commanders were able to observe the results of four raids on GAZ. The images clearly showed that 'Carmen' was dead – most of the production buildings were badly damaged, some of them completely burned out.

On the night of 9 June, the Luftwaffe command planned to conduct a fifth consecutive air attack on Gorky. But this time the weather made its own adjustments to the German plans. In the evening there was a heavy downpour that flooded the runways of the entire Bryansk-Orel air hub. P. Mobius of 9./KG 27 recalled:

One flight to Gorky from Olsufevo was upset by a rainstorm that took place there in the afternoon and damaged the grass surface of the airfield. Of course, then the aircraft tried to taxi to the start line. However, when they were all stuck around the runway, this flight was cancelled. The aircraft had damage to the propellers and fuselages.

However, some of the bombers still managed to take off and even flew the first 300 km to the target. But then suddenly there was an order to cancel the mission. Dropping bombs on the first available spare targets, the bombers turned back.

At about 22.30 Moscow time Soviet air surveillance posts (VNOS) recorded the crossing of the front line by two groups of enemy aircraft, numbering about thirty-six planes. At 23.07 an air alert was declared in Gorky, with air defence assets brought to combat readiness. The inhabitants went for the shelters, however, there was no attack. Later, the headquarters of the air defence corps district received reports that, after dropping bombs on Michurinsk and Ramensk, the planes had turned back for some reason. According to the entries in the Fliegerbuch of Hans Grotter from 5./KG 51, his Ju 88 A-4 '9K+JN', dropped bombs on the railway station in Michurinsk. The plane took off from Bryansk at 20.25, and landed at 23.55 after 210 minutes of flight.[29] In Gorky, General Alexey Osipov breathed a sigh of relief and at 23.57 ordered the 'all clear' signal.

Thus, despite the cancellation of the fifth raid, it is safe to say that during Operation *Carmen II* its goal, the destruction of the Molotov automobile plant, was achieved. The plant had been totally disabled for a long time. The reasons for the undoubted success of the Luftwaffe, in addition to the high level of training of bomber crews and tactical skill in managing large groups of aircraft, lie in the monstrous failure of the Soviet air defense. The bloody Stalinist regime was not able, even with a sufficient number of anti-aircraft guns and interceptor aircraft, to organise the high-quality training of professional personnel in this complex technique. The total incompetence, ignorance and outright stupidity of various chiefs and commanders could not be compensated for even by self-sacrifice and the will to win that was demonstrated by ordinary soldiers of the Soviet air defence. Untrained and incompetently managed female anti-aircraft gunners could not resist the battle-hardened professionals of Luftwaffe bomber aviation. The situation was further aggravated by the total technical backwardness and poor quality of Soviet equipment and weapons.

The effectiveness of Soviet air defence was almost zero. Luftwaffe losses amounted to just two bombers in 474 flights. Another two aircraft were seriously damaged, but were able to return to their air bases.

'Zementbombers' over Seshchinskaya

At this time, the Soviets were feverishly preparing retaliatory measures that would weaken the onslaught of the Luftwaffe. In such cases, the Russians always resorted to a proven means – air attacks against German air bases. Pe-2 reconnaissance planes spent whole days frantically ploughing through enemy airspace, looking for clusters of German bombers. As a result, after comparing all the aerial photographs, the command of the Soviet air force made a stunning discovery. The bombers that made night raids in the Volga Region were not based in the deep rear, but on the Orel ledge, that is, under the very nose of the attack aircraft of the 1st and 15th Russian Air Armies! Most of the 'vultures' were found at Seshchinskaya, Orel-West and Bryansk airfields. However, Russian air intelligence did not find the concentration of He 111s in Olsufevo, where almost all of KG 27 was based.

In the early morning of 7 June, when the only wheel workshop in the country was still burning down at GAZ, an urgent order arrived at the headquarters of the 1st and 15th Air Armies – in the period from 20.30 to 21.00 Moscow time to inflict massive attacks by Il-2 attack aircraft on five Luftwaffe air bases at once. However, the weather suddenly intervened. During the day there was heavy rain, and the dirt runways of the Soviet field airfields became completely unusable. As a result, the attack did not take place, which gave many of the crews the opportunity to live one day longer.

Therefore, the first major air attack on German airfields was made by long-range bombers (ADD). On the night of 7 to 8 June, according to the plan, 102 aircraft flew to Seshchinskaya, eighty-seven to Bryansk and another

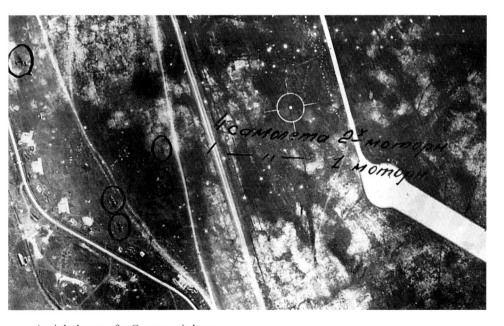

Aerial photos of a German air base.

Pilot Alexander Putin gets a task.

seventy-five to Orel. Due to difficult weather conditions, thirty-eight crews were unable to achieve their goals and dropped bombs on various alternate targets. Only 244 aircraft attacked the bases, with pathfinders dropping lighting and incendiary bombs, marking the target for the rest of the planes. On their return, the crews reported eight German bombers destroyed. In fact, one Ju 88 A-4 from II./KG 51 'Edelweiss' was destroyed in Bryansk, and in Seshchinskaya light damage (10 per cent) was caused to one Ju 88 D-1 of 4.(F)/121. None of the flight and ground personnel were injured.

Meanwhile, the headquarters of the Russian attack aircraft aviation divisions developed what they thought was a 'brilliant' plan for an assault. Taking into account previous experience, they decided the attack should be made at an angle of 25–30° from a height of 600–700m. The attackers would open fire from guns and machine guns from a distance of 400–600m. The method of attack was supposed to vary 'depending on the location of aircraft on airfields, the degree of their camouflage and terrain'. To destroy aircraft standing on the ground AO-10, AO-15 and AO-25 fragmentation bombs, as well as AO-2.5 cluster bombs, should be used. It was believed that the fragments would be guaranteed to put the planes out of action. For 'finishing' on the second approach machine guns, cannon and, to begin with, unguided rockets should be used. The last groups of attack aircraft were to destroy ammunition depots and fuel depots. They carried high-explosive FAB-50 and FAB-100 bombs with time-lapse fuses and ZAB-2.5 incendiary bombs.

The commander of the 198th Assault Aviation Regiment (198th SHAP), Major Karyakin, had received orders the day before – on 7 June – to attack the large Seshchinskaya air base. For many pilots, this order caused a nervous shiver. There were too many stories of terrible anti-aircraft fire and attacks by dozens of Messerschmitts. It was said that half the crews did not return from sorties to Seshchinskaya, it was a bad place on the map. In addition, the target was at the limit of the range of the Il-2.

The raid was then moved to the next day. Pilot Alexander Efimov later recalled:

> All evening we were busy preparing for the mission. We discussed the route, and especially carefully analysed the actions when approaching the target and at the beginning of the attack. We carefully studied the photo of Seshchinskaya airfield. We mapped out what target to attack, how to manoeuvre, where to go after the attack. At the end of the day, the commander of the regiment gathered everyone, and the pilots once again discussed in detail the order of execution of the combat mission. Then Karjakin gave the floor to Major Bondarenko. He was a remarkably calm man. We were going to smash the airfield Seshchinskaya – fascist hornets' nest. The mere thought of the importance of the upcoming flight sent a shiver down my spine, but Mikhail spoke to us so calmly and matter-of-factly that one might have thought we were preparing to fly there on a courtesy visit.[30]

Efimov himself received an order from Major Karjakin, paired with him before the attack to conduct weather reconnaissance on the route to the target. Although he wrote in his post-war memoirs that 'this was also an important matter', no doubt any pilot would rather fly out to scout the weather than storm a well-protected German air base. Thus, the commander of the regiment did not choose for himself the most difficult mission.

The planes of two other regiments from the 233rd Attack Aircraft Aviation Division – the 62nd SHAP and the 312th SHAP – were to participate in the raid. In total, thirty-six Il-2s were allocated for the strike. After setting the task, a representative of the 172nd IAP told the attack pilots about the order of meeting up with the escort fighters. The escort consisted of twenty-seven Yak-1s and Yak-7 fighters from the 233rd IAD and 309th IAD.

The morning of 8 June was overcast. Clouds hung low over the airfield, and it drizzled at times. The pilots lived under constant threat of death and did not plan their lives for more than one day, so this raised the hope that the flight would be postponed. However, in the late afternoon, the weather improved, and at 20.20 they received the order – to attack Seshchinskaya!

The weather scouts were the first to take off. Efimov continued the story:

> While the pilots were taking their places, we with the commander of the regiment, without waiting at the start, went to take off. We began to climb. We noticed that as we moved westward, the clouds rose higher and thinned noticeably. Here and there the sun was coming in through the windows. That's the front line. The commander reports the weather on the radio … Flying west, periodically changing course. Our division will be flying over here soon. Above us, a group of four 'Messers'[31] suddenly passed. The commander sharply tilted the plane and went down in the direction of the forest. But the enemy did not notice us…
>
> We take a reverse course and at extremely low altitude pass the front line. And here on opposite courses, above us in a familiar order of battle, sweeps an armada of stormtroopers with blue propeller fairings – our regiment. A little to one side are the yellow propeller fairings – planes of the 312th Regiment. The column of the 62nd Regiment – aircraft with red propeller fairings, are close.[32]

However, the raid did not turn out as planned, and the usual story repeated itself. Some attack aircraft were unable to rendezvous with the escort fighters, others got lost, and some made forced landings due to technical failures. As a result, instead of thirty-six Il-2s, only thirteen approached the enemy's 'hornets' nest'. Their crews were not happy about this because the smaller the group, the more likely it was that the enemy fighters would attack and shoot down a specific aircraft. Nor was the surprise of the attack achieved. On the approach to Seshchinskaya two groups of Il-2s, led by Major Bondarenko and Captain Malinkin, came across a powerful barrage of anti-aircraft guns. German guns seemed to be everywhere, in every clearing. Simultaneously up to a hundred bursts broke out in the air, accompanied by a booming roar. Then the familiar silhouettes of Bf 109s appeared in the sky at different heights. When the Soviet planes began their attack, anti-aircraft guns opened fire on specific aircraft.

As a result, the Il-2 pilots had to drop bombs in horizontal flight from a height of 1,200m. There was no question of precise aiming, however, some pilots reported that they had 'coming in on a low-level flight, they fired from onboard weapons at the aircrafts standing on the ground'. Freed from their 'cargo' the clumsy attack aircraft, which the Germans gave the nickname 'Zementbomber', hurried back to their airfield. However, all the pilots knew that they were now facing the most dangerous part of their mission. Coming out of the zone of anti-aircraft fire, the Zementbombers inevitably fell to the firing squad of Luftwaffe fighters. But this time the attack aircraft were lucky, because after them twenty-six diving Pe-2 bombers from the 204th Bombardment Aviation Division (204th Bad) of Colonel S.P. Andreev accompanied by forty-two La-5 fighters appeared over Seshchinskaya. They distracted the attention of the Germans.[33] Still, some Bf 109s and Fw 190s attacked the Il-2s, which were flying towards the front line in small scattered groups and singly.

The Il-2 of Junior Lieutenant S. Petrov, which carried just one crew member, was damaged by a 20mm shell, but the pilot still managed to turn his aircraft towards the front line at low speed and get out of the zone of anti-aircraft fire. Due to engine problems, Petrov had fallen behind his group and was returning to his airfield alone. Not far from the front line, his aircraft was overtaken by a pair of Bf 109s. The first machinegun burst missed, but the second hit the centre of Petrov's plane. He dropped to low level and was able to reach his own territory. However, the Bf 109s were not far behind. Machinegun fire disabled his rudder and the plane crash-landed on the edge of a meadow. It ploughed through the ground for about 50m, with its propeller blades curling, and stopped. The pilot was afraid that the Germans would kill him in the open, so he immediately got out of the cockpit and climbed under the wing.

The two-seat Il-2 of the Hero of the Soviet Union Major Mikhail Bondarenko was seen by a single German fighter soon after it turned for home, and the Luftwaffe aircraft then made seven attacks on it. Knowing about the presence of the rear gun, the German only attacked from behind and below. The Il-2's engine was damaged, the rudder control cables broken, and the pilot and gunner were injured, the latter seriously. With great difficulty Bondarenko reached the front line, and then immediately made a wheels-up emergency landing.[34] Three other Zementbombers were also badly damaged and made forced landings. Three fighters from the escort were shot down, and three more were damaged and landed without undercarriage.

As for the results of such a dramatic air attack, the Russians reported twenty Luftwaffe aircraft destroyed and fifteen damaged on the ground. The headquarters of the 1st Air Army, taking into account the reports of the Pe-2 crews, reported that 'at the Seshchinskaya airfield, up to thirty-five enemy aircraft out of sixty to seventy were destroyed and damaged, partially confirmed by photo control'. In addition, according to Soviet information, three Bf 109s, two Bf 110s and two Fw 190s were shot down in aerial combat around the target. In fact, III./KG 55 'Greif' and III./KG 1 'Hindenburg', based at Seshchinskaya, did not suffer at all! Only one German anti-aircraft gunner was wounded.

On the same day, forty-two Il-2s and fifty-six Yak-1, Yak-7 and La-5 fighters were to participate in an air attack on Luftwaffe bases in the Orel area, according to the plan of the 15th Air Army headquarters. Some of the fighters were allocated to block airfields and prevent the take-off of German fighters, the rest for the direct escort of attack aircraft.

At 19.30 twelve 'Gorbatyj'[35] from the 614th SHAP took off from Mtsensk. They were accompanied by twenty-two fighters from the 315th IAD of Colonel V.Y. Litvinov. The target of the attack was Orel airfield, where there were no German bombers at all, only fighters, transport and liaison aircraft.

At 19.58 six Yak-1s from the 65th Guards IAP appeared over the German airfield at Mezenka and tried to prevent aircraft taking off. The pilots then reported that they saw about thirty twin-engine bombers on the airfield and 'burned' five of them. The pair, consisting of Sergeant Bozhko and Lieutenant Koventsov, were then attacked by two Fw 190s, one of which they shot down. At the same time, one of the Yak-1s was also hit and made an emergency landing.

Then fighters from the 63rd and 64th Guards IAP arrived in the vicinity of Orel. The German observation posts detected the enemy's approach in time, and Fw 190s were scrambled. As a result, almost all the Soviet fighters were bound up in combat. The air battle, due to the low cloud cover, took on the character of fleeting, scattered skirmishes. Aircraft with stars and crosses spilled out of the clouds, then went back into them, with tracer lines cutting across the sky. From time to time burning planes flew through the air and parachutes opened.

Subsequently, the Soviet pilots claimed six downed Fw 190s, which were recorded in the accounts of Captain Kubarev, Senior Lieutenants Manoshin and Koventsov, Junior Lieutenants Alexeev and Popov, and Sergeant Sudozhkin. The Soviet air force's own losses in this battle amounted to one Yak-1, Yak-7 and La-5. But the Germans achieved their main objective; instead of protecting the attack aircraft, Russian fighters were completely bound up in the dog fighting and used almost all their fuel.

By this time, a dozen Il-2s from the 614th SHAP were approaching Orel. Their crews stared in vain at the rainy, leaden sky, hoping to see the silhouettes of their fighters. However, they were 'busy' and the attack aircraft had to carry out a dangerous mission without cover. As a result, German anti-aircraft artillery and JG51 fighters shot down all twelve 'Zementbombers', none of which could even make it back to their own lines. All twenty-four pilots and rear gunners were missing, including the regiment's navigator and assistant commander for air gunner training. The leader of the 315th IAD fighter group then reported that 'only four Il-2s were flying from the target towards Mtsensk, one of which was shot down by anti-aircraft fire, these planes were never seen again'. The fighters themselves also suffered heavy losses: seven pilots did not return from the mission.

Despite losing nineteen aircraft out of thirty-four, and thirty-one pilots out of forty-eight, the strike group did not achieve any results. Orel air base was not damaged, with all the bombs exploding in the nearby streets and

Russian Il-2 aircraft attack Luftwaffe air base. (Photo from Boelcke Archiv)

125

Explosions at a German air base during an air attack by Russian planes. (Photo from Boelcke Archiv)

waste ground in the city. The combat account of the pilots of JG 51 in the period from 19.02 to 19.40 recorded thirty-seven downed Soviet aircraft (ten Il-2s and LaGG-3s, seven Il-4s, four La-5s, two Yak-7s, and one Yak-1, MiG-1, MiG-3 and P-39).

According to the Luftwaffe, that evening the commander of II./JG 51, Oberleutnant Adolf Borhers, showed the highest performance, shooting down two Il-2s. Leutnant Joachim Brendel of I./JG 51 and Feldwebel Bernard Fehtel of 10./JG 51, both shot down two Il-2s. One was a Zementbomber recorded on the accounts of Spaniards from 15.(Spain)/ JG 51 – Teniente Juan Ramon Galivan (at 19.21) and Luis Asqet-Brunet (at 19.14). Other Spanish pilots also distinguished themselves: Gonzalo Nevia shot down 2 LaGG-3s (at 19.15 and 19.20), and Bernardo Menenes, Julio Manuel Munor and Rafael Galleja each shot down one LaGG-3 (between 19.16 and 19.25). JG 51 lost only one fighter all day! Fw 190 A-3 Wrk Nr 5327 was shot down in the area near Orel-Grazhdanskij airfield and pilot Teniente Alejandro Gonsales Perez was killed. This aerial victory was claimed both by Senior Lieutenant V.N. Kubarev and Junior Lieutenant A.I. Popov from the 65th GIAP, who claimed to have shot down an Orel-Grazhdanskij Fw 190 over the airfield, and Senior Sergeant N.A. Sedyushkin from the 63rd GIAP, who claimed to have downed an Fw 190 south of Orel-West airfield.

'Military fate' was more favourable to the twelve Il-2s of the 948th SHAP, whose target was to become an airfield near the village of Khomuty (24km south-west of Orel). After taking off from Prohodnoe and meeting their escort fighters, they headed for the target. However, they were 'lucky' as the path was blocked by solid clouds. The commander of the regiment, Major Hrabryh, decided to abort the mission and turn back. This saved the lives of many inexperienced crews.[36]

Then, on the night of 9 June, another 160 Soviet night bombers attacked Luftwaffe airfields but again this did not bring any tangible results to the Soviets. Only two ground personnel were injured at Orel-West airfield. At the same time, twenty-one Russian aircraft, or 13 per cent of the total number of those involved in the raid, did not return to their bases.

The air defence of German air bases clearly showed what effect a harmonious combination of high-quality advanced equipment and brilliantly trained personnel could produce. Thus, the concentrated and fanatical attacks on German air bases, which were intended to destroy the core of the Luftwaffe's bombing squadrons, were completely thwarted.

Chapter 5

The Entire Volga Region is on Fire

'Everything is bad'

In the first decade of June, the Eastern Front continued to be quiet. The Russians were trying to unravel the Germans' plans, which were still a mystery to them. Moreover, the beginning of air attacks against targets far from the front only further confused the slow-witted Soviet command. Stalin was nervous and forbade his generals to be active. The only exception was the Kuban bridgehead. On the morning of 5 June, units on the North Caucasus front launched another offensive, albeit with limited objectives. The 37th and 56th Armies were tasked with capturing the heavily fortified strongholds of Pobeda and Podgorny, which covered the approaches to the larger resistance points located in the villages of Kievskoye and Moldavanskoye. The attack was preceded by strong attacks from Russian bombers and attack aircraft. The 4th Air Force completed 479 sorties, and 113 more carried out by naval aviation. Pilots and anti-aircraft batteries reported they had shot down twenty-three German aircraft. In fact, the Luftwaffe did not suffer any losses over the bridgehead during this period. The Russians themselves lost thirteen aircraft. By 22.00, after fierce fighting, the Russians managed to advance 1 to 1.5km and reached within 400m of houses on the north-eastern outskirts of the village of Moldavanskoye.

On 6 June, the Russian air force flew 738 sorties, reporting four downed aircraft. On this day, the Luftwaffe did suffer serious losses on the Kuban bridgehead: four Bf 109s from JG 52, one Ju 88 D-5 from 4.(F)/122 and one Fw 190 of 5./Sch.G1. After the twin-engine bombers were withdrawn for air attacks against industrial centres, attack aircraft and fighters were given the main burden of supporting the 17th Army in the Kuban. However, the Soviets also significantly weakened their aviation grouping, moving aviation regiments to be re-equipped and to other sectors of the front. The Russians never succeeded in gaining air superiority over the bridgehead. Fighting on land did not bring them success either.

Meanwhile, the Luftwaffe planned its next missions, and the Soviets took measures to strengthen their air defence and discipline. On 8 June, the State Defence Committee adopted secret resolution No. 3534ss 'on air defence of Gorky factories'. According to this document, 100 additional small-calibre anti-aircraft guns, 250 large-calibre machine guns, 100 searchlights and seventy-five barrage balloons were allocated. At the same meeting, Stalin ordered the immediate dismissal of Alexey Livshits, director of the Molotov plant, and the appointment of the previously dismissed Loskutov in his place. The next day, GAZ received an order from the People's Commissar of medium engineering, Sergey Akopov: 'In accordance with the resolution of the State Defence Committee of 8.06.43, to remove comrade Livshits from the post of Director of the Gorky automobile plant 'Molotov', as he failed to do his job, and to return as Director to GAZ the former Director of comrade Loskutov I.K.' This decision was dictated only by the desire to punish Livshits, but also for objective reasons. After the destruction of the wheel shop Livshits was already in a state of depression and could no longer perform his duties.

In the city of Gorky, following the results of the first series of air attacks the commander of the corps area air defence, General-major Alexey Osipov, issued an order on 9 June in which he wrote:

> The enemy, using, in some cases, our lack of organisation and lack of skill in firing, continued methodically to destroy the most valuable military facility – automobile plant 'Molotov'… Each raid spent tens of thousands of expensive ammunition and they did not give a sufficient result due to the ineptitude of organising a fight with an air opponent.

On the same day, the Bureau of the Gorky regional office of the Bolshevik Party discussed measures to improve the air defence of the city. This regional office had been located in the former governor's house in the Nizhny Novgorod Kremlin since the civil war of 1917–22. The ancient fortress built by the Italian architect Petro Francesca at the beginning of the sixteenth century looked quite dilapidated. The walls were in bad repair in many places, two towers collapsed in the eighteenth century and were not restored. Before the war, some of the walls and towers were being prepared for demolition in order to build a large square in the centre of the city with a huge monument to the Bolshevik Yakov Sverdlov. Instead of wooden roofs, square and round towers were covered with ugly iron caps, and three of them had been removed. In 1942, anti-aircraft machine guns were installed on these towers. People lived on the territory of the Kremlin, and there was a tram depot. The entrance to the governor's house was through an arch cut in the wall nearby. In the past tsarist governors passed through it in carriages and were saluted by police officers on duty. Now, in June 1943, cars with the Stalinist nobility went through the arch one after another.

The servants of Stalin – Beria, Shcherbakov, Pronin, Gromadin and Merkulov – gathered to sum up their inspection. The commission's conclusions were not original and sounded very threatening. The rescue service (MPVO) was significantly strengthened and moved to round-the-clock duty. In addition to the existing eleven paramilitary fire brigades, it was decided to form five more teams with a total of 375 people. Another ten paramilitary fire brigades were created at the factories. To create water reserves, they ordered small rivers to be dammed to create fire reservoirs.[1]

Those present voiced the problems of preparing for air attacks at many enterprises. The report of the inspection at the Lenin radio telephone factory in Gorky stated:

> Everything is bad. The territory is littered with garbage, there are not enough buckets and shovels, crates with sand are filled with debris. In shop No. 4, there is one bucket for 16 barrels of water, and 14 shovels for 42 boxes of sand. Some members of the duty teams leave their posts during an air raid and run away from the factory. In shop No. 20, there are no buckets for 10 barrels of water. The existing bomb shelters can accommodate 1,900 people (54 per cent of the number of workers in one shift)…

This picture of complete mismanagement and disorder was typical of Russian military reality.

Due to the lack of water when extinguishing fires, it was decided to urgently reactivate the old water abstraction intake of the Molotov plant. It had long since been decommissioned and the exit to the river was covered with sand. On 6 June, the crew of the dredger *Volzhsky-15* received an order to move from Zvenigorod (near Kazan) to Gorky. For several days a cargo steamer towed the boat upstream. Arriving at the site, *Volzhsky-15* spent several days digging a channel to the old water abstraction intake.

A.I. Starikov, at that time the fourteen-year-old son of one of the team members, recalled:

> The left bank of the Oka, behind which one of the first giant buildings of the industry automobile plant 'Molotov' was located, consisted of a sandbank up to a hundred metres wide and towered over the water for at least one and a half metres. For the first few days, the work went on without air attacks, and the channel was dug quickly. We cleaned the receiver and started the water pump. The automobile plant was suffocating without water.

When the work was completed, the dredger was transferred to the right bank of the Oka. The ship's crew, along with their families, took up residence in the cabins of a small fire watch station that had been specially assigned to the ship.

But it was not possible to hide this fact from Luftwaffe. On 9 June, at 18.27 local time, two Ju 88 D reconnaissance planes flew over Gorky 'on schedule'. The aerial photos they took clearly showed that the Russians were trying to put the old water abstraction intake station into operation, and this fact was taken into account when planning the next air attack.

Air defence units were hastily prepared to repel possible new attacks. On 6 June, a division of small-calibre guns from the 90th Reserve Anti-aircraft Artillery Regiment was transferred to the Avtozavodsky district. Then, on 8 and 9 June, a separate division of large-calibre guns, a division of the Gorky anti-aircraft artillery school, and a division of the Chkalovsky anti-aircraft artillery school headed by Major M.P. Biryukov[2] arrived. An anti-aircraft machinegun regiment, as well as the 1580th ZenAP, armed with 20mm and 37mm guns, were deployed directly to cover the GAZ workshops. The latter were intended for shooting at low-flying and diving aircraft. Additional ammunition supplies were brought to the positions.[3]

When attempting to repel four Luftwaffe air attacks, a complete failure of the previously adopted large-calibre anti-aircraft barrage scheme was discovered. Due to the insufficient distance between the lines of fire curtains, the opening of fire on the second and subsequent echelons of enemy bombers was delayed. The air defence corps area command had to change the barrage pattern. The batteries were regrouped, and the defences in the main areas where the German bombers had flown were strengthened. Instead of three lines of fire curtains, two were prepared. The internal line of fire curtains were placed 2 or 3km from the border of the plant and the external ring was 6 or 7km outside the inner ring.[4]

Meanwhile, German pilots were preparing for new raids on Volga Region cities. On 7 June, some aircraft from KG 27 flew to their main base in Melitopol, in southern Ukraine, to pick up mail and stock up on the ripe cherries that were plentiful there. After spending a day at this 'resort', on the evening of 8 June, the He 111s flew back to Olsufevo. However, some of the crews remained in Melitopol, deprived of the 'pleasure' of bombing Gorky. Navigator Hans Reif of 3./KG 27 wrote in his diary:

> Tuesday, 08.06.1943. I think our crew was quietly retired. After last week the main part of the crews flew to Orel for three days to carry out raids on the centre of the military industry – Gorky (former Nizhny Novgorod), on the Volga, east of Moscow. Today the rest of the crews have already flown without us, probably for eight days to the airfield between Roslavl and Bryansk. With old, tested crew members, it would be fun for me, it would be interesting to fly together, even if it is dangerous to perform these flights.[5]

Reif fought on the Eastern Front from the end of 1941 and participated in all the major battles on the southern flank from the Crimea to Stalingrad. He belonged to the category of German pilots who perceived war as a kind of cruel 'sport', a competition with other crews for awards and achievements. Those such as Reif could really perceive raids on cities in the deep rear as 'entertainment', a kind of long-distance biathlon, where the risk to one's life only added to the adrenaline.

Next – Yaroslavl

As the lull on the front continued and the results of Operation *Carmen II* were encouraging, the Luftwaffe leadership decided to continue in the same vein.

On the evening of 9 July, it was again time for intense activity at the airfields in the Bryansk and Orel sectors. Ground personnel prepared planes for departure, the tanks were filled to the top with fuel, and powerful high-explosive bombs were suspended under the wings. Pilots and navigators were given their instructions. This time their target was Yaroslavl, specifically the rubber plant. Along the way, it was decided to attack minor targets in the cities of Uglich, Konstantinovsky, and Komsomolsk with small forces. III./ KG 27 'Boelcke' Hauptmann Karl Meier, II./KG 3 'Blitz' and I./KG 100 'Viking' were scheduled to take part. For the first time, II./KG 53 'Legion Condor' led by Major Herbert Wittmann participated in the operation after arriving from Luftflotte 1. Take-off, as usual, was scheduled for 20.00 Berlin time. According to the pilots' Fliegerbuchs, He 111 H '1G+EL' took off at 20.10 from Olsufevo, He 111 H '1G+AL' at 20.15 also from there, He 111 H '1G+SA' at 20.20 from Bryansk, He 111 H '1G+FS'at 20.32 from Olsufevo, and so on. A total of 132 bombers took part in the first major air attack on Yaroslavl.[6]

Aerial photos of Yaroslavl. The arrow indicates tire plant.

In contrast to the Gorky raid, the route to Yaroslavl ran north-east had to pass almost entirely through the Moscow air defence front. It was accepted that in such cases the commanders of Kampfgeschwaders and Kampfgruppens had to independently plot the most optimal and safe flight path to the target and back from their point of view. Some decided to fly west of Moscow via Gzhatsk–Volokolamsk–Kimry–Uglich; others preferred to bypass it to the east, via Kolomna–Yegoryevsk–Orekhovo–Zuyevo–Alexandrov–Rostov Veliky and then along the railway to Yaroslavl.

However, the mission did not go according to plan. Sixteen bombers were forced to abort and return to the base due to technical issues and bad weather. For example, He 111 H '1G+DP' took off at 20.15 from Olsufevo, but engine problems were detected. After flying about 400km, the plane turned back. Another seven aircraft struck a reserve target, the Serpukhov railway station. But the main problem was that, due to limited visibility, some of the planes went off course and instead of Yegoryevsk went to Podolsk and in the south-eastern suburbs of Moscow. The command of the Moscow air defence front again decided that this was an air attack on the capital. At 22.52 an air alert was declared in the city, which lasted a record three hours.

The 1st Air Fighter Army (formerly the 6th IAK PVO) flew sixty-three sorties during the night, involving fifty-nine night fighters from the 12th Guards, 16th, 28th, 34th, 126th, 177th, 178th, 309th, 429th, 445th, 488th, 562nd and 565th IAP. There were thirteen aviation regiments in total.

At 23.07 Moscow time, radio operators directed the Yak-7B of Junior Lieutenant Sapolatin to an He 111, which was flying at an altitude of 4,200m through light searchlight field No. 11 on a course of 135°. According to the pilot's report, after the first attack, the bomber began to descend. However, Sapolatin did not observe the fall of the enemy plane himself, and at 01.05 he returned to the base. Senior Lieutenant Semenov from the 16th IAP, flying his Yak-7B at an altitude of 5,000m, received a signal at 23.05: 'The enemy is flying a course of 360° – attack immediately!' Soon, in the area of Pavlov Posad (55km east of Moscow), the pilot noticed the dark silhouette of an unlit He 111. According to the pilot, after the first attack, the target abruptly changed course by 90°, and after the second the plane caught fire and fell near the village of Rakhmanovo.

Here is how the log of combat operations describes an air battle conducted by Junior Lieutenant Pismenniy in a Yak-7B of the 429th IAP:

> Patrolling in the light searchlight field No. 11 in the period 23.07–23.10, the fighter was directed to the enemy's He 111, which followed a course of 30–45°. After receiving the

information, the pilot turned a course of 220° and went to meet the enemy aircraft. After 2 to 3 minutes, the fighter pilot found it 400 metres above him. The fighter attacked the target at an altitude of 4,200 metres from the rear.[7] The enemy, noticing the machinegun track, turned a course of 30°. During a U-turn, the fighter hit the air jet of the enemy aircraft's engines. Coming out of the air jet, the pilot made a secondary attack from below.[8] From a distance of 80–100 metres, he fired two bursts of machine guns. The lower gunner of the He 111 returned fire. Half a minute later, the left engine of the He 111 flashed, the plane banked to 90°. The enemy bomber went into a vertical dive and crashed into the ground, burning in the area of Gzhatsk.

The battle was less successful for the commander of the 3rd Squadron of the 126th IAP, Captain Baranyuk:

At 23.10, Captain Baranyuk flew an La-5 plane to patrol in the searchlight field No. 12. In the area of Pushkino[9] at an altitude of 4,000 metres, the fighter pilot noticed 2 enemy aircraft illuminated by searchlights. One flew a course of 140°, the other a course of 220°. He began the pursuit of the enemy aircraft which was heading 220° – to Moscow. At an altitude of 6,000 metres, he made an attack, raising the nose of the aircraft. At the time of the attack, anti-aircraft artillery was firing at the enemy aircraft. After the first attack, Captain Baranyuk's plane went into a corkscrew. When exiting the corkscrew at an altitude of 5,000 metres, the fighter lost its target.

At the same time, one or two German planes dropped bombs on Moscow to lighten their weight and speed their exit from the zone of powerful air defence. They fell in the city centre near the building of the Moscow Council (municipality) and on Stromynka Street in the Sokolniki district. So, in fact, by chance, the last bombing of the Soviet capital during the war took place.

Because of the problems, only 109 German aircraft reached the main target of the attack. When the bombers bypassed Moscow and flew in a north-easterly direction, their heading was sent to the headquarters of the Rybinsk-Yaroslavl divisional area of air defence, led by Major General of artillery I.S. Smirnov. At 23:30 Moscow time, air raid sirens began to wail in Yaroslavl, and soon there was a staccato roar of anti-aircraft gunfire. Seventeen minutes later, at 23.47, the first bombers appeared over the city, dropping lighting bombs. This was followed by a hit on the water abstraction intake, after which an attack on industrial targets began.

The defence of Yaroslavl was carried out by ninety-four anti-aircraft guns, fifty-five anti-aircraft machine guns, and seventeen fighters from the 147th Air Defence Fighter Division under the command of Colonel Ivan Krasnoyurchenko. The main target of the attack was Yaroslavl tyre plant No.736, located in the north-western part of the city. Despite a strong and fairly accurate barrage from anti-aircraft guns, the German planes stubbornly went to the target, dropping high-explosive and heavy incendiary bombs. These easily broke through the wooden roofs of buildings and exploded on the upper floors or directly among machines and equipment. Then fiery jets of flammable liquid poured out of the sky. The viscous combustible mixture was almost impossible to extinguish, and everything that came in its way instantly caught fire. Workshops and warehouses were completely filled with combustible materials, which further fuelled the blaze. Soon, fire trucks arrived at the plant and they, together with the shop unitary teams, tried to tackle the fires, but there was no water in the network, and the routes to artificial fire reservoirs were blocked by fires and wreckage.

By 01.00, most of the industrial buildings had turned into huge bonfires. The last group of planes dropped bombs on the Yaroslavl Motor plant, the SK-1 synthetic rubber plant, the Vspolye railway station, and the railway bridge over the Volga. The bridge was not affected, but the industrial enterprises were significantly damaged. Several bombs fell on the Yaroslavl tobacco factory, where a warehouse containing 140 tons of tobacco was destroyed and burned down. Cigarettes were in extremely short supply in the USSR, and this airstrike was a terrible setback for smoking citizens!

The thermal and power station (TJEC No.1) was also affected. The old machine shop burned down, and the new machine shop and the concrete overpass that fed fuel to the bunkers were destroyed. There was a danger of the station shutting down due to the lack of fuel delivery. A participant in these events, K.N. Furmanov, later recalled:

> During the war, I was the head of the boiler shop and at the same time the head of the emergency recovery team. Our team was assigned the territory under the boilers in the ash room. Deafening explosions shook the building… we realised that high-explosive bombs had exploded somewhere very close. It was reported that the bomb hit the smoke pump. It was necessary to go up there, to a height of more than 30 metres,

in the dark on the stairs, shuddering from the explosions. The view of the ruined chamber was terrible. Everything seemed to be on fire, even the phone booth and the oil tank. Because of the smoke, you couldn't see where the sand boxes were, or where the hydrants were. But the training in the units was not wasted: everyone did exactly what was necessary at the moment.

The bombing of the station and the resulting fire killed the head of the Department of Labour A. Mitroshin, the head of another department, G.I. Vahnjuk, fitter A.P. Morozov and stoker M. Yakhnin. Four people were injured.

During the raid, telephone stations and the city telephone network in the Kirov, Stalinsky and Kaganovich districts of Yaroslavl were also severely damaged. In total, 190 tons of bombs of all calibres were dropped. According to the calculations of the Russian MPVO service, about 1,500 bombs fell on Yaroslavl and the surrounding areas during the one-and-a-half-hour raid.

On the way back from Yaroslavl, some German crews again lost their course and ended up over Moscow and its environs. At least sixteen bombers passed through the anti-aircraft artillery fire zone, and sixty-two flew through the searchlight fields (twenty-eight were illuminated). In fact, the event looked like a random air attack on Moscow without dropping bombs. In the city and its surroundings, ten anti-aircraft artillery regiments fired 7,776 rounds at the aircraft. The Russians even fired in panic from particularly powerful captured German 105mm anti-aircraft guns (fifty-nine shells were fired). Anti-aircraft artillery in the areas of Noginsk, Kashira, Serpukhov, Kolomna and Ivankovo also conducted a hurricane fire, shooting another 8,439 shells, a quarter of which were 37mm. In total, while reacting to this quasi-raid on Moscow, the anti-aircraft gunners spent more than 16,000 shells!

At 00.48 in the light searchlight field No. 11, a bomber returning from Yaroslavl was attacked by a Yak-1 fighter of Senior Lieutenant Konstantinov from the 429th IAP. The pilot performed one attack and said that the enemy aircraft was left smoking and went down, but he didn't see the fall. Another He 111, which was coming through the light searchlight field on a course of 220° at 01.21 was attacked by the MiG-3 of Junior Lieutenant Rodin from the 16th IAP. After the first attack, the bomber abruptly turned away and went into the clouds.

Incompetent Russian generals reported to Stalin that the Germans had tried to raid Moscow that night, 'but they were not allowed to pass, and they went to Yaroslavl'. In fact, this raid showed convincingly that the air defence of the capital, which had taken two years to construct and had been infinitely strengthened, was completely ineffective! Dozens of planes passed in the immediate vicinity of the city and above it at a 'working' altitude of 4,000m, and some even twice. At the same time, Russian night fighters made sixty-three sorties but reported only three downed planes, with another one claimed by the gunners. The 1st VIA PVO's own losses were two Yak-7BS from the 445th IAP, the pilot of one being seriously injured.

In fact during the raid on Yaroslavl three aircraft were lost:

- He 111 H-16 Wrk Nr 160518 '1G+MM' (crew: pilot Feldwebel Fritz Haug, navigator Unteroffizier Alois Ebner, flight engineer Obergefreiter Rudolf Kohler and flight mechanic Unteroffizier Georg Geissler) of 4./KG 27 was missing;
- He 111 H-16 Wrk Nr 160398 '1G+CA' (crew: pilot Feldwebel Willi Ebbinhaus,[10] navigator Unteroffizier Heinz Schroter, flight engineer Unteroffizier Alfons Hoffmann and flight mechanic Feldwebel Hermann Petersen) of 4./KG 27 was missing;
- He 111 H-16 Wrk Nr 167690 '5J+FR' (crew: Oberleutnant Otto-Bernd Schubert, navigator Unteroffizier Wilhelm Kuhne, flight engineer Unteroffizier Herbert Wehrner, flight mechanic Unteroffizier Heinz Werner, side gunner Unteroffizier Heinz Kretzer) of 6./KG 4 was missing.

It was not possible to identify which of these planes were shot down in the area of the target and which were shot down on the flight route. In the vicinity of Moscow (in the Pavlov Posad area), only one crashed He 111 and five dead crew members were found. It was probably He 111 H-16 Wrk Nr 167690 '5J+FR'.

Most of the German bombers safely passed through the anti-aircraft fire zone and returned to their air bases. According to the records in Fliegerbuchs of pilots from KG 27, He 111 H '1G+FS' landed in Olsufevo at 00.55, the duration of the flight being 263 minutes. The crew reported that the bombing was carried out from a height of 3,800m, and the message noted anti-aircraft fire, searchlights and night fighters. He 111 H '1G+EL' landed at 01.50 after 340 minutes, and He 111 H '1G+AL' landed at 01.45 after 330 minutes.[11]

Simultaneously with the air attack on Yaroslavl, several Do 217 E-4s from the experimental Staffel of II./KG 101, based at Pleskau (Pskov), raided the city of Rybinsk. They used bombs with rocket boosters. As a result, the power station of the city's aircraft engine plant was damaged, the boat factory was severely destroyed, as well as the Severnyi village where most of the workers lived. At the same time, anti-aircraft fire damaged Leutnant Heinz Frommhold's bomber, but it managed to reach its base on a single engine.

In the morning, the residents of Yaroslavl did not recognise their city. Smog from burning rubber hung over the banks of the Volga, obscuring the June sun. Fragments of bombs and anti-aircraft shells littered the streets everywhere. Clouds of smoke and steam rose over the Yaroslavl tyre plant.

All production buildings were severely damaged by explosions and fire, with the exception of buildings 'Z' and 'E'. The main body of 'A' was almost destroyed. The 'I', 'D', 'V', 'B', 'G' and 'F' buildings were significantly damaged. Thus, despite the difficulties of the mission, Luftwaffe put seven production facilities and a factory laboratory out of action. Heavy equipment in workshops No. 2, 3 and 4 was severely damaged and required dismantling and major repairs.

Structures and communications for supplying steam, air, water and electricity failed. The fire caused sixteen rolls and calenders[12] to burst, 40 per cent of the equipment's heavy bearings transmission to melt, and the foundation frames of two heavy calenders (friction and manufacturing of rubber sheets) to burst. Heavy fire and direct hits from bombs destroyed, damaged and deformed many pieces of heavy machinery. Nineteen of the twenty-three electric motors that drove heavy equipment, along with the 6 kilowatt starting equipment, were damaged so badly that they required disassembly, major repairs and replacement, the rest minor repairs. Of the six magnetic stations, four were completely burned down, and the remaining ones needed major repairs. Three-quarters of the plant's cable facilities were destroyed. The 220v and 500v power grids failed, and all the small- and medium-sized electric motors of the starting equipment were damaged.[13]

When the Yaroslavl plant buildings were still smoking, the People's Commissar of the rubber industry, Timofey Mitrokhin, chief engineer of Glavshinprom (the main department of the tyre industry of the USSR) M.I. Ivanov and other responsible employees arrived at the scene of devastation. They saw a terrible picture: everywhere they could see the charred skeletons of supporting columns, collapsed floor structures with burned, mangled fittings, broken down electric motors and other equipment. The entire territory of the factory was littered with collapsed structures. On the morning of 10 June, the attack on Yaroslavl was reported to the

State Defence Committee and personally to Stalin. Soon General Mikhail Gromadin, the commander of the Soviet air defence, who was in Gorky, learned about the bombing of a new target. The population of the country received scant information about the new air attack from the newspapers. *Izvestia* reported:

> On the night of June 10, a group of German planes tried to raid Yaroslavl. Several enemy planes broke through the barrage to the city, randomly dropping incendiary and high-explosive bombs. The resulting fires of residential buildings were quickly eliminated. There are victims among the civilian population. Anti-aircraft artillery shot down 6 bombers.

The command of the Rybinsk-Yaroslavl divisional air defence district drafted a report in which it was stated that of the sixty-five bombers sent to Yaroslavl 'about 20 broke through'. In fact, the VNOS posts and radar operators 'made a mistake in calculations', understating the number of aircraft involved in the raid by almost two times.

On the afternoon of 10 June, Russian air surveillance posts recorded the approach of a high-altitude reconnaissance aircraft. Between 13.44 and 16.55, the aircraft, identified as a Ju 88, flew the route Sychevka–Pogoreloe Gorodishche–Novo–Zavidovo (there he was unsuccessfully fired at by anti-aircraft guns)–Kimry–Kalyazin–Yaroslavl at an altitude of 10,000–12,000m. The plane returned along the route: Kalyazin–Kimry–Klin–Volokolamsk–Sychevka. The scout recorded the results of the air attack on Yaroslavl.

Seven fighters took off to intercept, some of which reached an altitude of 10,500m, but could not catch up with the target. Over the city of Sychevka, the reconnaissance plane was pursued by pilots of the 34th IAP; Shagalov, Shishlov, Barashkin and Bukarev. Junior Lieutenant Afanasy Iontsev's MiG-3 was the closest to the target. He took off from the Alferovo air base at 16.00. In the area of Teryaev Sloboda, at an altitude of 10,500m, the pilot saw a target above him, on a course of 270°. The sun was shining in his face and he could not keep track of the plane. Iontsev had overtaken the target on the left and was now watching it from behind on the right. The scout flew slowly south-west, gaining altitude. The German crew figured out the interceptor's manoeuvre and began to turn to the left, trying to keep it under them. Above Shakhovskaya station, the MiG-3 reached 11,400m, and the target was 100m above it. Iontsev could not get any higher, and his fuel was running low. 'Stalin's Falcon' then decided to destroy the target by ramming and positioned himself under the scout. However, at that moment flames burst out in the cockpit, burning the pilot's face. With that, Iontsev took to his parachute.

The pilot immediately lost consciousness as a result of his sudden bale out and oxygen starvation, but not before he managed to pull the parachute ring. In an unconscious state, he landed 155km west of the city of Sychevka, near the village of Medvedka. This was not far from the front line in the area of the German stronghold of Velizh. Iontsev was blown there by the wind from a height of 11,000m. The pilot was found and sent to the front-line hospital, where he only regained consciousness on the morning of 11 June. He was already being considered as 'not returned from a mission' back at his aviation regiment.

Iontsev (if his story is true) did the almost impossible – in an old interceptor he managed to achieve a fantastic height of 11,400m and almost shot down the elusive scout. The pilot claimed to have seen a Ju 86 P-1, an elusive stratospheric reconnaissance plane that flew several times over Moscow. In fact, it was an experimental Ju 88 D-6 of 4.(F)/121, equipped with a GM-1 injection system, which enabled the aircraft to gain altitude and escape Soviet fighters.

By this time, the MiG-3 fighter was almost obsolete. Production of the type was discontinued in early 1942 but the remaining examples were repaired many times and continued in service. Until the arrival of the British Spitfire, the MiG-3 remained the only high-altitude interceptor in the air force of the Red Army.

'A thunderstorm of incredible power'

On 10 June, German reconnaissance planes did not fly over Gorky. This caused optimism in the air defence headquarters, but the tension was palpable. When the hand of the clock approached 10 pm, everyone became noticeably nervous. There was also tension in the streets of Gorky. Many of the residents were smoking anxiously, eyeing the darkening sky warily. In the south-west of Gorky, citizens, fearing a German raid, hurried to leave the city. Grim columns of women and children with bags and carts moved to the safety of the suburbs. The gunners arranged the boxes of shells more comfortably and checked the mechanisms of their guns. Closer to night, it got colder, down to 16°C, and a weak north-east wind was blowing.

At 22.30, air surveillance posts recorded the passage of German aircraft. This time, the Luftwaffe was more cautious. The bombers followed a compact front 25 to 30km south of Kashira, bypassing Ryazan from the north. At the same time, another group passed through Stalinogorsk, south of Ryazan.

Two high-explosive bombs were dropped on peat extraction sites in the Krivaldino area (10km east of Shatura). As a result, two elevating crane were broken. Soon it became clear that the planes were again flying in the direction of Gorky.

At 23.00, VNOS posts in the Murom area reported: 'The hum of aircraft engines is heard.' At 23.24, General Alexey Osipov ordered an 'air alert' signal. The city alarm was taken by the city's districts and duplicated by means of notification within seven minutes. According to observers, fifty He 111s and Ju 88s were coming to the city. A total of eighteen group and single targets were recorded flying along the route Murom–Pavlovo–Gorky at an altitude of 4,000–6,000m. According to German data, eighty-six aircraft participated in the raid.

Shortly after midnight, more than 100 photoflash bombs lit up over Gorky. The first targets of the attack were again water abstraction intakes on the Oka River. A.I. Starikov, the son of one of the members of the crew of the dredger *Volzhsky-15*, standing at the high right bank of the river, recalled:

> I, as a potential employee, had my own cabin in the hold, where I slept soundly that terrible night. Through a dream I heard an incredible storm. The incessant roar of thunder and the bright flashes of lightning gradually gave me some uneasiness, and I began to wake up. When I awoke from my dream, I realised that something terrible was happening.

Running out on deck, the teenager saw an impressive sight. From the direction of the Gorky automobile plant, the roar of exploding bombs could be heard shaking the air, and anti-aircraft shells were exploding from above. The sky was lit up with bright, brief flashes. And in the sky, as if suspended, photoflash bombs burned like huge chandeliers. They illuminated the entire surface in the immediate area.

Starikov recalled:

> On the high bank, high above us, an anti-aircraft battery was firing. Either the shells did not reach the desired height, or the anti-aircraft gunners made a mistake when

choosing the direction of fire, only they exploded over us and showered shrapnel on the deck, and no downed aircraft appeared. Bomb blasts were visible in many places in the city. Then, with an unpleasant howl, a stream of bombs fell on the channel dug by our dredger, the restored water abstraction intake, and two land mines exploded at our dredger on the left side. My father was there, on watch, and I was worried about him. Fortunately, the ship was not damaged, but the boats alongside were torn off and carried down the stream.

The bombers again attacked the already heavily damaged and incapacitated Molotov plant. As a result of a direct hit by two SD70 bombs and one Brand C250A, a large fire broke out in the dilapidated engine assembly shop No.2. The roof collapsed and 200sqm of thermal insulation covering the walls was burned. In the grey cast iron foundry, powerful explosions destroyed the cooling conveyor, and severely damaged the roof trusses of the model warehouse and conveyor No. 3. A strong fire broke out. Two SC50 bombs destroyed the barracks of one of the units of the NKVD regiment for the protection of the plant, killing one person. In mechanical assembly shop No. 4, a high-explosive bomb broke through three floors and destroyed the canteen of the technical sector. A strong fire broke out in a warehouse of American cars, where about thirty cars were burned. A powerful explosion near the thermal power plant destroyed a power line running in the direction of the river harbour. Plenty of air bombs of different calibres exploded in already destroyed workshops, where it was not possible to specify the damage. Several bombs fell on the aircraft engine plant No. 466.

German planes dropped 215 high-explosive and about 100 incendiary bombs on residential areas, the river harbour and the old water abstraction intake station, according to the Russian rescue service (MPVO), seventy BrandC50A and BrandC50B bombs fell on the village of Zeleny, as well as seventy small incendiary bombs weighing a kilogram. There were large fires that engulfed entire streets. As a result, twelve barracks, school No. 24 and 300 wooden sheds were destroyed and burned. The surviving buildings were heavily damaged. According to official data, seven people were killed and four others were injured. In the harbour, the port office, six warehouses (including three containingcement), as well as four cargo transporters and a centrifugal pump were destroyed.

In shallow water, a barge with a displacement of 125 BRT was sunk by bombs. twenty-five high-explosive bombs were dropped on the village of Monastyrka. Two exploded near the building of the local municipality, the rest fell among the houses. A barracks burned down near the site where vehicles acquired through lend-lease were unpacked, and a fountain of water gushed out of the broken water main. On one of the streets an earth bomb shelter containing eighty residents caved in. Although the local MPVO team started digging immediately, three of them suffocated and died.

Fires at the Molotov automobile plant and in the residential sector were extinguished by eighteen fire pumps and two fire trains, and fires in the harbour were fought by a fire steamer and a boat. Small fires and incendiary bombs were extinguished by self-defence groups. The engine workshop No. 2 burned the longest, and the fire was only localised and eliminated by 04.00.

During the attack, other areas and facilities of the city of Gorky were also affected: the food concentrate plant, the 25 let Oktyabrya ship repair plant, the Molitovsky pier, the No. 718 Engine of the Revolution plant, Myza airfield, and many residential buildings. Thirty-three incendiary bombs fell in the grounds of the mental hospital in Lyakhovo, located on the hilly right bank of the Oka River. The patients coped with the consequences of the bombing very successfully, and firefighting units and groups acted smoothly, promptly detecting all the fires, delivering buckets of sand and extinguishing all the bombs. Only seven chicken coops were burned to the ground, killing the chickens. Twenty more incendiary bombs fell into a ravine behind the mental hospital fence.

According to Soviet information, during the fifth raid on Gorky, German bombers dropped 330 high-explosive and more than 200 incendiary large-calibre bombs. Anti-aircraft artillery fired 23,033 large and 3,943 small-calibre rounds, and 12.7mm machine guns fired 2,722 rounds.[14] The anti-aircraft gunners claimed ten downed planes; at the same time the Russians were sure that they were being attacked not only by Ju 88s and He 111s, but also by a whole group of Fw 200 'Condors'!

Fighters of the 142nd IAD also actively participated in repelling the raid, but only one pilot managed to intercept an enemy bomber. On orders from the division's command post, at 23.29 Captain Voronovich took an La-5 fighter to patrol the sector south-west of Gorky. Soon he found a single He 111 on the bright part of the horizon, on a collision course. The pilot decided to attack him from the front, but the bomber quickly slipped past,

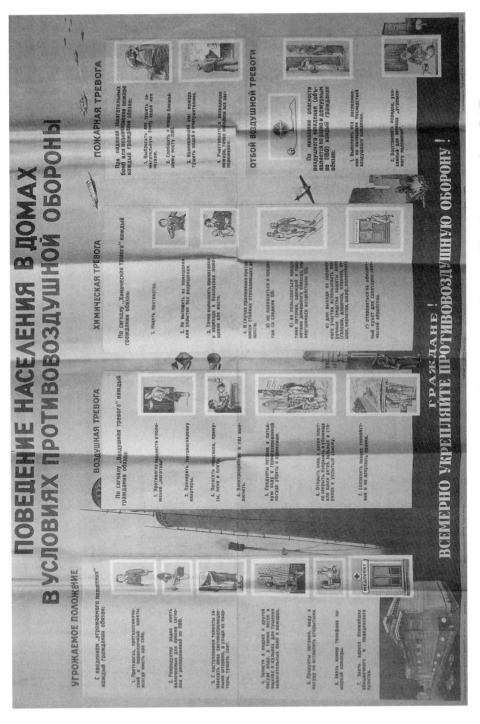

Soviet poster showing the actions of people during the air alarm. (History Museum of Russian car-producer GAZ)

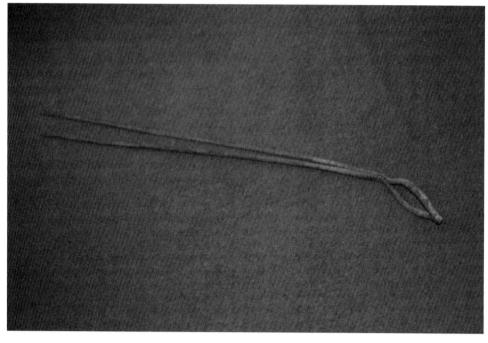

Metal tongs used for capturing and extinguishing incendiary bombs.

and Voronovich did not have time to open fire. Quickly turning 180°, he went to the rear of the enemy plane. In his report, he later wrote:

> I conducted an attack on the left, from behind,[15] from a distance of 50–70 metres, followed by an exit for the attack on the right, from below.[16] The firing was conducted from a distance of 30–40 metres, then, coming to the left side, carried out the 3rd attack from a distance of 20–30 metres. After the third attack, the left engine of the enemy aircraft caught fire. The fourth attack was made on the right, from behind at the same height.

Approaching the He 111, Voronovich opened fire from a distance of 20–30m, but almost simultaneously he was fired on from the upper turret of the bomber. Then, when the distance between the fighter and the target was reduced to a minimum, the German pilot turned to the right, slowed down and the La-5 passed it. As the planes drew level, the German sidegunner fired at the pursuer with his machine gun, achieving several hits. This forced the Soviet pilot to abruptly change course and stop the attack, while the

He 111 went down. Returning to the airfield, Captain Voronovich stated that he saw the Heinkel crash into the ground, and he was credited with a victory.

After 01.00 Berlin time, the tired German crews returned to their bases. He 111 H '1G+AL' of 3./KG 27 landed at Olsufevo at 01.10, having been in the air for exactly five hours. Five minutes later, He 111 H '1G+DP' from the 6th Staffel landed, the duration of flight was also five hours, during which the aircraft covered 1,600km. He 111 H '1G+FS' of 8./KG 27 landed at 01.31, having spent 305 minutes in the air. He 111 H '1G+EL' of 3./KG 27 was a little late in arriving, landing at Olsufevo at 02.00, with a flight time of almost six hours.

The repulse of this air attack was personally directed by the commander of the air defence of the Soviet Union, Lieutenant General Mikhail Gromadin. At dawn, he sent a telegram from Gorky to Joseph Stalin, in which he outlined the frightening details of the raid:

> On the night of June 10–11, 1943, the enemy raided the city of Gorky. The raid involved 135–140 aircraft, including 35 four-engine FW 200s, the rest Ju 88s and He 111s. The raid was carried out from airfields: Orel-69, Bryansk-30, Karachev-24, Senda-17. According to radio direction finders, the bombing was carried out from a height of 4,000–5,500 metres. Direction finders did not detect diving. The dropping of luminous bombs was performed from a height of 5,500–6,000 metres. The bombardment was conducted with a mass dropping of lighting bombs, which were successfully destroyed: at high altitudes by large-calibre artillery, and at low altitudes by small-calibre anti-aircraft artillery and machine guns.

Further, to show the 'effectiveness' of air defence, Gromadin reported to the dictator about 'minor damage' to two workshops at the Molotov plant and seven houses in the residential sector. He attributed ten downed German planes to anti-aircraft artillery, four of which were allegedly 'found' on the ground at the time of the 'clear a' signal. The number of victims was also determined as 'minimal', with the report giving a dubious figure of fifteen dead.

According to German data, during the air attack on Gorky that night, only one He 111 H-6 Wrk Nr 7681 '5J+MN' of the commander of 4./KG 4 'General Wever', Hauptmann Paul Krohmer, went missing. This was a heavy loss for this Kampfgeschwader. Krohmer was an experienced veteran and

Destroyed kindergarten in Avtozavodsky district city of Gorky.

Fire station in the city of Gorky.

had led the 4th Staffel from 10 October 1942. The fate of Krohmer (as well as the rest of his crew: navigator Feldwebel Wilhelm Dersch, flight engineer Unteroffizier Dietrich Waschow, Flight Mechanic Feldwebel Horst Petigk and Flight Gunner Gefreiter Adolf Wasserburger) remained unknown. Until 12 July, 4./KG 4 flew without an official commander. It was only after this that Oberleutnant Gerhard Morich took over the post. The Luftwaffe had a tradition: after a unit's commander did not return from a mission it would wait about a month and hope that he would be able to avoid the brutal Russian captivity and return.

After this attack, the Russians had to defuse a large number of unexploded German bombs. Some of them had technical defects, but there were also bombs filled with sand instead of explosives. This was the result of sabotage at the military enterprises of the Third Reich. Thirty-four unexploded high-explosive bombs were found in the Avtozavodsky district, including twenty-four SC250. Another seventeen such 'gifts' were found on the streets of the village of Monastyrka and twenty-seven on the grounds of GAZ. Soldiers of the 22nd Engineer Battalion NKVD neutralised these bombs. In just a week, from 5 to 12 June, they defused 134 bombs of different calibres. In addition, in different parts of the city they found 146 found entrance holes, mostly from large incendiary bombs.

However, not all German bombs were harmless. On the morning of 11 June, the banks of the Oka River turned silvery from the huge number of dead fish. Whole dead shoals floated belly up under the Oka bridge, carried away by the current in the direction of the city of Kazan.

The answer of Stalin's Falcons

On 10 June, the Soviets continued their attacks against Luftwaffe air bases. A total of 193 aircraft (forty-four twin-engine bombers, fifty-four attack aircraft and 135 fighters) were allocated from the 1st Air Army to these raids. Part of the fighters were again intended for escort, the rest for 'cutting off' enemy fighters and blocking airfields.

In the evening, twenty-three Il-2s from the 571st and 566th Attack Aircraft Aviation Regiments raided Bryansk airfield. They were escorted by fighters from the 18th Guards IAP and the 168th IAP. The fighters were already on their way to the target and were met by German fighters and engaged in a difficult air battle. Attack aircraft, despite the powerful anti-aircraft fire, dropped bombs, but, as usual, they were inaccurate. Then, at the moment of turning back on their course, they were attacked by fifteen Bf 109s and Fw 190s from JG 51. As a result, eighteen Il-2s were shot down, and only five crews managed to bring their bullet- and shell-riddled aircraft back to their airfields.[17] The failure of the attack was blamed on the commander of the 168th IAP, Major K.A. Pilschikov, who was arrested and put on trial by a military tribunal. However, the main point is that the kamikaze-style self-sacrifice of Russian attack aircraft was completely ointless. On 10 June Ju 88 A bombers from II and III./KG 51 'Edelweiss' were stationed at the Bryansk airfield, but none of them were damaged.

Twenty-three crews of the 62nd and 312th Attack Aircraft Aviation Regiments were assigned to attack the Seshchinskaya air base again. The planes arrived at the target at 20.20 Moscow time, when the bomber crews were having dinner, preparing for another raid on the Volga Region. Their reception was 'very hot'. The approaching 'Zementbombers' were met by fire from dozens of anti-aircraft guns of different calibres and heavy machine guns, including those located at the Seshchinskaya station and in the village of the same name. The firing from hundreds of weapon sripped through the evening sky. The shooting was carried out in three tiers, and around the air base there was a continuous cone of explosions at all altitudes. Russian attack aircraft pilots had not received such a 'welcome salute' before. It was clear that in such circumstances no choice of specific targets was possible. The pilots dropped all the ammunition at once on the target area, then immediately turned to the side.

A direct hit from a projectile on the Il-2 of Second Lieutenant A.G. Kuznetsov tore off the right wing, and his aircraft fell to the ground like a stone. Two more attack aircraft were damaged. Several Fw 190s attempted to attack the group as they were moving away from the target, but they were prevented by escort fighters that had a large numerical superiority. The Germans preferred to avoid the battle and disappear into the clouds. And yet before that, they managed to knock out two 'Zementbombers', which made forced landings.

At this time, the bulk of IV./JG 51's fighters were busy destroying the aircraft of the 224th Attack Aircraft Aviation Division and the approaching Pe-2 dive bombers. As a result, while the Il-2 pilots, who were looking around in fear, were rushing back to their territory, Pe-2s from the 204th Bombardment Aviation Division were dying behind them one by one. The nine planes led by the squadron commander, Major I.G. Ageev, were all shot down and twenty-seven members of their crews were killed or captured. It was a complete rout.[18]

The next day, Russian reconnaissance planes tried to photograph the results of the attack, but saw only clouds and haze in the area of the target. According to German data, on 10 June both objects of suicidal Russian attacks (Seshchinskaya and Bryansk air bases) did not receive any significant damage. But the irretrievable Soviet losses during the attacks amounted to forty-one aircraft, including nineteen Il-2s, eleven Pe-2s, four La-5s, four Yak-7s and three Yak-1s. Once again the JG 51 pilots distinguished themselves by shooting down most of the lost Russian planes. Oberfeldwebel Hans Pfahler of 12./JG 51 shot down four Pe-2s and one La-5 within fourteen minutes. The commander of 10./JG 51, Oberleutnant Horst-Gunther von Fassong, shot down three Pe-2s within nine minutes. Cavalier Knight's Cross recipient Leutnant Heinrich Hofemeier of 3./JG 51 shot down three Il-2s in eight minutes. Oberfeldwebel Gunther Kossatz and Unteroffizier Gunther Josten of I./JG 51 shot down three more 'Zementbombers' each in six and nine minutes.

In total, I./JG 51's pilots claimed to have shot down twenty-one Il-2s, two Pe-2s, two La-5s and one Yak-1 (in the period from 19.16 to 19.46); pilots of III./JG 51 claimed seven Il-4s and two La-5s (in the period from 19.13 to 19.25); and pilots from IV./JG 51 accounted for twelve Pe-2s, two Il-2s and two La-5s (in the period from 19.03 to19.36).

Spanish volunteers also distinguished themselves, and counted five downed Soviet aircraft on this day: Vicente Aldecoa, LaGG-3 (19.20); Luis Azquet-Brunet, LaGG-3 (19.04); Juan-Ramon Galivan, Il-2 (19.12); Javier-Maria Güibert, LaGG-3 (19.15); and Gonzalo Hevia, LaGG-3 (19.15). These aerial victories roughly corresponded to the actual losses of the Soviets. The only discrepancy relates to the types of Soviet aircraft. The Spaniards probably confused the Yak-1/Yak-7 with the LaGG-3.

According to Soviet data, from 5 to 10 June, its aircraft undertook 3,360 sorties against Luftwaffe air bases, destroying from 140 to 170 aircraft. In fact, the Russians managed to destroy only one Ju 88 on the ground! Two other aircraft were slightly damaged. At the same time, the attackers' own losses amounted to 106 aircraft. According to the operational department of the Red Army air force, the combat survivability of the Il-2 during raids on enemy airfields in May–June 1943 averaged one loss per 15.2 sorties.

On the night of 11 June, Russian long-range bombers again undertook major raids on Bryansk and Orel air bases, with the crews reporting the destruction of 150 aircraft! Its own losses, including from German

He 111 bombers at the airfield. Summer 1943.

Commander III./KG 27 Hauptmann Klein and commander KG 27 Oberst leutnant von Beust. Air base Olsufevo, June 1943. (Photo from Boelcke Archiv)

anti-aircraft artillery fire, amounted to nineteen aircraft. Interestingly, the German night fighters claimed only two downed aircraft. Success was achieved by Hauptmann Rudolf Schoener of St.I./NJGr.100 and Oberfeldwebel Christian Rorrs of I./NJGr.100. Again, the claims of Soviet aviation were in vain; in fact, again there was no serious damage to German airfields.

It was only on the night of 11–12 June that the Soviets achieved their first small success in their attempts to thwart the Luftwaffe. Groups of night bombers comprised of Pe-8s, Il-4s (DB-3s), North American B-25 Mitchells, Li-2 and TB-3s carried out 486 sorties to attack the air bases at Shatalovo, Seshchinskaya, Bryansk, Orel and Borovsk. At the same time, German airfields were also attacked by U-2 light night bombers. As a result, the Russians managed to disable fourteen German aircraft.

Three Fi 156 reconnaissance aircraft from NAGr.5 were destroyed (they were mainly engaged in reconnaissance of partisan positions in the Bryansk forests). Another three Hs 126 Bs from the same group received damage of between 15 and 40 per cent. Two Bf 110 G-3s from 1.(H)/16 were also badly damaged. Of the ground personnel, eight were killed and seventeen others were injured. WeFlugSt 'Schatalowka' suffered the most damage! This meteorological unit lost six Ju 88 A/Ds and as a result actually lost its combat capability. After these losses, in order to continue weather reconnaissance over the Volga Region, the Germans had to borrow aircraft from their neighbours. As a result, on 12 June, two Ju 88s from Wekusta 76/1 (operating on the southern flank of the Eastern Front) were sent on a business trip to Shatalovka air base.[19]

Attacks by Russian armoured attack aircraft, specially designed to defeat such targets, were completely useless. What happened to the hundreds of bombs dropped by 'Zementbombers' that never made it to German airfields? The answer is simple: they fell on nearby towns and villages, on fields and gardens, often on the heads of their own civilians. In the report on the operations of the 1st Air Army for June 1943 regarding the ineffective bombing, there was a disappointing conclusion: 'It should be noted that in the operation to strike enemy airfields, we suffered extremely large losses, especially 10.06, which could have been avoided with better organisation of combat work.'

Russian U-2 biplanes, light night bombers, were the most troublesome for the Germans. Sometimes German planes returning from a raid were about to land and would meet them in the dark. And to combat these 'sewing machines' (as they were called by German soldiers from the characteristic sound of their low-powered engine), some units allocated their own night fighters. P. Mobius of 9./KG 27 recalled:

> Sometimes in the morning twilight we encountered slow-moving enemy aircraft. These were 'worrying' planes that bombed the airfield. Although we all talked about organising a night hunt for these 'boxes', I believe that Oberleutnant Walter Grasemann[20] was the only one who remained over the airfield and in his He 111 shot down several Russian planes.

New victim

On the evening of 12 June, Russian air observation posts again recorded the flight of a large group of German aircraft from Orel and Bryansk. But this time they flew much to the south of Tula, over Yelets and then over Lipetsk. At first, the Russians thought it was a new raid on Gorky. But it soon became clear that the bombers were heading east – towards the cities of Kuibyshev or Saratov. When, at 23.40 local time, the planes flew near the city of Balashov, it became clear that their new target was Saratov. Soon information was received about another group of bombers that had taken off from Stalino (in the Donbas) and was approaching Saratov from the south-west.

Like previous targets, this city met the first massive air attack unprepared. By June 1943, the air defence of Saratov and its surrounding areas was provided by the Saratov divisional air defence district under the command of Colonel M.V. Antonenko (chief of staff Lieutenant Colonel N.A. Tikhonov). It consisted of two anti-aircraft artillery regiments (the 720th and 1078th ZenAP) and two separate anti-aircraft artillery divisions (the 89th and 501st OZAD). They were armed with 192 large-calibre guns (76mm and 85mm), seventy-two small-calibre guns, and ninety anti-aircraft machine guns. In three separate batteries there were four SON-2 gun-pointing stations. In addition, the air defence force included the 43rd Anti-aircraft Searchlight Regiment, which had ninety-eight searchlights, three separate VNOS battalions, and a separate communications platoon. Notification of all parts of the divisional area was assigned to the main post of VNOS, and anti-aircraft artillery units to their observation posts. To control the airspace there were two RUS-2S Pegmatit radar stations, which were subordinate to the commander of the 144th Fighter Aviation

Division of Air Defence (142nd Air Defence IAD). There were also forty-eight barrage balloons in Saratov.[21]

Large-calibre anti-aircraft artillery was located in three combat sectors. The 1st (Northern) sector covered the city of Saratov and its enterprises. The 2nd (South-West) protected objects located to the south of the city (Uleshovskaya and Uvekskaya oil storage facilities). Sector 3 (South-East) covered the railway bridge over the Volga and the city of Engels, located on the eastern bank. The 20mm and 37mm anti-aircraft guns were mainly for the defence of the thermal and power station (TJEC), the Kirov oil cracking plant and the bridge over the Volga. In the defence of other cities in the Saratov region (Balashov, Rtischevo) there were several dozen anti-aircraft guns and machine guns. In the area of Saratov, the 3rd Brigade of River Ships of the Volga Military Flotilla was based, which carried out anti-aircraft and mine defence of the Volga.

Major I.P. Suvorov's 144th IAD had two fighter aviation regiments (the 405th IAP and the 963rd IAP). They were armed with forty-one aircraft and had twenty-three night fighter pilots. For night fighters, five battle night zones were set up around Saratov, which were adjacent to the anti-aircraft artillery fire zone.[22]

Combat personnel of the 144th Air Defence IAD

Regiment	Air base	Number of aircraft
405th IAP	Anisovka	12 Yak-1
	Nikolaevskij	7 Yak-1
963rd IAP	Razbojshhina	12 Hurricane, 1 Yak-1
	Balashov	9 Hurricane
Total:		41 (21 Hurricane and 20 Yak-1)

As in other Russian cities, 'traditional' Soviet disorder flourished in Saratov. The city did not have enough firefighting equipment, and there was a shortage of qualified personnel for service in the paramilitary fire protection at all sites. The service was carried out mainly by elderly citizens and disabled people. In Saratov, the blackout was massively violated at enterprises and in the residential sector. Fire reservoirs collapsed and turned into swamps. Shelters and the earth bomb shelters were filled with water, and these were often were used by the population as rubbish dumps. The city lacked concrete bomb shelters. On 17 April 1943, the NKVD department sent a message to the Saratov regional office of the Bolshevik party, stating: 'The state of the local air defence of the city does not meet the requirements of the situation. The planned activities of the city headquarters of MPVO are not carried out from month to month, especially for blackout, emergency recovery work and equipment of shelters, which puts the city of Saratov at risk in case of possible raids by enemy aircraft.'

And now the threat had become a reality. On 9 June, the Saratov city defence committee adopted resolution No. 179 'on blackout in the city of Saratov', which required the military and civil prosecutor's office to establish strict control over the observance of the blackout regime in factories and transport. At the enterprises, shelters were hastily put in order, sand and water were stored. But very little was done until 12 June.

At 23.50, local time, air raid sirens howled in the city, and twelve minutes later the first bombers approached the anti-aircraft artillery fire zone. Colonel Antonenko ordered the regiments to launch a barrage and the night fighters to take off. Ten ships of the Volga military flotilla protecting the railway bridge also started shooting from the river. Balloons rose silently into the sky. At 01.20, the operators of the RUS-2 radar station reported that the enemy was already over the city. And almost simultaneously, dazzling white photoflash bombs ('chandeliers') flashed high in the sky, snatching numerous factory buildings, residential buildings, oil tanks, and silhouettes of ships on the roadstead out of the gloom. For a moment all the townspeople stood in suspense, listening to the roar of guns and the dull bursts of shells. Soon the howl and whistling of falling bombs cut through the air. Bright flames erupted in the southern part of the city.

The main blow was inflicted on the Kirov oil cracking plant and the Uvek oil storage facility. He 111s dropped bombs from a height of 3,000–4,000m, and Ju 88s by diving. The air attack took place without preliminary reconnaissance, so the Germans were not aware of the weather in the area of the target. Therefore, when the bombers reached Saratov, there was dense cloud cover over the city, which prevented the mission from being completed. A large part of the 150 and 600 high-explosive and incendiary bombs fell past the attacked object. As a result of the raid, two earthen oil storage areas containing mazut, a low-quality fuel oil, ignited. The Krasny Tekstilshchik factory was also damaged, and one residential building and a school were destroyed. According to Soviet data, 36 people were killed, including members of the fire paramilitary guard and the civilian population.[23]

Air defence units were caught off guard and acted inefficiently. The searchlights performed twenty-four group searches, but because of low cloud cover, only one target was illuminated. However, anti-aircraft guns did not have time to fire at this single target. The gunners claimed two downed aircraft, but the Luftwaffe actually suffered no casualties. Night fighter sorties were also unsuccessful. Commands for take-off were given late, and the distribution of aircraft by patrol zones did not correspond to the air situation. The control system did not provide for the transfer of night fighters from one zone to another. All aircraft were concentrated in zones No.1 and No.4, and the Germans mostly flew through zones No.2 and No.5. As noted above, the interaction between anti-aircraft artillery, searchlights, and night fighters was poorly organised. Anti-aircraft fire zones and night fighter patrol zones were not clearly marked, and there was no way to determine the allegiance of searchlight-lit aircraft. This led to the fact that night fighters (the Russians scrambled eighteen interceptors in total) were often illuminated by searchlights and were fired upon by friendly anti-aircraft artillery fire. It turned out that the pilots of the 144th IAD were poorly prepared for action in night conditions.

I./KG 100, under the command of Major Paul Claas, participated in this raid. After the first three air attacks against the 'tank factory' in Gorky on the morning of 7 June, some of the aircraft returned to the old air base in Stalino. The other aircraft flew there in the following days. According to Helmut Abendvoth's flight record, his He 111 H '6N+EK', took off from Stalino at 19.47 Berlin time. The target of the attack was the oil cracking plant in Saratov. At 00.20, after 273 minutes of flight, the bomber returned.[24] That night, some of the bombers struck secondary targets. For example, a Ju 88 of 5./KG 51 'Edelweiss' bombed the railway station in Michurinsk for the second time in four days. Another proof of the inefficiency of the Russian air defence was the fact that the Luftwaffe suffered no losses in these long-range raids.

'Blood dogs led by von Beust'

On the evening of 13 June, a Ju 88 D of 1.(F)/100 once again performed aerial photography by flying over Gorky at a height of 8,000m. On the way back, a pair of MiG-3s from the 445th IAP tried to intercept the reconnaissance plane. They took off from Kashira airfield (south of Moscow). However, when the fighters approached, the experienced Luftwaffe crew changed their course in advance and disappeared.

One of the photos received showed the Strelka (the confluence of the Oka and Volga rivers) and the Oka bridge.[25] Interestingly, the Germans identified this object as the Eisenbetonbrücke Paschkoutnyj-Most (reinforced concrete pontoon bridge), although this name actually applied to an old wooden floating bridge that was dismantled in 1933. This outdated name and intelligence was probably extracted from old information about Nizhny Novgorod. The bridge was marked in the photo with the letter 'A', and specialist decoders from 1.(F)/100 described its parameters: five spans of 120m, a total length of 740m and a width of 21m. And this data fully corresponded to reality, i.e. the Germans were mistaken only in the name! The letter 'B' was designated the Kremlin, on the territory of which there were marked 'Arsenal', 'Palace of deputies' and 'military college'. In fact, these were the Arsenal, the House of Soviets and the school of radio specialists, respectively. German intelligence was clearly well aware of the location of all the important sites. The letter 'C' marked the territory of the former Nizhny Novgorod fair, the main parts of which were the 'main fair house' and the financial exchange building. The Germans probably did not know that the former 'main house' housed the Gorky city council. The experts deciphering the photo also highlighted mills near Kazansky railway station.

By the evening, the weather in Gorky was cloudy with a humidity of 51 per cent, but there was no rain. A north-easterly wind was blowing at a speed of 30mph. Until midnight, the city was calm, and many residents already hoped that the air raid would not happen tonight. However, these hopes were dashed and at 00.05 air raid sirens howled in all areas of the city, which had become a familiar messenger of approaching deadly danger.

At the headquarters of the Gorky corps air defence district, located in the old ravine between the spurs of the hills of the hilly part of Gorky, staff intently monitored incoming messages from VNOS posts and radars. The bombers carefully bypassed Moscow from the south and flew along the route Ryazan–Murom–Pavlovo–Gorky. The main mass moved in small groups at an altitude of 3,000–5000m. Single pathfinders on the way to the target periodically dropped photoflash bombs. When the first planes approached Dzerzhinsk, the 1291th ZenAP defending it began a barrage, then the 748th ZenAP began firing. But the bombers, despite the bursts of shells, continued to the target. This time, ninety-two aircraft participated in the raid. At the same time, some aircraft attacked secondary targets, for example an aircraft under the command of Hans Grotter, Ju 88 A-4 '9K+BN' of 5./KG 51, dropped bombs on Stalinogorsk.

The main target of the attack this time was the Leninsky district of Gorky, primarily the Engine of the Revolution factory, which produced 120mm

Aerial photos of the city of Gorky on June 13, 1943. The letter 'A' indicates the bridge over the Oka river; the letter 'B' – the Kremlin; the letter 'C' – the territory of the former Jarmarka and cargo port.

mortars, Katyusha rockets (the Germans called them 'Stalin's organs') and other military products. Diving Ju 88 As destroyed the water abstraction intake station on the Oka River (Pervomaiskaya vodokachka), completely interrupting the supply of water to residential settlements and businesses. Then, at 01.07, sixteen high-explosive and twenty heavy incendiary bombs were dropped on the Engine of the Revolution factory.

Four firefighters of the unitary team of workshop No. 12 – Kukushkin, Arakcheyev, Batyanov, Petrushenko – were at their posts, intently listening to what was happening on the streets. The first series of explosions was followed by a second, and then there was a sharp crunch from above, followed by a thud and a pop. After that, a bright flash lit up the entire room for a moment. The fighters saw combustible fluid that had sprayed within a radius of several tens of metres was blazing. Kukushkin and Arakcheyev grabbed buckets of sand and began throwing them in the fire, Batyanov and Petrushenko tried to pour water on the combustible fluid, but there were too many pockets of fire, and the sand quickly ran out. However, the fighters were not to be beaten and began to smother the flame with earth, sheets of iron and other non-flammable material. As a result, fire was prevented.

At the same time on the roof of the same building the firefighters Scheglov, Razzhivin, Zverev, Kudryashov, Petrov, under the leadership of superintendent Baturin, struggled with the consequences of incendiary bombs that fell on the roof of a neighbouring shop connected to workshop No. 12. The combustible liquid rolled like volcanic lava in several streams at once. The firefighters covered it with sand, hitting the flame with shovels, but the fire broke through from the other side. When people rushed there, the previously extinguished area flared up again. This battle with the fire lasted about an hour, while Razzhivin and Kudryashov regularly brought new sand up the fire escape. As a result, workshop No. 12 remained untouched by fire.[26]

Other buildings were less fortunate. In workshop No. 1, after a direct hit by a SC1000 bomb, the walls collapsed, and all the doors and windows were blown out. All the service spaces and toilets were destroyed. A second high-explosive bomb hit workshop No. 11, destroying all the walls and vestibules. The wooden building of the model shop, after being hit by incendiary bombs filled with a mixture of oil and petrol, was immediately engulfed in fire and completely burned down. At the same time, a large amount of equipment was lost: a motor crane, saw machines and machine tools. The flames completely destroyed the neighbouring workshop No. 13. In the foundry, which was the most important supplier of semi-finished products for artillery factory No. 92 and other enterprises, two cranes and railway gates were broken, while the metal structures of lanterns and window openings were damaged. In workshop No. 15, walls collapsed, crane tracks shifted, and the entire power grid failed. In the factory garage, too, there was a severe fire that destroyed the walls, an electric furnace, a repair shop, several cars and the entire stock of automobile parts and rubber that were available at the factory. The dining room was also badly damaged. An oil tank with a capacity of 1,100 m^3 was destroyed here, and boxes with ready-made parts for M-13 rockets were burned. Various damage was received by shop No. 2, the edging workshop, and glass and window frames were blown out in seven more workshops. The number of victims was small: three people were killed and twenty-seven suffered injuries of varying severity. In the workers' village, school No. 105 was destroyed during the bomb attack, and a bathhouse and barrack No. 3 were burned down on Shosseynaya Street.[27]

Twenty-two high-explosive and fifty heavy incendiary bombs were dropped on machine-tool factory No. 113 (which produced PPSh-41 sub-machine guns and gearboxes for T-34 tanks). As a result, six buildings were destroyed and one was damaged. In the main production workshop No. 6, 20 per cent of the roof, half of the partitions and openings and 40 per cent of the heating and ventilation system were destroyed by explosions and fires, the water supply and lighting were disabled, and all the windows and window covers were blown out. After numerous direct hits by bombs filled with combustible fluid the model and central material warehouses, mechanical workshop, equipment warehouse, main store adjacent parts (logistics warehouse) and the vegetable store burned down. Three gas-generating engines, one electric generator, 876 electric motors, twenty-two machines, thirteen fans, seven overhead cranes, five cargo lifts, two furnace machines, and all the equipment, materials and documentation of the *Stankogigant* newspaper were destroyed. In addition, a large amount of electrical equipment, measuring instruments, spare parts for electric motors and a locomotive vehicle were burned. Over 20 tons of non-ferrous metals were rendered unusable by the fire.

In workshops No. 2, 5, 9, 10 and 12 many incendiary bombs fell, but the fires were heroically extinguished by self-defence groups that were operating on many factory sites at once that night. For example, a fighter of the Tsybulsky control team, despite the close bomb explosions, remained on the observation tower until the last moment and passed the situation to the command post, until he was knocked down by an explosive wave from another bomb that fell on the plant. The doctor Snizhitskaya and the commander of Kukushkin's medical-sanitary platoon provided assistance throughout the bombing to the wounded in the residential building No. 9a on Pamirskaya Street, passing along the enterprise. Tataev and Dmitriev, soldiers from the emergency recovery team, dug victims out of the collapsed earth bomb shelters and saved many lives.[28]

The 25 Years of October ship repair plant, on the bank of the Oka River, was also bombed. Several explosions occurred in the bay, resulting in the sinking of one barge, and a second was broken up in shallow water. Forty-five high-explosive bombs fell on the Krasny Kozhevennik factory and the consumer goods shop was completely destroyed, where twelve workers were buried. The excavation of the building continued for forty minutes, after which the victims were sent to the hospital in serious condition.

The residential sector of the Leninsky district of Gorky was also severely affected. Fifty high-explosive and twelve heavy incendiary bombs fell on the village of Karpovka. Fires spread across entire streets, spreading from building to building, from shed to shed, fences and trees were ablaze. Fifty-six houses were destroyed by explosions and fire. One SC250 bomb hit the Karpov church, severely damaging the building and killing several priests. In total, more than 250 high-explosive and about 400 incendiary bombs of all calibres were recorded falling on Leninsky district. In the residential sector, according to Soviet data, twenty-seven people were killed, another fifty-two were injured and concussed.[29]

This time the Avtozavodsky district escaped with minor damage. The main blow fell on residential areas east of GAZ, where German planes dropped forty high-explosive and several hundred incendiary bombs. The entire banks of the Oka were engulfed in flames, and columns of explosions sent clouds of sand, mud and dust into the sky, mixing it in the acrid flames. The roar and crackle of burning wood mingled with the heart-rending screams of goats, whose pens were engulfed in flames.

Meanwhile, the last groups of bombers were approaching the city, including He 111s from KG 27 'Boelcke'. The commander of this Kampfgeschwader, Oberstleutnant Freiherr von Beust, personally directed the actions of the pilots, giving orders from his plane circling over Gorky. Each crew, after performing a bomb attack, immediately reported the results to the chief on the radio. Hartl of the 8th Staffel, who was in the KG 27 commander's crew on this mission, recalled:

> The calmness that von Beust radiated was unique! When an anti-aircraft shell exploded over Gorky directly next to our He 111, he calmly ordered me, as a radio operator: 'Hartl, write down the exact time.' When the fragments damaged the fuel system, he instructed the navigator to calculate the return flight taking into account the loss of fuel. Further, von Beust firmly stated: 'We remain here until the last plane of the squadron appears and Hartl receives a message that all the bombs have been dropped.'

In the Voroshilov district, located on the high (right) bank of the Oka River opposite the Molotov motor vehicle plant, the situation remained calm throughout the raid. The factories continued to work, although the workers listened warily to the sound of guns and explosions coming from the street. Self-defence groups and fire units were on alert. Off-work residents of the area crouched in the earth bomb shelters, while the bolder ones watched the air attack from a high slope. The bombing that was taking place on the Engine of the Revolution factory just 3km away was clearly visible. Huge clouds of smoke were carried away by the wind to the south-west, blocking the view of the Molotov plant and its surroundings.

At 01.45, the Voroshilovsky district of Gorky was suddenly bombed. At the No. 326 Frunze radio equipment factory, night shift workers heard a loud bang, then a crunch, interspersed with a crash. In the shops and workshops, plaster crumbled and glass rattled. Everyone realised that something huge had fallen on the plant. Subsequently, it turned out that the single-storey canteen building had been hit by a SC1800 bomb. Breaking through all the floors, it went a few metres into the ground, but did not explode. Several bombs exploded at Myza railway station. The tracks and station buildings were severely destroyed there.

The Zhdanovsky district, located in the old city (the hilly part of Gorky), was also bombed. Lyubov Dmitrieva, who worked as a nurse at the blood transfusion station, recalled:

> I was at the station at the time. Through the windows of the third floor, facing the automobile plant, we watched, as if spellbound, as 'lighters' dropped by the Germans fell.
>
> The chief doctor, E.N. Nechaev, came to us and said anxiously:'Girls, all go down, something is not calm in my heart, something will happen.'
>
> We did not listen to his advice and continued to stay in our seats. A few minutes later, he came in again and scolded us again. Only then did we rush down. As soon as we reached the second floor, we felt our building shake and shards of glass rained down.

Several explosions occurred in the area of Pushkin Park. Bombs exploded on the streets of Belinsky, Kostin and Vorovsky, on the Srednoj market and at the No. 5 Klara Zetkin hosiery factory. By a fatal coincidence, a military unit was marching along the street at the time of the bombing, and dozens of soldiers were killed and wounded. Nurses from the blood transfusion station were the first to arrive at the scene of the tragedy. Dmitrieva said:

> When we ran out of the station, we saw this picture: everything around us was burning, cracking. When we reached the place where the bombs were dropped, we saw craters and dead Red Army soldiers lying on the ground. We were moving wounded soldiers from the site of the explosion. The doctors bandaged them and then sent them to the hospital.

Meanwhile, the German planes were returning to their bases. At 01.25, Berlin time, when it was already 04.25 in Gorky, He 111 H '1G+AL' of 3./KG 27 landed in Olsufevo after 305 minutes of flight. At 01.40, after spending 319 minutes in the air, He 111 '1G+EL' from the same Staffel landed. W. Hartl of 8./KG 27 recalled: 'An hour after landing, we heard a Russian radio station that interfered with our broadcasts. The Russians reported on the radio: "Bloody dogs led by von Beust killed thousands of defenceless people," and so on.' This fact indicated that the Soviets were well aware of the German Kampfgeschwader and their commanders.

The management of MPVO in Gorky summed up the results of the next raid. Major General Antropov indicated in his report that out of a total of eighty bombers, allegedly '5 to 10 planes broke through to the city'. But then, thinking that no one would believe this figure, he signed '15–20 planes' by hand. Civilian casualties in the air attack were estimated at 253, of which fifty-five people were killed. Of course, this figure is very doubtful. Five enterprises were damaged in various ways, but the Engine of the Revolution factory suffered the most. Significant damage was caused to the residential sector of the city. As a result of the bombing, ninety houses and barracks were destroyed and burned down. Dozens of residential buildings were damaged.

It was morning in Gorky, but firefighting and clearing debris continued throughout the city. There were thirty-three fire trucks and four fire trains operating in five districts of the city. In the Zhdanovsky district, work to help the wounded, clear away corpses and clear the streets of debris continued until 08.00, after which it was possible to restore the movement of the tram No. 2. At Myza railway station, train traffic was resumed by 15.00. Soldiers of the 22nd Engineering Anti-Chemical Battalion of the NKVD began to neutralise numerous unexploded bombs. Just in the Leninsky district, by midday on 14 June, seventy-nine unexploded high-explosive bombs were found, including two SC500s, thirty-five SC50s and forty-two SC250s. This accounted for about a quarter of the bombs dropped by the Luftwaffe on the area. The record was set by the Red Tanner factory, where sappers found thirty unexploded bombs! In the morning, residents of the Kirov district found a crater with a diameter of 12m and a depth of 3.5m at the Mayakovskaya station of the children's railway. Not far from this place, a 50-litre tank was found, half a metre deep in the soil. A small incendiary bomb was attached to the side of it. Everything within a radius of 30m was spattered with a mixture of kerosene and oil.

Hauptmann Putz under interrogation by Marshal Novikov

The headquarters of the Gorky corps area of air defence claimed five downed bombers, of which three were brought down by anti-aircraft artillery. According to reports from the commanders of the batteries and regiments, the planes were hit over the city centre, Myza station and the town of Bor. Night fighters carried out thirty-three sorties with a total flight time of forty-one hours. At the same time, pilots reported that in the area of the cities of Pavlovo and Bogorodsk, they shot down two bombers, including one of them by ramming. One La-5 pilot, Senior Lieutenant Mikhail Belousov, did not return from his mission.[30]

In fact, Luftwaffe losses amounted to just two aircraft, with one of them being shot down by a night fighter south-west of Gorky. One of the pilots of 6./KG 27 wrote in his report:

> We were flying on the right flank of the right link. Suddenly, a single Russian night fighter flew almost vertically between us and the plane on the left flank, and then attacked our plane on the right. I immediately broadcast on the radio: 'Attention, a night fighter is nearby!' We repelled the attack with aimed fire. The night fighter launched another attack, this time from behind. I manoeuvred to give the skirmishers a better chance to fire, and we were able to repel the attack again with aimed bursts. Soon after, I noticed that the plane on the left flank went into a steep dive. His crew was reported missing.

The downed aircraft was He 111 H-16 Wrk Nr 7554 '1G+HH' of Feldwebel Gerhard Richter from I./KG 27, which took off at 23.00 from Olsufevo

Left: Commander of the 142nd Fighter Aviation Division of Air Defence Colonel Viktor Ivanov.

Below: Pilots of the 786th IAP PVO.

airfield. All five members of its crew – pilot twenty-five-year-old Richter, navigator twenty-eight-year-old Feldwebel Willi Hofmann, flight operator twenty-five-year-old Feldwebel Rudolf Kopper, flight mechanic thirty-year-old Oberfeldwebel Hans Hagenmeister and flight gunner twenty-three-year-old Obergefreiter Helmut Beckenbah – were declared missing.[31]

Fighter LaGG-3 29-series.

LaGG-3 from the 786th IAP PVO after an emergency landing.

The He 111 of Oberfeldwebel Ludwig Havighorst of 5./KG 27 was also attacked by a night fighter. Soon after the bombs were dropped, the air gunner and the radio operator simultaneously spotted the Soviet plane. The pilot, Ludwig Denz, immediately turned to the left, and as a result, the fighter skipped past, after which the flight gunner, Unteroffizier Blass, opened fire. Havighorst recalled: 'The downed plane turned to the side. From somewhere below, a jet of flame shot out of it, and, falling to the ground, it exploded.' The downed fighter was probably the La-5 of Senior Lieutenant Mikhail Belousov. Seeing a German bomber in front of him, the pilot radioed that he was going to ram, after which his connection was cut off.[32]

The He 111 H-16 Wrk Nr 160291 '1G+BM' belonging to the commander of 4./KG 27, Hauptmann Helmut Putz, also did not return from Gorky. Putz was one of the veterans of KG 27. The son of the famous German artist Leo Putz, he was the first KG 27 pilot to be awarded the German Cross in Gold in October 1941. A year later, on 19 September 1942, Putz received the Knight's Cross. By June 1943, he had completed more than 300 sorties.

On 13 June, the Putz bomber took off at 20.30 Berlin time. It is unlikely that the commander of the 4th Staffel thought that he would not return to his unit and would not be able to celebrate a successful flight in the officers' mess in the usual manner. He had many battles and operations behind him, and each time he had returned unharmed. However, even professionals and experts were sometimes shot down. Flying at a low altitude on the way back, the bomber was hit by anti-aircraft fire near the city of Tula. Unlike many of his colleagues, who managed to reach their territory with a single engine and almost severed tail, twenty-eight-year-old Putz made an emergency landing near the city of Kozelsk. The front line was only 50km away. Putz tried to escape, but was wounded in the leg by a Red Army soldier and taken prisoner. A similar 'military fate' befell the twenty-five-year-old radio operator Oberfeldwebel Eugen Schorn. The other two crew members – navigator Unteroffizier Rolf Hoffmann and flight engineer Oberfeldwebel Georg Kotzihik – were listed as missing.

Since this was the first time a Staffel commander had fallen into the hands of the Soviets, Putz was soon taken to Moscow, where he was personally interrogated by the commander of the Red Army air force, Marshal of the Soviet Union Alexey Novikov. The terrified pilot, whose brilliant career suddenly ended that night, did not tried to confuse his jailers and told them the truth. Putz told Novikov:

I participated in night raids on objects in Gorky and Yaroslavl from Olsufevo airfield, usually 30 aircraft each took off. As a detachment commander in KG 27, I twice commanded groups to Gorky (my plane was flying first) and once tried to bomb Yaroslavl, but because of a strong anti-aircraft barrage firing in the area of Moscow returned back. In the last raid on the night of June 14 I was hit by anti-aircraft fire on the way back from Gorky and the plane made an emergency landing.

Unlike other captive pilots who insisted that they had mainly fought in the west, and that this had been only their first or second sortie on the Eastern Front, Putz said he had carried out more than 300 sorties there, including 130 to 140 at night, and he had flown another sixty hours at night before getting to the front. He revealed:

Usually the task for a night mission is given to the crew 2–3 hours before departure. Night flights to long-range targets were performed at altitudes of 1,500–3,000 metres, but on the night when we were shot down, we were flying at an altitude exceeding 4,000 metres. Night flights are always performed by single crews …

The 'military fate' of Helmut Putz and Eugen Schorn was not the most cruel. They remained alive, and the Soviets took into account their truthful testimony during interrogations. Schorn was sent to PoW camps No. 27 in Moscow, No.28 in Potma, and then in Taganrog and Rostov. Travelling as a prisoner in Russia, he saw many times the cities and stations where he used to drop bombs. Schorn survived his harsh Russian captivity and was released on 28 April 1949. Putz also returned to Germany after the end of the war.

Night attack Hurricanes

The 'military fate' of the crews that participated in the air attack on Saratov that night was just as unpredictable. Sixty He 111s from KG 55 and I./KG 100 took off from Stalino air base. According to records in the Fliegerbuch of Feldwebel Helmut Abendvoth, his He 111 H '6N+EK', took off at 19.50 and returned at 00.19. The duration of the flight was 269 minutes, which was four minutes less than a day earlier.[33] Similar to the raids on Gorky,

Aerial photos of the city of Saratov. In the lower left corner – Saratov oil cracking plant 'Kirov', in the centre – Saratov Aviation Plant № 292.

German bombers flew to Saratov on the same unchanged 'schedule' and on a direct course, without manoeuvring. The distance from Stalino to Saratov was about 700km.

After reaching the Volga north of the city, the planes crossed it from west to east, then turned to the target. The main target of the attack was again the Kirov oil cracking plant. This time the weather was clear, which ensured the success of the mission. As a result of high-explosive and heavy incendiary bombs, large pockets of fires broke out. A total of 37,000 tons of oil products were burned. In the neighbouring village of Knyazevka, a large fire also broke out, engulfing several streets at once. As a result, 100 houses were destroyed and fifteen people were killed.[34]

During the bombing, He 111 H-16 Wrk Nr 110071 'G1+AR' of Unteroffizier Gerhard Kruger of 7./KG 55 'Greif' was hit by anti-aircraft artillery fire. The crew, which included navigator Feldwebel Karl Schuholz, flight engineer Unteroffizier Hermann Opplinger, flight mechanic Unteroffizier Alfred Eckert and flight engineer Unteroffizier Gotthard Hoyer, reported on the radio that they were continuing to fly on one engine, but the aircraft never returned to base. After flying about 200km to the west, Kruger made an emergency landing. This event took place in a sparsely populated area between the cities of Balashov and Borisoglebsk in the Khoper river valley. The crew managed to leave the landing site unnoticed and hide. For four days, the pilots made their way west, hoping to reach the front line and return home. They managed to swim across the river and reach the Kalach upland. But there the pilots were captured by the Russians.

Similar was the fate of another bomber – He 111 H-16 Wrk Nr 150273 '6N+IL' Oberleutnant Gerhard Puklitsch (navigator Hauptmann Helmut Fritzsche, flight side gunner Unteroffizier Schtreiher, flight operator Oberfeldwebel Schwarz) from I./KG 100. Puklitsch later recalled:

> After the raids on the Gorky automobile plant 'Molotov', conducted from Seshchinskaya (Central sector of the front) at night between June 3 and 6, 1943, our I./KG 100 moved back to Stalino on June 7. From there, we had to make night raids on industrial facilities in Saratov, especially on the oil cracking plant 'Kirov' and the ball bearing factory. The target for 13.06.1943 was the oil cracking plant. And, having already been over the oil cracking plant 'Kirov', according to the order, special attention had to be paid to its power plant. This was

the second air attack on this target, and we were prepared, as we had been the night before, for a strong air defence and numerous searchlights.

After a normal start, made at 19.46 in the evening twilight, the flight took place without any accidents. When it was quite dark, we crossed the front at an altitude of 3,200m in the area of the Shakhty and continued the flight in the light of the moon and with good visibility. There was only a little cloudiness below. A large railway bridge over the Volga River, located south-east of the oil cracking plant, was provided as a reference point for reaching the goal. From this point we had to attack the target, making an approach to it from the opposite side from the moon. The oil cracking plant is located south of Saratov on the edge of the airfield, which is also adjacent to the ball bearing factory. These facilities, because of their great importance for the military industry, were accordingly protected by air defence. And already during the approach to the target area, a hurricane of anti-aircraft artillery fire was opened and searchlights were turned on.

After passing over the bridge, we turned left to approach the target. Now the air defence was focused on the machines that were approaching the target. At this time, photoflash bombs ('chandeliers') also hung over the target, so it became as light as day. Our bombers are approaching the target. Bomb hatches are open. Due to the small length of the specified target, the oil cracking plant power plant, we drop 8 bombs with a short interval, which exactly fit into the target. We repeat this operation 3 times, entering the target from the same direction. The gunner repeatedly captured the results on camera.

During the last approach, the target was already in the dense smoke of fires, which greatly complicated visibility. Anti-aircraft guns, both before and now, fire from all barrels, and in addition to bursting large-calibre shells, we see traces of trails from small and medium-calibre shells. Searchlights are everywhere, one of which has slipped past our plane several times. And suddenly one of them seized us and began to hold us. Three more, four more, and then a dozen searchlights joined in, so that we were now guided by a beam of bright light. The light in the cockpit is so bright that we put on sunglasses, called 'frog eyes' by the pilots, to complete this approach to the target. Now, however, the batteries opened fire on our lit plane. We are rattled by the blast waves coming from the detonating projectiles. And then two powerful shocks hit us. The left motor loses power and starts to burn.

A long plume of smoke follows us. Now it is urgent that I shut down the damaged engine. To do this, I turn off the ignition, turn on the fire extinguishing system, and set the propeller to planing mode. But it turns out that nothing can be done, because the mechanism for changing the pitch of the propeller blades is clearly damaged. The aircraft is pulling hard to the left, and I'm trying to rebalance it.

Meanwhile, we managed to bring down the flames on the left engine. At that moment, the gunner shouted: 'There's a fighter behind us!' At the same time, we see the tracks of its ammunition rushing past us. An attacking Russian fighter immediately opened fire with machine guns on a radio operator and gunner of our aircraft. Only thanks to incredible efforts, we managed to break away from the night fighter that attacked us several times and again send the plane on the right course. This was probably due to the fact that our side gunners may have hit the enemy fighter, because at some point it suddenly turned sharply away and left us alone.[35]

Russian night fighters from the 144th IAD Air Defence carried out nineteen sorties to intercept German bombers that night. The pilots reported seven air battles. At 23.00 (Moscow time), Captain Titov in the Hurricane in zone 3 intercepted a He 111, which was illuminated by searchlights at an altitude of 1,500m. The night fighter carried out three attacks from behind and above from a distance of 200–250m. Titov's report said: 'After three attacks, the enemy's left engine began to smoke, he came out from the rays of the searchlight with a sharp decline at an altitude of 800–900m, and visual contact with it was lost.'

At 23.10, Sergeant Chumichkin, in a Yak-1, intercepted a He 111 in zone 2 at an altitude of 3,000m. The Russian fighter opened fire, but its weapons soon jammed. The German crew returned fire, then disappeared into the clouds using a sharp manoeuvre.

At 23.25, Captain Nizhnik, in a Yak-1, discovered a German plane flying at an altitude of 1,800m in zone 3. The target was illuminated by a searchlight. The report said:

> Being at the same height, Captain Nizhnik got close to the enemy up to 200–300 metres and made two consecutive attacks from behind – on the left, then on the right.[36] He fired from a cannon and machine guns from a distance of 200–250 metres. After the second attack, the He 111's left engine caught fire. The enemy aircraft came out from the rays of the searchlight with a sharp decline and, masking himself against the dark background of the terrain, he left the pursuit.

This is not a drawing of a young child! This is a diagram of the battle of the Hurricane fighter from the 963rd IAP with a German bomber He 111 at 22.45 on June 14 (from the combat log)!

At 23.30, in zone 4, Lieutenant Nikolayev, in a Hurricane, intercepted a Ju 88, which was illuminated by floodlights at an altitude of 4,000m. Approaching the bomber from behind, from above on the right, the night fighter carried out its first attack from a distance of 150–200m. According to Nikolaev's report, the bomber tried to break away by sharp diving and manoeuvring. His Hurricane carried out seven more attacks, using up all the ammunition. The Ju 88's left engine caught fire, after which contact with the target was lost.

At 23.38, Captain Kabetsky, in a Yak-1, saw a He 111 in zone 3, which was illuminated by a searchlight at an altitude of 2,000m. Kabetsky attacked from the front, then turned around and performed two more attacks from behind. However, the pilot was soon blinded by both the flashes of his weapon and the searchlights, so lost visual contact with the target.

A similar interception was performed by a Hurricane piloted by Lieutenant Sobolevsky. He also reported three attacks against a He 111, after which the left engine smoked but it managed to escape in the dark.

At 23.50, Captain Holyavka, in a Hurricane, intercepted a He 111 in zone 3. Approaching the target at a distance of 100m, Holyavka opened fire from behind, from above on the right. After that, Holyavka carried out two more attacks from a distance of 100m, simultaneously firing from all his weapons. The pilot claimed that the Germans did not shoot at him, and after the third attack, the bomber caught fire and fell south of the railway bridge over the Volga. At 00.12 his Hurricane landed at its air base having completely spent its ammunition. It is difficult to determine which of all these night fighters attacked the Puklitsch bomber.

Incredible adventures Germans on Medvedickie Jary[37]

Barely out of the area of anti-aircraft fire, He 111 H-16 '6N+IL' headed south-west at an altitude of 2,000m. The crew found themselves in the same position as He 111 'G1+AR' of 7./KG 55. Puklitsch added power to the right engine, but the plane was still difficult to control and did not want to keep altitude. As was envisaged in such cases, the pilots began to throw overboard everything 'unnecessary', including armour plates, machine guns and ammunition. But the damaged bomber was still gradually losing speed and altitude... After an hour and a half of an incredibly difficult flight, the He 111 had still not even reached the Don, and the front line was still about 500km away. The situation was desperate, and the radio operator was constantly transmitting the signal 'SOS', the course, altitude and speed of flight to their base.

In the end, the pilot made the difficult decision to make an emergency landing on Soviet territory. This meant minimal chances of escape and very high chances of falling into the hands of cruel Russian executioners! Puklitsch recalled:

> The engine power minimum, the fire extinguishing system is on, the flaps are extended and the landing lights are on. The land is fast approaching – it is this is freshly ploughed land. Impact, the plane skidded on its belly and finally stopped. A cloud of dust rose inside the cabin. The glazing of the nose of the plane broke, and the lower compartment of the rear gunner came off. Fortunately, no one was injured. There was an eerie silence. At this point, the right engine caught fire. Probably during the impact on the ground, fuel or oil got on the hot exhaust pipes, which caused the ignition. We immediately left the plane and started throwing earth at the fire. This gave a positive result – the fire was extinguished. Without moving, we listen to the darkness. It seems to be quiet. We rush back into the cockpit, destroy instruments, radio transmitters, and target maps, and save flasks, a bag of provisions, firearms, a signal pistol, and ammunition. We manage to find green and white cartridges, as well as several ES6 cartridges, the shot that was the sign of identification to date. The red rocket cartridges were buried in a pile of debris, so we couldn't find them.[38]

According to their instructions, after an emergency landing on enemy territory, the crew had to destroy the aircraft and its equipment. But the pilots did not do this, so the flames would not give away their location. Puklitsch made the correct decision to immediately leave the landing site and get as far away as possible. The 'military fate' had been favourable to the crew so far as they had already been lucky twice. First, despite the damage, they managed to fly far away from the target, and secondly, they landed in a deserted area. It was dark, which gave them a good chance of disappearing. Having gone quite far from the plane through the weeds and tall grass, the pilots hid under a bush.

THE ENTIRE VOLGA REGION IS ON FIRE

As the authors were able to establish, the landing occurred north-west of the Knyazhensky farm, 25km west of Mikhailovka railway station. The trajectory of the landing approach took place over the Medvedickie Jary hill along the valley of the Medveditsa River. There were no settlements in this area, so no one noticed the landing of the bomber.

The German pilots spent the next day under the bushes and itwas full of different events. First Puklitsch, Fritzsch, Schtreiher and Schwarz were attacked by clouds of merciless Russian mosquitoes, and then a Ju 88 D spy plane flew through the sky. A Russian peasant on a cart drove along a nearby road, then a policeman on a motorcycle. Twice the pilots were drenched by a warm June downpour. After that, they began to think about a rescue plan. The reality was terrible! They calculated that it would take at least four weeks to walk to the front line. The only real chance to return 'home' would be in the case of evacuation by plane. However, this would require a lot of luck and careful preparation.

Puklitsch continued:

> When the sun set in the west, the navigator Hauptmann Fritzsche and the flight radio operator Oberfeldwebel Schwarz went on patrol, and I with the side gunner Unteroffizier Schtreiher began to look for a suitable place to land the plane.
>
> We concluded that the field road and the strip of steppe plain bordering it would be quite suitable for night landing. We gathered again at our hiding place. The immediate surroundings seemed deserted, and we decided to stay here until our comrades began to search for us. We hoped that we would be able to draw their attention to us during their next flight to the target. We calculated the estimated time of flight. We began to while away the waiting time by collecting dry grass for fires. There was a full moon in the sky, not counting individual clouds. Visibility was good.
>
> At the end of a few hours, almost exactly on time, a low rumble from afar announced the approaching formation. The planes were flying very high, and we let them get closer. Then we fired a rocket with a light signal ES 6 from the previous day. Then another. No reaction. The heavily loaded planes passed over us smoothly. And we assumed that the planes would first deliver the bombs to the target, and on the way back they would search for us.

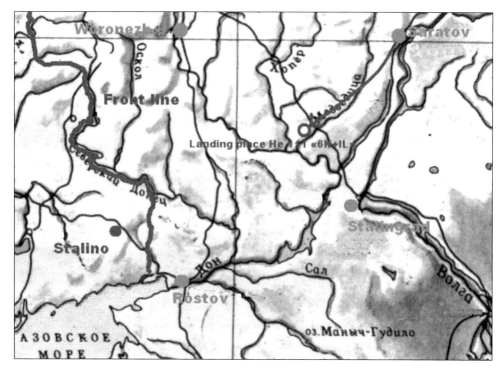

Scheme of emergency landing of the bomber He 111 H-16 '6N+IL' W.Nr. 150273 Oberleutnant Gerhard Puklitsch from I./KG 100 after the raid on the city of Saratov on the night of June 13-14.

Puklitsch was right. Bombers from I./KG 100 again flew to Saratov on the night of 14/15 June. According to Soviet data, the planes were going to the target in groups of six to nine aircraft, the approach to the target was carried out from the western direction, and the bombing was carried out from a height of 1,500–3,000m. The low altitude was due to adverse weather conditions. Above Saratov there was significant cloud cover with breaks at an altitude of 1,500m, visibility was about 1km. However, most of the crews were able to find the target and complete the mission. Bombing caused more damage to the Kirov oil cracking plant, with another 4,000 tons of oil products burned. In a report from the Saratov regional office of NKVD, it was reported that 'enemy aircraft acted with impunity due to the lack of air defence equipment'.[39] The anti-aircraft artillery of the Saratov divisional air defence district continued to conduct mainly barrage fire, wasting thousands of shells.

But the Russian night fighters were very active that night. From 22.30 to 00.00 in the sky around Saratov twenty-five aircraft patrolled constantly.

The pilots reported ten air battles, with two downed and one damaged bomber. Apparently, one German plane was shot down by Senior Lieutenant Goncharenko (Yak-1), and another was shot down by a pair consisting of Senior Lieutenant Ponomarenko and Captain Tanyashin (both in Yak-1s). According to Soviet data, one bomber fell in the area of Umorye, the second 18km south-west of Saratov. One 'damaged' bomber was recorded by Lieutenant Nikolaev in a Hurricane. In fact, the raid passed without losses for the bombers.

On the way back, the German crews were assigned to search for the Puklitsch crew. The radio signals they had transmitted the previous night had been picked up by many German radio stations, and throughout the day work was in full swing at Stalino airfield. During the day, several I./KG 100 crews flew in search of the downed aircraft. First of all, it was necessary to establish the position of the forced landing, in order to narrow the search area. For example, He 111 '6N+OK' took off twice at 11.00 and 13.07 to search in the north-east direction.[40]

By comparing different data, the I./KG 100 headquarters was able to accurately determine the square where the downed crew could be located. Therefore, the flight route was chosen exactly over this area. It was decided to conduct the main search on the way back, when the planes would be released from their heavy bomb load.

Meanwhile, the Luftwaffe operation was running its course. At 07.20 (Moscow time), a Ju 88 D reconnaissance plane suddenly appeared over Saratov. At an altitude of 7,500m, it flew over the city on an east–west course and began to move away to the south-west. At 07.35, two Hurricanes flown by Captain Titov and Senior Lieutenant Holyavka from the 963rd IAP and two Yak-1s flown by Starshina Vorona and Sergeant Gromilov from the 405th IAP took off to intercept. However, their mission ended in failure. 'In the process of pursuit, Captain Titov, Senior Lieutenant Holyavka and Sergeant Gromilov did not catch up with the enemy due to weak engines,' the Russian report said. In the Atkarsk area, Starshina Vorona got close to the enemy aircraft at 300–400 metres and fired 3–4 turns. The enemy aircraft entered the cloud cover, and visual contact was lost.'

At 22.20–24.00 (Moscow time), thirty He 111s carried out an air attack on the Kirov plant. According Helmut Abendvoth's Fliegerbuch, his He 111 H '6N+EK' from I./KG 100, took off from Stalino at 20.07 Berlin time. The target of the raid was again designated as the oil cracking plant. At 00.47, after 280 minutes of flight, the bomber landed back.[41] The target had been hit again and a large fire broke out at the plant. Several bombs exploded at Uvek railway station. Russian night fighters carried out thirteen sorties, but only Junior Lieutenant Kiselyov and Captain Holyavka both flying Hurricanes, managed to establish visual contact with the target and execute attacks. In both cases, the bombers quickly disappeared into the darkness. At the same time, Holyavka's fighter was fired on by side gunners, and while manoeuvring it came under fire from Soviet anti-aircraft artillery. The Hurricane received shrapnel hits to the rudder and propeller. Despite serious damage, the reliable British fighter landed safely back at base. He 111 H-16 Wrk Nr 8348 of III./KG 55 was damaged by anti-aircraft fire above the target. The bomber reached its air base and made an emergency landing. The damage was 25 per cent, and injured the pilot, Obergefreiter Otto Meyer.

After a successful attack, the Germans launched a rescue operation in the Hoper river valley. Puklitsch continued:

> After calculating the time again, we waited, continuing to collect dry weeds for fires. Finally, from the east, I heard the hum of an engine. No doubt it was the hum of engines of the He 111. It was moving in our direction lower than the other planes returning from the mission. We fired the ES rocket and flares again, and lit marker fires of dry grass. The plane switched on its side lights and began circling at a low altitude. Will he come down?
>
> Tirelessly, we continued to throw dry grass into the fires and give light signals with our pocket lanterns, drawing the onboard code of our plane 'IL' with their beams. The plane also responded with light signals, and we thought we were understood. The plane had been circling here for half an hour when another joined it. Together, they flew with their lights on for another half hour, making a large diameter fly by, then a small one. But there was no intention of landing. Suddenly, in the distance from the north side, we heard machine-gun fire, which was probably conducted from our aircraft. However, we did not put out our marker fires. Well, now we could expect that the Russians would appear soon. The planes, following a straight line above us and waving their wings, made it clear that they were flying away.[42]

All this 'light show' gave the Puklitsch crew hope for a quick rescue. They had been lucky for the third time because, incredibly, they had been found!

Would they be lucky again, or would the capricious 'military fate' turn away from them?

It is clear that low flying aircraft, launches of flares and marker fires could attract the attention of Soviet observation posts and local residents. And the pilots had to spend at least another day in the rear of the evil enemy. Puklitsch recalled:

> The barking of dogs from a distance made us act immediately. We hastily extinguished our fires and set off in the old direction. Because of the fires we had built, and because of the noise of the planes, we had no doubt that the Russians now knew where to look for us. For an hour we ran across the steppe as fast as we can, taking only short breaks. The moon had set, and it was quite dark. Orientation is possible only by compass. From time to time we stop and listen carefully. All around is utter silence. Go on!
>
> About an hour after midnight, we stumbled through a furrow in a mown field. We instinctively fall to the ground. Where there is a field, there are villages. Carefully, we cross a field that seems large enough. On the other side of it we found a steep ravine overgrown with bushes. Typical terrain for this area. Hiding in the bushes, we decide to spend the day here. We spread out for guard duty.

Here the pilots decided to hide until dark. They still had two ES6 signal cartridges and one each for the white and green signals. In the evening, they scouted the area and gathered straw for fires. Then they began to wait for the night with incredible tension.

As darkness fell over the inhospitable Russian plains, the hum of an airplane was heard from the south-west, coming and going. Soon the pilots realised that this was the typical sound of a He 111 bomber. Then they saw the 'spade's'[43] distinctive silhouette against the moon. The crew fired an ES6 rocket, but the plane did not react to it and flew past. Then they lit a fire and fired a green rocket. After that, their comrades noticed the signal, and the bomber flew in their direction.

After inspecting the area, the pilot slowly made a landing. With the brake flaps fully extended, the plane touched down gently, near to the signal fire. When Puklitsch ran to the cockpit, Hauptmann Fronert leaned out and calmly asked: 'Is that you?'[44]

In this episode, the 'vast Russian expanses', which the Germans liked to mention in their memoirs, helped them a lot. It is difficult to imagine that a German crew would have been able to live in England unnoticed for a couple of days, lighting fires and firing missiles, and later be evacuated from there on the same type of bomber!

As it turned out, the operation to rescue the crew was carefully planned. Three planes were sent to search for it, with one to land and the other two to remain in the sky. If the landing He 111, '6N+MH', damaged its landing gear or could not take off, the two crews could be taken out by other bombers. At the same time, all three planes were prepared for the operation: armour plates and all unnecessary equipment were removed from them.

Puklitsch continued his dramatic story:

> I quickly run ahead and, shining a flashlight, accompany the plane back to the fire, where the take-off should begin. At the edge of the field, the plane turned, the lower hatch opened, and we quickly climbed inside. Squeezing past the radio operator, Unteroffizier Hessderfer, I hurry forward to the commander of the aircraft, Feldwebel Ekschtat, to instruct him about the features of the area. In view of the fact that there were no orientation lights outside now, we would have to keep a compass heading for take-off. It is very important to hold our course until we leave the ground, as the slightest deviation can lead us to the dangerous ravine in which we spent the last day.
>
> At the beginning of the run-up, we pick up our radio operator, who was the furthest from the plane, and the plane is already at full throttle acceleration and … deviates to the left. My blood froze in my veins as I saw the edge of the field rapidly approaching in the light of the searchlights, with a dark ravine beyond it. What Feldwebel Ekschtat did in his '6N+MH' now, a loaded, fully fuelled and armoured He 111 would hardly have been able to do: the Feldwebel abruptly pulled the wheel, lifted the plane over the ravine, and then slowly let it go, continuing to increase the speed sufficient for take-off. We breathed a sigh of relief. This take-off, not to mention the very courageous landing made at night on unknown enemy territory, was a first-class flight achievement.[45]

This was no exaggeration: 'military fate' had helped the German pilots five times! Despite damage from anti-aircraft fire, they managed to escape from the target area. They force-landed in a deserted area. They were not detected by the enemy. They were found by their comrades among the 'vast Russian expanses'. And then they were evacuated. Without at least one of these conditions, the entire rescue mission could not have taken place. This was a fairly rare, though not an isolated, incident in the history of the Luftwaffe on the Eastern Front. Puklitsch and his comrades soon arrived safely at Stalino air base.

The Russians found He 111 '6N+IL' lying north of Knyazhensky farm only three days after it landed, however, they could not determine when this had occurred. The Soviets assumed that the plane had been damaged by a night fighter over Saratov between 14 and 15 June.

At dawn on 16 June (at 06.00 Moscow time/04.00 Berlin time), a German reconnaissance plane flew over the southern outskirts of Saratov. He again made a long detour and appeared from behind the eastern bank of the Volga. The Russians were again caught off guard and the fighters that took off to intercept it failed to find their target. At the same time, the air surveillance posts identified the intruder as an He 111, although in reality it was a Ju 88 D. The scout delivered photos that showed widespread destruction. After several days of continuous bombing in the Stalinist and Oktyabrsky districts of Saratov, the water supply, lighting, and telephone network had completely failed, and the population fled in panic to the surrounding villages.

Delighted with their obvious success in destroying the Russian military industry, the Luftwaffe command decided not only to continue raiding strategic targets, but also to extend these to a wider area.

On 16 June, a tragic incident occurred involving Kampfgeschwader 55 'Greif'. During the flight to Seshchinskaya air base the commander of 6./ KG 55, Major Johannes Lorenz, landed on Russian territory for an unknown reason. His He 111 H-6 Wrk Nr 8182, came down south of Vyazma on the banks of the Ugra River. This happened in the vicinity of the headquarters of the Russian 33rd Army. Navigator Feldwebel Hans Leitner and side gunner Obergefreiter Karl Dworack tried to escape, but were killed in a shootout with the staff guard. Lorenz and the radio operator, Obergefreiter Bernhard Mencke, surrendered.

In the following days, secondary targets became targets of air attacks. On the night of 17/18 June, bombers from I./KG 100 raided the city of Kamyshin, located on the Volga midway between Saratov and Stalingrad. A local oil storage facility and a glass container factory were destroyed. Along the way, the planes dropped bottom mines into the river. On the same night, a single He 111 carried out an air attack on the city of Syzran, located on the right bank of the Volga River west of the city of Kuibyshev (now Samara). Ten high-explosive bombs and one heavy incendiary bomb were dropped on this target.

Another group of planes went to the Caspian Sea on a mission to attack oil tankers on a roadstead 12ft deep. This was a deep-water port in the northern part of the Caspian Sea, where oil products were loaded from large sea tankers to river vessels. Among the participants in this mission was He 111 H '6N+MK'. According to the Fliegerbuch of Feldwebel Helmut Abendvoth, his plane took off from Stalino at 19.42. When the bomber reached the sea, it dropped one SC500 high-explosive bomb and four SC250 bombs on Russian vessels in turn. The He 111 returned to the air base at 02.42, having spent seven hours in the air. At the same time, the crew reported the sinking of at least one vessel.[46]

These raids can be considered the end of the second phase of the Luftwaffe air 'Blitz' against the Volga Region. In the period from 9 to 18 June, bomber aircraft finally deactivated the 'Molotov' motor vehicle plant in Gorky, destroyed the Kirov oil cracking plant in Saratov and the Yaroslavl tyre plant. In addition, several medium-sized enterprises and large oil storage facilities were severely damaged. Luftwaffe losses during the second phase amounted to eight bombers (all He 111s) and seven crews, of which three aircraft were shot down or damaged during raids on Gorky and Yaroslavl, and two over Saratov.

'With such a "bounced landing"…'

Shortly after the first air attacks on Saratov, the commander of Soviet air defence, Lieutenant General Mikhail Gromadin, arrived in the city. He took part in a meeting of the Saratov regional office of the Bolshevik party, then started checking the combat readiness of the air defences. During the inspections, it turned out that the order of battle of anti-aircraft artillery was built incorrectly, and the calculation of the barrier fire curtains was inaccurate. The available gun-aiming stations were used inefficiently and were not sufficiently controlled through calculations. Thus, the bitter truth about the complete inefficiency of Russian air defence was revealed again.

At a later meeting, measures were discussed to improve interaction between air defence and rescue service units (MPVO), and to supply water by rail, trams and steamers. Separately, the issue of catching German agents who fired signal flares in the direction of bombing targets was considered.

The fight against the distributors of false and panic rumours was launched. On 19 June, the Saratov city defence committee adopted resolution No. 182 'On fighting fires caused by enemy incendiary air bombs'.

A similar activity of incompetent management, unable to protect their city, was observed in Gorky. On 17 June, a meeting of the Bureau of the Gorky regional office of the Bolshevik Party was held. The main issue was the ongoing Luftwaffe air attacks. First Secretary (party head of the region) and chief of the city defence Committee Mikhail Rodionov noted the successes achieved by MPVO formations in the aftermath of the last raid:

> As the fight against fires at the machine-tool factory and the Engine of the Revolution factory showed, the situation there was saved by artificial reservoirs that were dug the day before the bombing. There, the water pipes, as well as at the automobile plant 'Molotov', failed immediately, and if it were not for artificial reservoirs the plants would have burned down.

At the same time, the issue of combat readiness of air defence units was considered. On this occasion, Rodionov said:

> Recently, we were with comrade Gromadin and Gerasimov in Pravdinsk. The 722nd Fighter Aviation Regiment is based there. Communication is bad there: there are two aircraft on duty on alert, but in order for them to get up in the air, a messenger must come running and tell them about it. There is no wire. Pilots are poorly fed, little practice, little training. We looked at how they land, with such a 'bounced landing' that it is not clear how the planes do not fall apart. And this is how they land during the day!

The massive German use of heavy incendiary bombs with combustible fluid came as a complete surprise to the Soviet command and business leaders. The head of the main Department of MPVO NKVD, Lieutenant General Osokin, wrote in his order No. 32/7692:

> The last enemy raids on industrial targets and cities have used new types of incendiary bombs with flammable liquid, a composition that increases the area of simultaneous ignition of both horizontal and vertical surfaces of buildings… At

individual facilities the incorrectly produced blackout by closing the light apertures (tight closing of large openings with boards) created serious difficulties for dismantling and removing of blackout devices during firefighting… when heat is formed overlaying combustible materials.

There was a need to create new firefighting equipment. The initiative was taken by plant managers. For example, the director of the Kirov Oil and Fat Plant in Gorky, Andreyanov, wrote to Mikhail Rodionov:

> Recent raids by enemy aircraft have shown that production facilities have suffered more from incendiary bombs of a new design… Extinguishing these incendiary bombs with existing fire extinguishing means is somewhat difficult. I propose to organise the production of foam fire extinguisher (foam sprinklers) with a capacity of 15–20 litres with a hose and a spray gun.

However, the development took many months, and by that time the Luftwaffe could have burned all the cities of the Volga Region!

Moreover, the Germans were not the authors of the technique of using large-calibre incendiary bombs with combustible fluid, but used the techniques of British bomber aviation. The Germans had experienced the enormous destructive impact of incendiary bombs, which was significantly greater than that of conventional high-explosive bombs.

The Soviet leadership took urgent measures to restore the destroyed factories. On 16 June, the Gorky city defence committee considered measures to alleviate the consequences of the bombing of the No. 718 Engine of the Revolution plant and to quickly restore the Molotov motor vehicle plant. The general contractor was hastily chosen, Stroygaz No. 2 Construction Company, headed by N. Hvackij. Two hundred people from the Soyuzprommehanizatsiya Construction Company and two Red Army battalions were allocated for restoration work, and a decision was made to mobilise 3,000 people from the city's able-bodied population.[47]

The same issues were discussed in parallel at the highest level in Moscow. On 14 June, People's Commissar of foreign affairs, at the same time Prime Minister, Vyacheslav Molotov (the Molotov plant was named after him) signed an order to transfer 500 repaired electric motors with a capacity of 4–10kW from Moscow to the People's Commissariat of medium engineering (Ministry of industry), especially for the Molotov plant. On 16 June, the State Defence Committee ordered the People's Commissar of railways (Minister of Transport) Lazar Kaganovich to transport all cargo going to the Molotov plant and Stroygaz No. 2 Construction Company by military transports. All railwaymen were required to take any cargo to the motor vehicle plant without hindrance. The People's Commissariat of the river fleet, headed by the People's Commissar Shagnov, must also freely accept and provide urgent transportation of all cargo and baggage intended for the restoration of the Molotov plant. The head of the main Directorate of the civil air fleet, Astakhov, received an order to deliver 150 tons of the most important cargo for GAZ by transport aircraft during June and July.

On 16 June, the State Defence Committee headed by Stalin met again to discuss the Volga Region air defence. There it adopted secret resolution No. 3588ss 'On strengthening the air defence of the most important industrial centres, bridges and power plants'. According to this document, 390 85mm anti-aircraft guns, 655 37mm and 20mm guns, and 14,000 DShK anti-aircraft machine guns were ordered to be allocated for the designated targets! The city of Izhevsk, located 600km east of Gorky and never subjected to Luftwaffe air attacks, was to receive most of this arsenal. This important industrial centre was to receive 100 large-calibre anti-aircraft guns! The cities of Ufa and Perm were to receive forty-eight guns of all types. This suggests that Stalin was greatly frightened by the scale of the Luftwaffe air attacks and feared for the fate of the cities of the deep rear.

At the same time, the fate of the commander of the Gorky corps area of air defence, General Alexey Osipov, was being decided. At a meeting of the State Defence Committee, Stalin asked the commander of Soviet air defence, General Mikhail Gromadin: 'What is the commander of the Gorky corps area of air defence?' If Gromadin had answered that Osipov was personally responsible for the destruction of the Molotov plant, he would have faced severe punishment, perhaps even the death penalty. But Gromadin suddenly came to the defence of his subordinate: 'Osipov is a very honest and knowledgeable commander, one of the oldest anti-aircraft gunners in the country. Osipov certainly made mistakes, but he can be completely trusted …'

The intercession of General Gromadin bore fruit, and the penalty was 'soft'. After the meeting, the incompetent Osipov was removed from his post and appointed head of the anti-aircraft artillery school. Major General of Artillery Nikolai Markov was appointed the new commander of the Gorky corps air defence area. He was not a particularly successful military leader either. In October 1942, Markov had been appointed commander of the Grozny divisional air defence area. But by that time the main protected site, the Lenin oil cracking plant in Grozny, had been completely destroyed by the Luftwaffe. In the spring of 1943, Markov was appointed commander of the Rostov divisional air defence district. Its units were unable to prevent the repeated destruction of the Bataysk railway junction. Markov was sent to Gorky after the Molotov plant and other facilities had already been destroyed.

In addition, Stalin decided to form a Coordinating Committee for air defence. It included the chief of the General Staff A.M. Vasilevsky, the commander-in-chief of the Red Army air force A.A. Novikov, the commander of Long-Range Aviation A.E. Golovanov, the commander of the air defence of the USSR M.S. Gromadin and others. This committee held only one meeting, on 26 June. Later, the resolution of the State Defence Committee No. 3660ss 'On measures to improve the management of air defence forces' was adopted. Its essence was to create two air defence fronts: the Western one, with headquarters in Moscow, and the Eastern one, with headquarters in Kuibyshev. The border between the fronts ran from north to south along the Arkhangelsk–Kostroma–Krasnodar line.

The Western Air Defence Front was supposed to cover Moscow, the Moscow and Yaroslavl industrial districts, Murmansk, as well as front-line facilities and communications of the active army. It also included the Moscow air defence army, which was formed on the basis of the former Moscow air defence front. In total, the Western Air Defence Front included eleven corps and divisional air defence areas and fourteen fighter aviation divisions. The Eastern Air Defence Front, consisting of seven corps and divisional air defence areas and eight air divisions, was assigned to defend important sites in the Urals, the Middle and Lower Volga Region, the Caucasus and Transcaucasia. Control over the actions of the air defence forces was assigned to the command of the Red Army artillery.

Chapter 6

The Finishing Blow

On the Caspian Sea

At the beginning of the third decade of June, the prolonged lull continued on the Eastern front. The Soviets received the most contradictory information about the Wehrmacht's plans and intentions. The longer this pause lasted, the more nervous Stalin and his generals became. And large-scale air attacks against industrial targets only added to the nervousness. 'What are they up to this time?' – this is the main question that the leadership of the Soviet Union and most of the commanders and soldiers of the Red Army asked themselves endlessly.

On 17 June, the Russians received more 'valuable' intelligence information from various sources. These reported that the 17th Army was preparing to attack the Kuban. On the basis of interrogations of prisoners and defectors, it was concluded that the Germans had specifically transferred fifty Tiger heavy tanks to the Novorossiysk sector in order to use them to eliminate the bridgehead in the Myshako area. In addition, Russian intelligence established that between 20 and 25 June, the Wehrmacht was going to launch a major offensive, with the main attack being made on Rostov-on-Don, and the auxiliary one on the Kuban bridgehead. The operation would allegedly be supported by a large number of tanks, aircraft, and even the fleet. On the same day, a Pe-2 reconnaissance plane flew over the Kerch Strait and recorded increased two-way traffic between the two banks. The Russians decided that this might indicate the transfer of troops to the Kuban bridgehead and preparation for an amphibious operation. Soviet attack aircraft pilots were ordered to be on alert for attacks on German ships and landing craft in the Sea of Azov. 'According to intelligence data, the enemy continues to concentrate its forces off the coast of the Taman Peninsula and the Sea of Azov,' the 230th Attack Aircraft Aviation Division reported in the combat log on 19 June. During the day, the movement of individual boats and several barges was observed in the direction from north to south-west along the coast. According to the testimony of a prisoner of war of the Romanian army, the enemy in the Novorossiysk area was preparing an offensive in early July. And in addition, there were large reserves of chemical substances – chemical weapons and chemical divisions. The Soviets were confident that the Wehrmacht offensive would begin with the mass use of chemical warfare agents. This false information created additional panic in the officers and soldiers.

On 20 June, the Russian intelligence service, terrified by its own fears, assumed that the German attack would begin with massive chemical bombardments and artillery bombardments with projectiles containing toxic substances. Then the landing of amphibious troops from ferries and landing barges on the coast of the Sea of Azov would begin. Immediately after that the Wehrmacht would launch a simultaneous attack from the Mius River on Rostov-on-Don and from the Kuban bridgehead on the cities of Krasnodar and Tikhoretsk. In the future, a strike at Kursk was expected, and then a large-scale offensive with uncertain goals. At that time, Stalin seriously feared a repeat of the offensive in the Caucasus and even on Moscow!

The Luftwaffe was still in a favourable position. The start of Operation *Zitadelle* was postponed until the beginning of July and there were no major battles on the entire front. The Kampfgeschwader were preparing for the next phase of the operation to destroy Russian industrial centres. Now it was decided to conduct air attacks against medium and small enterprises, as well as against oil traffic in the Caspian Sea.

On the night of 19/20 June 1943, German bombers carried out another air attack on Saratov. The main blow was inflicted on the Kirov oil cracking plant, as well as on oil loading vessels that were at the berths. As a result, according to German data, two ships were sunk and two more damaged.

During the raid, a group of He 111s from KG 55 'Greif' was attacked by Russian night fighters. As a result, one aircraft from the 7th Staffel had its left engine disabled. A member of the bomber's crew recalled:

> We are hanging out over Saratov, 800 kilometres on the other side of the front. The 'old man' directing the raid changes course and altitude over this damned hole, because we feel like a stationary target for anti-aircraft artillery in this clunker. It is only a matter of a few seconds – and this has already happened: the searchlight has captured us, and as if this was all that was needed, at the same moment a bundle of yellow machine-gun

tracers passes over the plane. 'There's a night fighter behind us'– the radio operator's cry is cut off as a deafening blow throws us into corners. Our 'suitcase' dives like a fiery comet.

The left engine is burning, and on the left and right we are still passing through sheaves of machine-gun tracers. Trembling hands try to find the parachute ring on his chest, but it fails. Before our eyes, the arrows of the devices are spinning. The air stream is buzzing around us. At any moment, the last explosion in our lives can be heard. Suddenly, a huge force, like a weight weighing a hundredweight, presses us into its corners. The 'old man' levelled our 'suitcase'. The altimeter shows 1,000 metres. There was no more time to lose. What about the engine? It no longer burns, its airscrew only rotates slowly. The fire must have been knocked out during the frantic dive.

During the Russian anti-aircraft fire, a serious head wound was received by radio operator Oberfeldwebel Hans Kobbenhagen. His radio was a useless

85 mm anti-aircraft guns 52-K in position.

Anti-aircraft artillery fire control device (PUAZO-3).

pile of metal and wires. The entire electrical system of the aircraft failed, and the crew members had to manually pump fuel into the only working engine, on the reliability of which their fate now depended. At an altitude of 1,000m, the damaged He 111 barely flew over the inhospitable Russian plains.

The German pilot continued his dramatic story:

> Now everything depends on reliable navigation. However, how to fly the plane if the exact location is unknown. Nevertheless, we must use a single engine, if at all possible, to somehow try to reach the front line before dawn. If we are lucky, the Red corporal will sleep near his anti-aircraft guns. If they are awake, they will take us down from the sky like a lame duck. Unfortunately, there could be no doubt about it. Well, and if we can get past, we can't be sure that at dusk our own gunners aren't trying to shoot us down and draw a new ring around their barrels.[1]

The crew threw everything unnecessary out of the plane, including some fuel. Thanks to these actions, it was possible to stabilise the flight. Soon the dawn began to break and the navigator was able to navigate by ground reference. When the He 111 approached the front line, a thunderstorm began, thanks to which the bomber imperceptibly crossed this dangerous place. As a result, the Germans managed to fly to their air base and land safely. 'Military fate' this time turned out to be favourable to them. But not to everyone…

He 111 H-16 Wrk Nr 160523 of 5./KG 27 was also attacked by a night fighter. The bomber was able to fly to German territory and make an emergency landing. However the plane had received 50 per cent damage, one person was killed, and another was seriously injured.

The specialist Kampfgruppe I./KG 100 'Viking' did not participate in the raid on Saratov that night; it was on other missions. One Staffel flew to mine the Volga, the other two Staffel to bomb ships in the Caspian Sea.

'My brother hinted to me that he included me in the crew that is installing mines: there are few anti-aircraft guns, no night fighters. He said you need to adapt to the conditions of night flying,' recalled side gunner Klaus Fritzsche.[2] This young pilot had only recently started service in I./KG 100. His brother, Helmut Fritzsche, and other crew members were those who had been successfully evacuated from Soviet territory a few days earlier after their emergency landing. Klaus had not yet had time to fight, and he had just started to get used to the Eastern Front, unaware that he was in the thick of the events of the Luftwaffe's largest strategic operation. Fritzsche continues his story:

> Suddenly the commander of the group – a major – comes up to me, 'I want to check what kind of radio operator you are. Join my crew.' Flying where? The Caspian Sea, of course. On the previous night, his radio operator had been severely wounded by a shard from an anti-aircraft shell.

This was Major Paul Claas, who commanded I./KG 100 from October 1942. By this point, it had already completed 310 sorties, including 103 against targets in the UK. On 14 March 1943, Claas was awarded the Knight's Cross. He already had experience flying over the Caspian Sea, which he received during air attacks against oil tankers in October–November 1942. During this period, the crews of I./KG 100 managed to sink several ships. This was the familiar Claas theatre of operations. Unlike large cities, oil tankers did not have a strong air defence, and over the sea there were no Russian night fighters.

The already mentioned Helmut Abendvoth also made a long flight to the Caspian Sea. His He 111 H '6N+MK', took off at 19.30 Berlin time.

The details of this departure in the Abendvoth flight book are recorded illegibly. It is only clear that the flight lasted about seven hours, and the He 111 dropped six high-explosive SC250 bombs on the Russian ships.

Fritzsche recalled:

> The night is quiet, there is no wind or clouds.The flight over the mouth of the Mius and Manych to the Volga delta is calm. No anti-aircraft guns, no fighters. But we must be careful. American P-39 Airacobras with Russian pilots fly here. And for their better orientation, on the ground during our flight, fires are lit in the direction of movement.
>
> We are approaching the Volga Delta, where, according to scouts, there are a good hundred floating objects on the roadstead that need to be destroyed. Our plane with the commander onboard is the first to fly into the affected area, located at an altitude of 1,000 metres. Immediately, frequent anti-aircraft gunfire begins, and the commander gives the order to stop the raid to avoid unnecessary risk. The moon illuminates the sea, and any vessel can be clearly seen on its shiny surface. Leaving the danger zone, we see a large-tonnage vessel. We circle, trying to determine the deck weapons. They don't shoot at us. 'Down low,' the commander orders. 'Put an end to his swimming!'
>
> Everything else passes before my eyes like a movie that I watch from the viewer's seat. We go into a dive, and I hear the commander shout: 'I didn't switch off the safety catch, the bomb didn't detach from the plane!' And at the same time, anti-aircraft fire begins again. We feel a strong blow, I feel pain in my leg, the right engine fails, various measures are taken to stabilise the single-engine flight, but without success.
>
> 'Attention! Landing on water,' says the pilot. Noise of contact with water and … silence. The plane floats. There is time to throw out and inflate the rubber boat. All four crew members take seats in it, each with a bag of emergency supplies. Put it in the boat with four machine pistols, a signal pistol with cartridges, an emergency radio transmitter, a mast, a sail and a medical kit. The useful area of the boat is small, and with such a load there is no place for people. So we're

sitting on board, one foot on a pile of rescue supplies, the other in the water. Looking for oars, it turns out that one is missing. This means that two rowers will row ahead on the left and right, and the third with another oar will keep the course.

Boarding and placement on the boat is safely completed in a matter of minutes. The still-floating plane begins to sink. The tail rises from the water, and slowly, under the gurgling sounds, our proud 'eagle' disappears under the water.[3]

That is how, in an instant, the fate of the pilots at the front changed abruptly. One accidental hit by an anti-aircraft shell deprived the bomber's crew of a pleasant sleep in a comfortable barrack and the usual morning coffee in the officers' messo. Claas and his companions found themselves in a rubber boat in the middle of the distant Caspian Sea. And, exactly 600km from the front line in the deep rear of the hated enemy. The situation could not be worse! This was not England, where PoWs could expect to be treated with dignity. No, they were in the territory of a special enemy, which the Nazi propaganda portrayed as inhuman and savage, like Tolkien's orcs from Mordor!

At least Claas and Fritzsche were still alive. And there was still hope that they would be discovered and evacuated. Even if they were hundreds of kilometres from their territory, they hoped for salvation. Having determined their direction using the compass, the crew rowed their boat to the west. While Claas and others were sullen, Fritzsche admired the nature and the atmospheric phenomena. Soon the sun began to rise in the east, and the sky was painted with unimaginable colours. Unlike his comrades, the young Klaus had no front-line experience and did not understand the essence of the nightmare he was in. He did not know the likely consequences of a possible encounter with people whom Nazi propaganda compared to 'orcs'.

Fritzsche continued:

> The sun has risen. We are trying to determine the speed of our boat. The result is disappointing: about 2 kilometres per hour. The sail will be no use, since there is not the slightest wind. And how many kilometres from the western shore of the Caspian Sea we are, even the commander has no idea. We are starting to send 'SOS' on the international frequency of disaster at sea, 500 kilohertz. As a radio operator, I warn that the Russians are listening to this band as closely as the

Germans, but the commander does not pay attention to this. I'm surprised, because it's fraught with the danger that we will be detected by Russian vessels, if there are any nearby. Three hours later, the sound of a diesel engine is heard in the distance, and soon after the noise of engines is heard from all sides. We think that these are fishermen who have had a good night's sleep and are fishing. There are no boats in sight, and we continue to row. Eventually, around noon, a fairly large fishing motorboat approaches. There are a lot of people on it, each with a machine pistol and a rifle in their hands.[4]

Seeing people who looked like evil 'orcs', the pilots experienced a bad feeling that the war, and perhaps their lives, were definitely over. Moreover, unfortunately for the Germans, it turned out that there were militant Kalmyks on board. They differed from the Russians not only in appearance, but in primitive living conditions, and therefore had no idea about the Geneva Convention. Soon the Germans' fears were horribly confirmed. The crew was stripped naked, subjected to severe beatings and torture, and the commander was killed and thrown overboard. As it turned out, the reason for such ill-treatment of the PoWs was the sinking of a floating fish factory the previous night. Many women and children had been killed on this ship, which was sunk by I./KG 100 bombers. Claas and his crew had been captured by the relatives of these victims. In addition, the Knight's Cross, which was hanging around the commander's neck, played a fatal role. From propaganda articles and posters, all Russians knew that this was the highest military award of Nazi Germany. Thus, the presence of the medal decided the fate of the I./KG 100 commander. This is not the end of the story with regard to military awards.

When the Kalmyks delivered Claas's uniform to the commander of the Volga military flotilla as a trophy, on it hung four Iron Crosses. They had obviously been taken by angry fishermen from other German pilots. This allowed the Russians to claim that a 'Nazi ace awarded four Iron Crosses'[5] was shot down. The Russians, since the time of the tsarist Empire, had a strange tradition of awarding the same person several identical orders. In this case, this idea of multiple awards was routinely transferred to the Germans.

There are several alternative (Russian) versions of the dramatic death of Paul Claas. According to one report, he committed suicide by hitting his head on the bilge eyebolt. According to other information, Claas and his crew tried to board a fishing boat by force of arms in order to sail it to Iran! But supposedly the fishermen repulsed the attack and slaughtered Claas with carving knives. Apparently, the capture of such an important German so impressed the poorly educated locals that this event became an occasion for active myth-making.

Fritzsche and two other surviving Germans were handed over to the leadership of the Caspian flotilla, where the attitude towards them turned out to be much more humane! Russian sailors let the pilots smoke their cigarettes and even took them for questioning like VIPs in a ZIS-101 limousine! Similar vehicles were used by members of the Soviet government and the chiefs of large offices of the Bolshevik Party. Then the Russians gave the pilots a walking tour of the city of Astrakhan. Perhaps the reason for this contrast in attitude to PoWs was the fact that the Germans had been transferred out of the hands of angry local residents, Kalmyks, into the hands of professional military man. Meanwhile, the 'military fate' provided new tests for the unfortunate crew. While in Astrakhan, the Germans witnessed their colleagues from I./KG 100 conducting an air attack on the city. The pilots did not know that there, below, where their bombs fall, were recent colleagues and comrades. There 'at the top' was even a brother of Klaus Fritzsche – Helmut! This was the evil irony of 'military fate'. However, even in this case, the Russians showed mercy to the German prisoners and saved them from 'friendly fire' by sending them to a bomb shelter.

During subsequent interrogations, the pilots tried to misinform the enemy, claiming that they were from the crew of a reconnaissance plane and had arrived in the Caspian Sea from the Crimea. But the Soviets were well aware of which Luftwaffe units were conducting air attacks and what their missions were. Fritzsche described the Soviet officer who conducted the interrogation:

> In appearance, he looks like a representative of the academic intelligentsia. He greets me in pure German, and a conversation begins that has nothing to do with interrogation. About my family environment, the history and culture of Germany. He is interested in my education, and when he finds out that I have studied English, he easily switches to it. He treats me to white bread, fish, and a glass of vodka. I also relax. And so for more than an hour. Suddenly the major says: 'Mr Feldwebel, I have the impression that you have a good education and a high level of intelligence. I would like to know why you think Russians

are fools. According to the interrogation reports, you lied to us. Now I'll tell you what happened. You flew not from Kerch, but from Stalino, to undermine the Volga. Your commander – Major Claas – is well known to us, and I regret that he was killed.[6]

After the end of the interrogations, the pilots were sent, as expected, to prison camps. It is not known exactly who performed the duties as the commander of the specialised I./KG 100 immediately after the death of Major Claas. In any case, the commander of the 1st Staffel, Hauptmann Bätcher, officially assumed this position on 28 July. The example of the evacuated Puklitsch crew showed that German pilots could wander for a long time on Soviet territory. Probably, until 28 July, the Germans hoped that Claas could still return from enemy territory. However, hopes for a miraculous rescue were not fulfilled this time.

'Eerie forest of anti-aircraft guns'

On the night of 20/21 June, the Luftwaffe undertook a second major raid on the city of Yaroslavl. J. Wolfersberger of the 5th Staffel KG 27 'Boelcke' recalled:

> On June 20, the order came for a raid on the rubber plant in Yaroslavl. At the exact time indicated, we take off and hover again in our aircraft between heaven and earth, and death, our faithful companion, is with us again. Hours pass, there, to our left, flashes of anti-aircraft shells sparkle, in that direction in the immediate vicinity of Moscow. A city that once trembled when German soldiers were a few kilometres away.

A total of 112 aircraft participated in the raid.

Given the experience of ten days ago, when by accident many of the bombers happened to be over Moscow, the Germans plotted the flight path to the target more carefully. Most of the bombers flew in a narrow corridor 20km wide between the cities of Kaluga and Tula, then between Serpukhov and Kashira, between Mikhnevo and Yegoryevsk, then between Noginsk and Orekhovo-Zuyevo, then east of Aleksandrov and along the Moscow–Yaroslavl railway line. From time to time, leading aircraft (pathfinders) dropped photoflash bombs ('chandeliers'). Because of this, an air alert was declared in the city of Pereslavl-Zalessky (photoflash bombs scared the inhabitants). Nevertheless, the bombers only flew 60–70km from the Soviet capital, inevitably falling into the zone of anti-aircraft fire and the zone of action of night fighters of the 1st VIA PVO. Regiments and divisions defending the cities of Kashira, Kolomna, Noginsk, and Shatura fired over 2,000 anti-aircraft shells.

Russian night fighters completed fifty-two sorties, which involved aircraft from eight aviation regiments. The pilots reported seven air battles and one downed aircraft. At 23.18, a pair of Yak-1s flown by Major Alexey Katrich and Senior Lieutenant Konstantin Kryukov from the 12th Guards IAP managed to intercept a single Ju 88 near Kashira. Katrich recalled:

> In my zone, I manoeuvred at an altitude of 3,500–4,000 metres in order to be below the average altitude of enemy bombers. This makes it easier to detect the enemy against the sky at night, and to remain unnoticed on the dark background of the earth. The night was moonless, with a slight haze, cloudless, and on the northern and north-eastern part of the horizon there were some light bands that made it easier to observe in this direction. Twenty to 25 minutes after take-off, I noticed the silhouette of a bomber on the bright part of the horizon, going on a course of approximately 90 degrees.[7]

The pilot could not accurately determine the distance to the target, but given the time it took to approach, it was about 1½ to 2km. Trying not to lose sight of the target, Katrich started converging on an intersecting course and soon opened fire. Almost simultaneously, Senior Lieutenant Kryukov also began firing at the bomber. Katrich continues the story:

> I opened fire on the enemy aircraft at the same time as Senior Lieutenant Kryukov, unexpectedly, without seeing each other. This was obviously because both of us, having paid full attention to the enemy, relaxed our caution. Senior Lieutenant Kryukov, patrolling in the neighbouring zone, also found this plane and made a rapprochement at the same time with me. After our first attack, the enemy's tail caught fire, possibly due to damage to the oxygen tanks in the tail section of the Ju 88's fuselage, and now we had no reason to fear that we would

lose it. In order not to collide, we agreed on the radio to make attacks from different sides and not go to the opposite side after the attack.[8]

The bombers' side gunners desperately opened fire and managed to damage Kryukov's plane. However, the Soviet fighters continued to attack, and eventually the Ju 88 was engulfed in flames and went down. The bomber crashed near the city of Ozery, 120km south-east of Moscow. Later, the code and emblem on the fuselage were able to establish that the aircraft was from 8./KG 1 'Hindenburg'.

The raid, like the last time, did not go exactly according to plan. For various reasons, twenty-two German aircraft did not reach the target. Three of them dropped bombs on Tula, one on Ryazan, and another on Plavsk. The remaining ninety bombers continued to fly towards the target.

Above Yaroslavl, the German pilots were waiting for an uncharacteristically strong air defence. Russian anti-aircraft guns fired a powerful barrage, and at a high altitude there were raised barrage balloons. P. Mobius of 9./KG 27 recalled: 'After dropping bombs from a height of 3,000 metres, we suddenly saw the rays of the enemy searchlights ahead of the barrage balloons. We abruptly went up, gaining 4,000 metres, and then lay down on the opposite course.'

Another pilot from 6/KG 27 shared his impressions: 'During these raids, the bombing was carried out from 6,400m. There was a very powerful anti-air defence with heavy anti-aircraft guns. Practically a terrible forest of anti-aircraft guns!'[9]

In fact, there was no 'forest' of 'heavy' guns in the area of Yaroslavl. The regiments defending the city had only seventy-five 85mm anti-aircraft guns.

Despite the impressive lighting effect, the Russian air defence forces were still unable to prevent the bombing. Some 130 tons of bombs of all calibres were dropped on the city. As a result of the attack, a complex of warehouses and residential buildings where employees of the Yaroslavl tyre plant lived were destroyed. The rubber preparation workshop, the rubber warehouse, the resin warehouse, the soot and textile warehouse and other auxiliary structures were burned down. The Pervyj barrack settlement, which was located next to the factory, was almost wiped out. Bombs also destroyed house No. 11 along the Avenue Schmidt. The thermal and power station (TJEC) No.1 substation Severnaja was damaged, while the main engineer of the station, N.S. Tikhonov, was killed and five other employees were injured in the fire. Five workshops were destroyed at the synthetic rubber plant, three workshops at the regenerator plant, and four at the asbestos plant.[10]

After the bombing, the KG 27 planes made a second approach to the target to record the results of their bomb hits. 'We hit the target, as evidenced by the fires that have now arisen. Satisfied, we take a course to the departure airfield,' recalled J. Wolfersberger. Meanwhile, huge flames were rising high in the sky over the Volga, illuminating everything at a great distance. The glow of the fire was visible for many kilometres from Yaroslavl.

Night fighters of the 147th IAD PVO carried out twenty-five sorties during the raid and claimed two downed bombers. Senior Sergeant I.F. Ushkalov from the 959th IAP rammed a Luftwaffe aircraft in his Hurricane near the village of Davydovo, then took to his parachute. According to Soviet data, the plane he shot down was found near the village of Elenino. Presumably, another night ram was made by Senior Lieutenant S.S. Pichugin from the 439th IAP in his MiG-3. The Russian pilot was killed. Both pilots were awarded the Order of Lenin, one posthumously.

On the way back, some of the bombers flew the same route that was used to fly to the target. Another group of planes returned to their bases on a route that passed north of Moscow through Kalyazin-Kimry–Volokolamsk-Gzhatsk. The 257th and 237th Anti-Aircraft Artillery Divisions that defended the village of Ivankovo and the city of Mozhaisk targeted this group of bombers (909 shells were fired). One stray Ju 88 A flew directly over the outskirts of Moscow at an altitude of 5,000m. Another 229 rounds of 85mm calibre were fired at it. The searchlights illuminated eleven targets. Interestingly, even small-calibre artillery (25mm and 37mm) and 12.7mm anti-aircraft machine guns were fired at German bombers, which were totally ineffective at targets flying at that altitude.

The raid on Yaroslavl cost the Luftwaffe serious losses. KG 27 'Boelcke' lost three aircraft:

- He 111 H-16 Wrk Nr 160289 '1G+FN' of 5./KG 27 was shot down by a night fighter. All four crew members – pilot Oberleutnant Bruno Lembke, navigator Unteroffizier Walter Koster, flight engineer Unteroffizier Franz Fichtenbauer and flight mechanic Otto Burkhardt – were missing;
- He 111 H-16 Wrk Nr 160286 '1G+CP' of 6./KG 27 was shot down by a night fighter. All five crew members – pilot Leutnant Conrad Krebe, navigator Oberfeldwebel Artur Gerstenberg, flight engineer Unteroffizier Paul Kaminsky, flight mechanic Unteroffizier Fritz Ottmann and flight gunner Gefreiter Martin Schlett – were missing;

- He 111 H-16 Wrk Nr 8341 '1G+ER' of 7./KG 27 was probably shot down by anti-aircraft artillery. Its crew – pilot Feldwebel Karl Sinner, navigator Gefreiter Klaus Schwarz, flight engineer Unteroffizier Otto Weidlich and flight mechanic Unteroffizier Heinz Lorenzmayer – were missing.[11]

8th Staffel KG 1 'Hindenburg' lost two bombers:

- Ju 88 A-4 Wrk Nr 144456 Feldwebel H. Pannier went missing with all his crew (he was probably shot down by the night fighters of Katrich and Kryukov from the 12th Guards IAP);
- Ju 88 A-14 Wrk Nr 144453 received a direct hit from an anti-aircraft shell, probably while approaching the front line. The plane made an emergency landing in the location of its troops, and then completely burned out. However, its crew was not injured.

4./KG 3 'Blitz' lost one plane:

- Ju 88 A-4 Wrk Nr 3709 '5K+KM', Feldwebel Werner Kremp and Unteroffizier Albert Wagner were missing.

In addition, He 111 H-16 Wrk Nr 160170 '1G+AT' of 9./KG 27 was damaged in the night fighter attack. At the same time, two crew members were injured – radio operator Obergefreiter Franz Ronnau and flight mechanic Obergefreiter Karl Hoffmann, but the plane returned safely to base. Anti-aircraft fire damaged Ju 88 Wrk Nr 8770 of Oberfeldwebel A. Merckle of II./KG 51 'Edelweiss'. While landing at Bryansk, the pilot lost control and the bomber crashed. A flight gunner was injured. Another bomber from II./KG 51 (Ju 88 A-5 Wrk Nr 4603) made an emergency wheels-up landing at Smolensk and suffered 40 per cent damage.

It is difficult to reliably determine which of these aircraft were damaged and shot down directly in the vicinity of Yaroslavl, and which on en route to the target. In total, the Luftwaffe lost eight bombers (7 per cent of those that participated in the raid) and five crews. This was the highest loss sustained in the entire Blitz over the Volga.

However, the troubles of the German pilots did not end there. On the way back, one of the He 111s of 9./KG 27 suffered a serious problem, namely a propeller fell off 500km from the front line. Despite this surprise the crew remained calm. P. Mobius wrote in the report:

There was a vibration in the left engine, and the propeller, along with the propeller fairing, flew off and fell down. However, the engine fairing remained intact. It was impossible to maintain a height of 2,500–3,000 metres on a single engine. So we turned on the compressor and were able to stay at 2,000 metres.

N. Falten – another member of the crew of the same aircraft – later recalled:

We had to fly over enemy territory and the positions of their troops for another 500 kilometres. After we balanced the bomber, I prepared to drop the heavy armour plates. If the plane started losing altitude, we would throw them out. But this was not necessary.

The He 111 not only made it to the front line, but also landed safely at Olsufevo air base. Other tired crews were also returning from a dangerous raid. J. Wolfersberger recalled:

We fly past Moscow again, and soon there are signs of the front line ahead: fires, flares taking off and artillery fire. Then soon we see the signal lights of our airfield and land. We get out of the planes and go to the command post to make reports. Then we go to our barracks to relieve the stress of this combat mission with a healthy sleep.[12]

Between 06.43 and 08.00 on 21 June, a reconnaissance plane identified by the Russians as a Ju 88 flew along the Vyazma–Sychevka route – north of Klin–Ivankovo and then on to Yaroslavl. Its mission was to record the results of the last air attack. VNOS posts determined that the flight altitude was 10,000m. Four fighters were scrambled to intercept from the Central airfield of Moscow and Klin air base, but they were not able to attack the German because of its high altitude. On the way back, the reconnaissance plane flew along the route Kimry-Klin–Volokolamsk–Shakhovskaya-Vyazma station. Again, the fighters of the 1st Air Fighter Army were unable to intercept it, although four pilots made visual contact with the target. This time, its altitude was determined at 12,000–12,500m. The Russians concluded that the aircraft was an ultra-high-altitude Ju 86 P reconnaissance aircraft, but in fact again it was a Ju 88 D-6 of 4.(F)/121, equipped with a system for injecting nitrous oxide (GM-1).

'Without the help of Great Britain and the United States, we can't win...'

The relaxation and recuperation of the German bomber crews was short-lived. On the night of 22 June, KG 27 'Boelcke' again participated in an air attack on Gorky, the seventh since the beginning of the operation. The actions of the squadron were again personally directed by Oberstleutnant Baron von Beust, whose He 111 H '1G+AA', took off from Olsufevo at 20.31, Berlin time. This time, eighty-five aircraft participated in the raid.

In Gorky, after a week's break, the citizens hoped that the Germans would now leave the city alone. But closer to midnight, based on VNOS reports, it became clear that German bombers were flying there again. The planes followed the direction of the targets in groups of three or nine. The main mass flew along the route Ryazan–Sasovo–Kulebaki–Gorky, the rest following through Ruzaevka-Arzamas with access to the target from the southern direction. At the same time, Russian air surveillance posts again recorded a four-engine 'ghost' plane in the sky, identifying it as an Fw 200!

German pilots rest on the grass near a He 111 bomber. (Photo from Boelcke Archiv)

At 00.11 local time, air raid sirens began to wail again in Gorky, and residents who were not working longingly made for the shelters. Forty-five barrage balloons rose into the air. Following the sounding of the alarm in different parts of the city, signal rockets began to fly into the sky, which were fired by German agents. Observer Malkov from observation post No. 1 at the Molotov plant reported at 00.16: 'In the area of the second surgical hospital, a signal rocket was launched from the ground.' Then, at 00.24, a similar message was received from observation post No. 5: 'Behind the Severnyj Poselok settlement, east of Schastlivaya station, a red rocket was launched vertically from the ground.' This showed that, despite all the measures taken, the German saboteurs continued to be active in the city. However, the German pilots were perfectly orientated in the sky over Gorky and did not need the services of secret agents from the Abwehr and SD.

At 00.35 and 00.45, the observers reported: 'Everything is calm in the air'. But at 00.50 in the area of the village of Novinki, located on the high right bank of the Oka River, opposite the Gorky automobile plant, the sky was cut by the rays of three searchlights. A few minutes later, long beams flashed on the outskirts of the Avtozavodsky district of Gorky, and at 00.56, anti-aircraft guns were heard firing near the city of Dzerzhinsk. All this indicated that an air attack would soon occur. At the same time, Antonov, from observation post No. 2, reported: 'The drone of an airplane over the Oka River, two photoflash bombs, anti-aircraft fire in the southern part of the city!'

Around 01.04, the first photoflash bombs ('chandeliers') broke out in the sky, then within an hour German planes dropped more than 130 photoflash bombs. This time, the entire Zarechnaya district, located along the Oka River, became the target of the attack. The raid was carried out in echelons at intervals of seven to eight minutes. The Ju 88s bombed from a dive, and the He 111s from a height of about 4,000m. For example, He 111 '1G+AA' of KG 27 of Commander von Beust dropped bombs from 3,800m. Individual bombers again used combustible fluid.[13]

At 01.08, the grey cast iron foundry shop of the Molotov motor vehicle plant was hit by four bombs – two SC250s and two Brand C250As – but two of them did not detonate. However, the explosions and the resulting fire destroyed two pieces of foundry equipment and damaged four more. In addition, seven electric motors, two machine tools and five bridge cranes were damaged, with floor structures and the roof damaged.[14] Fires broke out in the armature-radiator housing from the impact of incendiary bombs, but the shop teams managed to quickly extinguish the fire, not allowing it to spread. The explosion tore off the barrier balloon, which went into free flight, simultaneously causing a short circuit in the power electric line going to the water abstraction intake station. The blast wave at aircraft engine plant No. 466 in workshops 6, 7, and 25 shattered all the glass in the windows and light apertures.

At 01.47, the German bombers switched their efforts directly to aircraft engine plant No. 466 itself, which was next to GAZ. Four SC250 bombs fell on the main building and the Assembly shop, of which one did not explode. As a result, finished products (components and unfinished motors) were covered with debris and damaged. In workshop No. 22, the floor structures of the roof were destroyed by a direct hit from a bomb. In workshop No. 5, two bombs broke through the roof and destroyed the water main. In workshop No. 3, as a result of direct hits, the roof collapsed, and there was a strong fire. Another high-explosive bomb hit workshop No. 7, and, breaking through the roof, exploded inside. As a result, the machine tools cold run-in was severely damaged. In workshops No. 3B and No. 3D, the explosions damaged four machine tools, destroyed the engine block assembly rooms and machining for engine crankcases. In the above-mentioned workshops, all the windows were blown out, the roof and floor structures trusses partially collapsed, and the main pipelines were seriously damaged. A BrandC50A bomb fell near the building, but there was no explosion, leaving only a hole in the ground. By a lucky chance, none of the factory workers were injured; at least, that was what was recorded in the official report.

At 01.02, nine photoflash bombs were dropped over the Engine of the Revolution factory, then two more 'chandeliers' of ten photoflash bombs flashed high in the dark sky. At the same time, an observation post located on a high tower recorded the launch of a signal rocket from the ground, carried out by a German agent from the river. The plant director Nikulin immediately ordered the evacuation of the workers to the bomb shelters. After a while, at an altitude of 300m, a dark silhouette of a bomber appeared and then the air was pierced by the whistle of falling bombs. Powerful explosions occurred in workshops Nos 1, 12 and 14, in the garage and other buildings of the plant. A large fire immediately engulfed the wooden building of the logistics warehouse. At 01.27, another bomber flew over the plant, dropping two high-explosive and one FLAM500 incendiary bomb. A powerful explosion thundered on the mezzanine of workshop No. 2, then a loud bang was heard inside and combustible fluid broke out and instantly flared. Eight minutes later, those on the observation towers clearly saw another plane coming in from the Oka River. It dropped bombs on the central tool warehouse, and another large-calibre incendiary bomb hit the already burning workshop No. 2.

The members of the firefighting part of the workshop unitary team, Shcherbakov, Glazov and Afanasyev, and the chief of staff of MPVO Gerashchenko were stunned by explosions. However, they did not leave their posts and resolutely engaged in an unequal battle with the rapidly spreading fire. From the experience of previous bombings, the fire department employees knew that combustible fluid should be extinguished with sand or earth instead of water. Soon, an emergency recovery team and soldiers from military units arrived to help them. All the fire departments immediately started extinguishing the roof of workshop No. 2. Water was pumped through long hoses from fire reservoirs, while buckets of sand were passed along a chain up the stairs. From his command post the plant director Nikulin continuously called the city headquarters of the MPVO rescue service, begging for help. Soon, eight fire engines arrived, which were immediately distributed to the objects. Then three more companies of soldiers pulled up.

The battle with the fire took place on the roof of the foundry shop, located next to the logistics warehouse, which was already burning like a giant bonfire. The forty-four-person workshop unitary team tirelessly extinguished countless fires that occurred here, there, or in several places at once. The workers covered them with sand and metal sheets, and constantly watered the roof with water, preventing the bitumen from warming up. The fire continued to advance, but at the crucial moment the critical situation was 'saved' by the complete collapse of the material warehouse building.

Fighting the fires continued as the early June dawn began. With heroic efforts, the foundry shop was saved from the fire, with the exception of the cupola furnace, which was destroyed by a direct hit from a high-explosive bomb. Most of workshop No. 2 was also saved, but three bridge cranes, one girder crane and fifteen machine tools were burned.

The factory's logistics and model warehouses were completely burned down with all the contents (materials, equipment, models and other valuables). The central tool warehouse, along with all the tools and accessories, was totally destroyed by fire. All the equipment for making rockets for the M-8, M-13, and M-31 multiple launch systems was destroyed. In workshop No. 12 the explosions destroyed the charge lift and the coke shed, and the roof of workshop No. 9 burned down. Workshop No. 3 was badly damaged. It collapsed half of the roof, partially burned and destroyed load-bearing structures, and burned out the wooden floor. In addition, the blast wave knocked out windows and frames in the main office of the plant. Across the site the water supply, power and electric lines lighting, heating system and air pipeline were destroyed. The number of victims was relatively small: four people were killed and forty were injured and burned.[15]

Other enterprises in the Leninsky district of Gorky were also affected: the plant of food concentrates and the Red October factory. The Zagotzerno base, located on the Oka River, was hit by a large number of large-calibre incendiary bombs, which caused numerous fires. Soon, three fire trucks and three fire trains arrived at the site. By then, however, the fire had spread throughout the buildings, sending huge flames into the sky. As a result, sixteen warehouses containing oats were completely burned, as well as more than 600 tons of wheat. The fire could only be extinguished by 07.00. Railway tracks and high-voltage electric lines were destroyed.

At the Novaya Sosna plant, which was a branch of the Gorky automobile plant, numerous high-explosive and incendiary bombs caused a large fire that engulfed several buildings at once. Six fire trucks were sent to extinguish them, and a fire boat approached from the river. But, despite all these efforts, the factory ffered great damage. The package shop, material warehouse, canteen and vegetable store were completely burned down. Of the eighty-three units containing the plant's main equipment, twenty-eight were destroyed.

Many bombs also hit the residential sector adjacent to the factories. The explosions completely destroyed nine houses and two barracks, and dozens of others were engulfed in flames. A large amount of combustible fluid ignited sheds, baths, fences and trees, and anything that could burn. Residents tried to organise firefighting, passing buckets of water along a chain and putting out the fire with earth, sawdust and anything that came to hand. Seven fire engines raced through the streets, trying to stop the spread of the fire, but there was a catastrophic lack of water, and access to artificial fire reservoirs was not available as many places were closed off by rubble and bomb craters. In addition, the thick smoke made it difficult for firefighters to navigate the labyrinths of narrow streets in the housing sector. As a result, thirty-seven single-storey residential buildings, the building of the 5th Militia Station, school No. 106 and a grocery store were completely burned down. Many other buildings were damaged. In total, thirty fire trucks were operating in the Leninsky district that night.

At 01.20, the Stalinsky district was bombed. Fifteen high-explosive and heavy incendiary bombs fell on aviation plant branch No. 2, which partially destroyed the woodworking shop. Three people were killed, two were seriously injured and three were slightly injured. The steam line, water supply and power lines were severely damaged.

A direct hit from a high-explosive bomb in the shop for the production of cases of the bus factory caused the collapse of ceiling structures over an area of 308 sq m and knocked out twenty-four window frames. In addition, the paint shop was completely burned down along with five vehicles. The director of the plant, Parinov, was killed. Fires in workshops where bodies were made were extinguished by MPVO soldiers. At a nearby lime factory, a Hoffman kiln was destroyed, and a tar pit and dormitory building partially burned.

At 01.45, one high-explosive bomb hit the flour warehouse of mill factory No. 1, and, breaking through the roof, exploded inside. As a result, a fire broke out that burned floor structures and part of the manufactured products. The flour conveyor was badly damaged. A second bomb fell at the shop of the workers' supply department, while a third exploded on the railway sidings. Another powerful explosion thundered on the coastal dam. Incendiary bombs filled with petrol, polystyrene and phosphorus hit railway cars standing under the loading area at a flour warehouse. Five of them were burned.

Several bombs exploded in the area of Moscow railway station. Water pipes and telephone lines were damaged in many places. At Gorky-Tovarnaya station, the technical inspection point for railway cars burned down after direct hits from incendiary bombs.

In addition, the Germans tried to bomb the road bridge over the Oka. This important strategic object was quickly covered by a smokescreen, which made it difficult for the pilots to aim. A SC1800 bomb fell near the bridge and the explosion was so strong that shrapnel riddled residential buildings on the beach, and glass, window frames and doors were blown out. More bombs exploded in the river, to the right and left of the bridge. One high-explosive bomb hit the floating jetty, which was standing near the cargo port. But the bridge itself, despite the nearby explosions, survived.

The Luftwaffe failed to hit all its intended targets. More than 100 high-explosive and fifty heavy incendiary bombs were dropped on the Krasnaya Etna metallurgical plant,[16] which produced parts for the Gorky automobile plant. However, the target luckily escaped serious destruction. Only the drawing shop that produced wire suffered from the fire. Almost all the bombs fell on residential buildings.

The last group of bombers struck the Voroshilovsky district, according to Russian data dropping seventeen high-explosive and forty-five different incendiary bombs. At the Lenin radio telephone factory No. 197 the explosion wave damaged electrical cables and feeders, and the factory bath was damaged. A pasta factory and the Frunze military and political school were destroyed.

In total, during the seventh air attack on Gorky, fourteen factories, a railway station and a river port received various damage. Seventy houses and barracks were destroyed, and as many more were damaged. The flames from the fires that were burning all over the city were visible for tens of kilometres away. The villagers understood that something terrible was happening in Gorky. According to Soviet data, on the morning of 22 June, as a result of the air attack, eighty-eight people were killed, while another 180 were injured and concussed.[17] In addition to the bombing that night, German planes scattered propaganda leaflets throughout the region. They reported the futility of further resistance. The German command called on the Russian people to quit their jobs and not fulfil the tasks of their government.

In their attempts to repulse the enemy raid, the anti-aircraft artillery expended 40,000 shells. Night fighters carried out thirty-four sorties and claimed to have shot down one bomber.

At 23:00, a La-5 fighter took off, piloted by Lieutenant Colonel Kovrigin, deputy commander of the 142nd Fighter Aviation Division. After gaining altitude, he headed to the area of the cities of Pavlovo and Vorsma and there began a search for enemy aircraft. The sky was bright on this night, and not only the riverbed of the Oka was clearly visible below, but the outlines of cities and towns could easily be seen. On his radio Kovrigin received periodic reports of approaching bombers that were about to appear in the patrol area. At 01.00, Kovrigin saw the silhouette of a He 111 on the bright part of the horizon, above him, at an altitude of about 3,500m, heading for Gorky. The pilot went to approach. Having reached the target, he decided not to open fire but to immediately ram. The bomber was rapidly increasing in size, and it seemed that a collision was inevitable. Kovrigin had probably already mentally imagined how he would return to the airfield as a hero and receive a medal. But at the last moment, the German pilot disrupted his plans by abruptly turning aside and the La-5 missed its target. After that, the bomber began to descend, while its flight gunner opened up with a machine gun. Kovrigin managed to maintain visual contact with the target and continued the pursuit. In his report he wrote that he 'made six attacks from a position strictly in the tail and from the bottom, from the side, from the right and left sides from a distance of 50–25 metres', after which one of the engines of the bomber caught fire and he quickly crashed. However, the pilot did not see the bomber hit the ground.[18]

According to German data, during the air attack on Gorky, a night fighter did shoot down one bomber – Ju 88 A-4 Wrk Nr 4560 'V4+GR' of Unteroffizier F. Wilfinger of 7./KG 1 'Hindenburg'. It sent a short radio message: 'Attacked by night fighter …'After that, the connection was cut off forever. The entire crew of four was reported missing.

Russian night fighters also suffered losses. At 00.48, a MiG-3 was shot down over Bogorodsk. During its emergency landing, the plane snagged power lines. Several electrical wires were severed, but the pilot survived.

On the way back, German bombers were attacked by night fighters, which were particularly intense in the area south of Tula. As a result, He 111 H-16 Wrk Nr 8234 '1G+CR' of 7./KG 27 was shot down. Flight mechanic Feldwebel Lotar Nasteinchik was killed, and four other crew members – pilot Leutnant Hans Schweingruber, navigator Obergefreiter Sigfrid Gottschalk, radio operator Obergefreiter Werner Wolf and flight gunner Obergefreiter Alfred Wagner – were injured. Despite this, the 'military fate' was favourable to this crew. The bomber was able to evade the chase and made an emergency landing in a field west of Dubrovka railway station (12km south-east of Seshchinskaya air base). The plane was completely destroyed, and Obergefreiter Wolf died in hospital the next day.

According to the staff of the Gorky corps area air defence: 'On the outskirts of the city 50 planes were seen and over the city 10 to 12 aircraft of type Ju 88 and He 111'. However, the NKVD office prepared a more objective summary, which indicated that, based on the number of bombs dropped, and according to surveillance data, at least forty aircraft flew over the city. On 22 June, the new head of the regional office of the NKVD of the Gorky region, Colonel Goryansky, sent a report to the People's Commissar of internal affairs, Lavrentiy Beria, in which he detailed the number of bombs dropped on the city.

Districts of Gorky	High-explosive bombs, kg				Incendiary bombs, kg			
	500	250	50	In total	250	50	1	In total
Avtozavodsky	1	8	4	13	4	20	15	39
Leninsky	1	11	36	48	2	104	-	106
Stalinsky	1	9	13	23	16	42	4	98
Kirovsky	8	36	50	94	22	28	-	50
Voroshilovsky	-	7	10	17	-	15	30	45
Total	11	71	103	191	44	209	85	338
Total weight, tons	5.5	17.7	5.3	28.5	11	10.4	0.1	21.5

A street in Gorky after the bombing. (Drawing by artist I.I. Permowski)

The mood of the population of the Gorky region after the latest Luftwaffe raid was depressed. It seemed that there would be no end to the bombing attacks, and that enemy planes would eventually destroy the entire industry. Everyone understood that the German air force had not been defeated in Stalingrad and the Kuban, as reported by Soviet propaganda. Many in

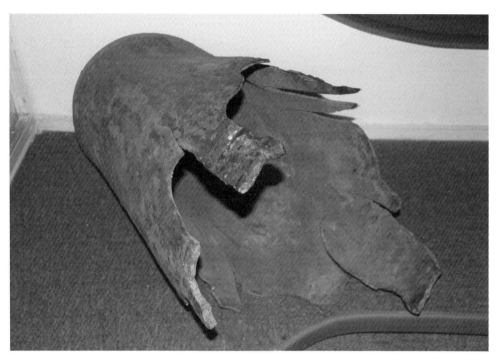

A fragment of the Luftmine BM1000 that was dropped on the city of Gorky.

positions of authority privately expressed the opinion that as the Germans struck blow after blow on the deep rear, the Luftwaffe had become even stronger. Nikolai Dobrotvor, a professor at the Gorky Pedagogical Institute, was in the village of Perevoz during the latest raid. He had gone there to give propaganda lectures on the current international situation. There, from the window of the district office of the Bolshevik party, the professor watched the attack on Gorky. The glow from the fires was clearly visible for 120km!

Professor Dobrotvor wrote in his diary:

> The picture is spectacular, but creepy. The village didn't sleep last night. The next day, German leaflets were found in the area. In the village they say that … without a second front, without the help of Great Britain and the United States, victory over Hitler's Germany is impossible. They view it pessimistically.[19]

Thus, the massive Luftwaffe air attacks on the industrial areas of the Volga Region of the USSR, in addition to the destruction of factories and plants, had a great effect on the morale of the local population.

The end of the Saratov Aviation Plant

On the morning of 22 June, two reconnaissance planes appeared in the Saratov region, one of which flew over the southern edge of the city and began to move away to the west. Ten Russian fighters from the 405th and 963rd IAP took off to intercept. At 08.30, Junior Lieutenant Chilikin, in a Yak-1, saw anti-aircraft shell bursts in the sky and, guided by them, made visual contact with the target.The pilot's report said:

> I reported the enemy to the command post of the aviation regiment and began to pursue it with a climb. In the area of Kologrivovka station, the enemy noticed me – his guns opened fire from a distance of 650–700 metres. When I saw the enemy aircraft firing, I proceeded to the side of the sun and continued to approach. At 08.46 north of the city of Atkarsk at an altitude of 8,200–8,300 metres, I made the first attack from behind on the right,[20] firing at the aircraft engines from a cannon and machine guns from a distance of 250–300 metres. Making a manoeuvre to the right, I made a second attack from behind on the right.[21] The fire was conducted from a gun and machine guns on the left engine from a distance of 250–270 metres. After the second attack, a stream of white smoke appeared from the enemy's left wing. The enemy returned fire and, changing course, continued to leave with a climb. The third attack was made from behind on the left. The fire was conducted from a gun and machine guns towards the left engine and the cockpit from a distance of 150–170 metres. The enemy sharply dived and at an altitude of 800–1,000 metres entered the clouds. On the dive, I made another attack, aiming at the tail from a distance of 400–450 metres. Due to a shortage of fuel, I landed at Petrovskoe airfield at 10.00.

Chilikin identified the target as an He 111, but he had actually attacked a Ju 88 D. The fact that he failed to shoot down the reconnaissance plane was explained by his command as 'poor fire training of the pilot'.

On the night of 22/23 June, the Luftwaffe carried out another raid on Saratov. This time, the target was the Uleshovskaya oil storage facility, on the bank of the Volga River, 5.5km north of the Kirov oil cracking plant and on the border of the Stalinsky and Oktyabrsky districts of the city.

According to Soviet data, fifty bombers took part. The first pathfinders dropped photoflash bombs ('chandeliers'), clearly marking the target for the following groups of bombers. Planes approached the target over the Volga and descended. Some dived directly into the fuel storage area and dropped bombs from a low altitude. Air defence was carried out by the 720th ZenAP. Russian machine-gun crews with large-calibre machine guns were positioned on huge tanks full of petrol. This arrangement of anti-aircraft machine guns was pure madness! As a result, several of these fighters, including women, were burned alive.

In total, fifty high-explosive and twelve heavy incendiary bombs were dropped at the Uleshovskaya facility. As a result, a huge fire broke out, lighting up the entire city. The flames rose hundreds of metres into the sky. The storage plant was almost destroyed, with 20,000 tons of oil products burning, as well as thirteen residential buildings on neighbouring streets. The bombing affected a sawmill, a leather factory and the air base of the No. 292 Razboyschina aviation plant. According to official data, fifty people were killed and injured.[22]

Russian night fighters carried out sixteen sorties, but all of them were unsuccessful. During the raid, Ju 88 A Wrk Nr 3757 from II./KG 51 'Edelweiss' was damaged, but its crew managed to reach the front line and made an emergency landing north-east of Orel-West air base. Later, its damage was estimated at 40 per cent. 'Military fate' was more cruel with the crew of Ju 88 A-4 Wrk Nr 8780 (also from II./KG 51). When landing at Bryansk, both engines suddenly failed. The bomber crashed and all the crew were killed.

On the evening of 23 June, the VNOS posts of the Saratov divisional air defence district again reported to the headquarters the approach of German aircraft. At 23.25 local time, another air raid alert was heard in the city. Air raid sirens were also sounded at Saratov Aviation Plant No. 292 (which produced Yak-1 fighters). However, the workers, according to the established procedure, continued to work. According to their instructions, evacuation was allowed only at the moment of 'immediate threat' of an attack on an industrial facility. Thus, the decision to send workers to bomb shelters depended on the intelligence and humanity of local bosses. The delay in issuing a termination of work order sometimes resulted in unjustified casualties among workers. Reports of changes in the situation were constantly being sent to the MPVO headquarters of the facility. At 23.32, the posts positioned on the towers reported that the hum of aircraft approaching from the south was clearly audible. These were again He 111s from KG 55 and I./KG 100. Another seven minutes passed, and directly over the aircraft factory hung 'chandeliers' of twelve photoflash bombs. Only then was the order given to evacuate the workers to the bomb shelters. Then, during the raid, pathfinders dropped about ten more photoflash bombs over this objective. Members of the MPVO teams took up their posts, including on the roofs of buildings.

The Germans again repeated their effective method of raiding industrial facilities. The first blow was inflicted on the water supply network and as a result, water pipes were damaged in several places. One of the high-explosive bombs hit the entrance of thermal and power station (TJEC) No. 1, another destroyed the floor structures of the oil pumping station. After that, the aircraft factory was completely deprived of electricity and water. Further, within forty minutes, German bombers attacked the target in three waves from a low level, dropping over 100 high-explosive bombs weighing 500–1,000kg and a large number of heavy incendiary bombs.

Fire protection measures at the Saratov Aviation Plant, as was usually the case at all the Soviet factories, were neglected. In addition, to hide the military purpose of this enterprise, it was built as a plant for the production of agricultural combines. Absurd Soviet secrecy led to the fact that, in accordance with this deception, the workshop floors were lined with wooden bars. Moreover, during the work, the wood had become saturated with technical oil. Thus, an excellent combustible material was formed and when the incendiary bombs hit it ignited immediately. As a result, there were six large fires at once, and the spread of the fire quickly became uncontrolled. Floor ignition, as had happened earlier at the Molotov plant, led to the load-bearing beams losing stability and settling. One by one, the floor structures began to collapse. Then the stocks of prepared aviation wood also caught ablaze (the main parts of the fuselage, wings and tail of the Yak-1 were wooden). Despite desperate efforts to extinguish the fire, it continued throughout the night. As a result, ten workshops were completely burned, three were partially damaged and two more were destroyed by direct hits from large-calibre bombs. The factory's railway tracks were severely damaged, and twenty-three railway wagons with raw materials were smashed and burned. As a result of the attack, more than 70 per cent of the production areas and more than 60 per cent of the equipment was destroyed. All the materials warehouses were burned down, and technical documentation for aircraft production was lost. The main logistics warehouse was also completely destroyed. The NKVD office reported to the Saratov regional office of the

Saratov Aviation Plant № 292 after the bombing.

Bolshevik Party: 'Air defence means were again unable to repel the attack of enemy aircraft, whose planes bombed the plant with impunity from a low altitude, almost putting it out of action.'[23]

Simultaneously with the raid on Aviation Plant No. 292, German bombers attacked vessels on the Volga, between Saratov and Kamyshin, including ships of the Volga military flotilla. The bombers dropped more than seventy bombs, but according to Soviet data not a single ship was damaged. At the same time, the river port in Astrakhan was also attacked by air. One of the sailors of the steamer *Goncharov* later recalled:

> That day in Astrakhan, we took on board cargo, put passengers on board and went to pier 8 for refuelling. At this time, the enemy air raid began. It was evening, and it was already dark. Hitler's pilots hung up 'chandeliers'and began bombing. Our *Goncharov*, manoeuvring between the bomb blasts, shook from the blast waves, in many places the canvas covering burst and parted, the boat suspended over the stern was torn off, all the glass was smashed out of the portholes. However, everything went well, we managed to get away from the enemy bombs.[24]

All these high-performance air raids passed without loss to Luftwaffe. Only one He 111 from of 9./KG 55 was damaged by anti-aircraft artillery over Saratov, but its crew was able to reach German territory and make an emergency landing. Two crew members were injured: radio operator Unteroffizier Erich Ludwig and flight gunner Unteroffizier Frahz Harl.

In the morning, first deputy People's Commissar of the aviation industry, Pavel Demetyev, head of the Department of the central office of the Bolshevik Party A.V. Budnikov and a representative of the air force command, J.L. Bibikov, flew urgently to Saratov. When they arrived at the airfield, they saw huge clouds of smoke and steam rising from the southern part of the city. Joseph Stalin's messengers realised that something disastrous had happened. Indeed, all that remained of the Saratov aviation plant were the burned walls of the buildings and the charred machine tools. A lot of new Yak-1s had burned on the conveyor. The Luftwaffe had achieved another success, completely disabling the sixth largest enterprise in the Volga Region. Moreover, this result was achieved during a single raid, at the cost of damage to one aircraft. The destruction was so large and widespread that part of the leadership of the People's Commissariat of Aviation industry suggested that the plant should not be rebuilt. The workers were planned to be distributed to other factories in the industry. At the sight of the piles of ashes and charred ruins, this seemed the most rational solution. But then, the arguments of reason were once again rejected, and for propaganda purposes it was decided to rebuild the plant.[25]

The last air attacks of the Russians and Germans

Meanwhile, the Red Army air force did not stop trying to bomb the German air bases from which the Volga region cities had been raided. On 18 June, Russian long-range bombers launched another air attack against Seshchinskaya air base. They again claimed a lot of destroyed aircraft and 'great destruction'. However, according to German data, as a result of this raid, only two bombers – He 111 H Wrk Nr 7344 out of 5./KG 4 'General Wever' and He 111 H-16 Wrk Nr 8301 from II./KG 55 'Greif' – were destroyed by direct hits on the flight line. This was the first major success of Long-Range Aviation forces! On 19 June, He 111 H-16 Wrk Nr 160922 of II./KG 55 was heavily damaged (55 per cent) during an air attack on Karachev airfield.

On 20 June, 187 Russian bombers attacked an airfield in the vicinity of Bryansk, where aerial reconnaissance recorded 'a large concentration of

German bombers'. As a result, Ju 88 A-4 Wrk Nr 3786 of II./KG 51 was damaged (25 per cent). Thereafter on 22 June, 152 Il-4s, TB-3s and Li-2s bombed one of the airfields near Orel. The same night, major air attacks were carried out on Olsufevo air base and Karachev. On the way back, one Li-2 was attacked by a German night fighter, but, despite the damage, was still able to return. At the same time, the Soviet bombers claimed two downed Messerschmitts (a Bf 109 and a Bf 110).

The next night, 109 Russian planes bombed Olsufevo again, dropping FAB-500 bombs. On the night of 26 June, Long-Range Aviation bombers again attacked this Luftwaffe base, but these raids did not produce any results. During the bombing and on their return to their bases, the Russian bombers were again attacked by German night fighters. According to the crews, these were Bf 109 fighters. For example, 50km from the front line, Captain Matvey Markov was shot down over Russian territory. The entire crew – pilot, navigator Lieutenant Ivashchenko, co-pilot Lieutenant Belousov, flight mechanic technician Lieutenant Afanasiev and flight gunner Sergeant Halyavinsky – died. These were some of the many victims of these senseless and inaccurate air attacks. Thus, the huge raids on German air bases in the Orel and Bryansk areas conducted from 5 to 26 June brought almost no results. At the same time, the attackers themselves suffered huge losses, far exceeding the damage suffered by the Luftwaffe during its long-range raids in the Volga Region.

By the end of June, the geography of Luftwaffe air attacks on deep rear targets continued to expand. Once again, the Soviet air defence command could only guess where and when the enemy would strike next. And the Luftwaffe, having got the taste for it, continued to select more and more new targets for their bombers.

On the night of 25 June, a major raid was carried out on Balashov railway junction (200km west of Saratov). The main targets were the station and airfield, on which were dropped 239 high-explosive and fragmentation bombs, and thirty-five heavy incendiary bombs. As a result of the resulting fires, ninety-two wagons containing military cargo were burned, and a large part of the railway was put out of operation. In addition, nine residential buildings were destroyed in the surrounding villages. In the aftermath of the raid, 150 people from the local and district fire departments, eighty fire crews with seven pumps, one fire train, as well as all the railway workers working at the station took part. The work was carried out all night, and then for another three days. The fires were extinguished in two hours, and train traffic was partially restored in six to seven hours.

On the night of 26/27 June, I./KG 100 carried out a raid on Astrakhan. The targets were ship repair plants in the Trusovsky and Stalinsky districts of the city. As a result of this and previous air attacks on the city, the III international shipyard, the 10th Anniversary of the October Revolution shipyard, the Lenin shipyard, the Karl Marx plant, the Rejdtanker shipyard, oil storage tank No.6, the Rybosudomotornyj plant, Plant No. 638, the Astrakhan Department of measuring instruments, the bakery plant, tobacco factory, canning factory, confectionery factory and other facilities were completely or partially destroyed.

Once again, the raid went completely unpunished. He 111 H-16 Wrk Nr 8928 of I./KG 100 was damaged over Astrakhan, but its crew managed to make it to Stalino, where the aircraft sustained additional damage (45 per cent) during an emergency landing.

At the same time, a small group of German aircraft conducted the ninth air attack against Saratov. Its goals were various industrial facilities and residential areas. As a result of the bombing, various damage was caused to the silicate brick factory, the timber processing plant and the Saratov thermal and power station. Bottom mines were parachuted into the Volga. The operation to mine this important waterway, which began at the end of April, had been going on for two months.

In the late summer evening of 28 June, residents of the city of Kuibyshev – the reserve capital of the USSR during the war – were suddenly awakened by an unusual noise. Air raid sirens wailed in the streets, and a voice from the loudspeakers announced anxiously: 'Citizens! Air alert! Air alert!' Many citizens immediately rushed to bomb shelters in panic. 'Here it is our turn came,'– such thoughts were in the minds of many residents as they rushed with their families to basements and earth bomb shelters. Soon, on the approaches to Kuibyshev, the roar of anti-aircraft guns was heard, and somewhere in the dark sky, shell bursts flashed. However, there was no bombing.

In fact, a small group of German planes were bombing the railway bridge over the Volga River in the city of Syzran, 70km west of Kuibyshev. As a result, the bridge was damaged, but no span collapsed. At the same time, air observation posts reported that mines were being dropped into the river by parachute in the immediate vicinity of the bridge. Soon this section was closed to navigation, and minesweepers appeared there that began to trawl the waterway.

On the afternoon of 27 June, Ju 88 D-5 Wrk Nr 430 491 '4N+NK' of 2.(F)/22, flown by Unteroffizier Walter Jobstfinke, appeared over Saratov.

Several Russian fighters were alerted, and this time the interception was successful. At 11.44, a pair of aircraft took off, consisting of a La-5 flown by the commander of the 405th IAP Air Defence, Major V.A. Shapochka, and a Yak-1 of Captain Kovzun. Major Vasily Shapochka was an unusual pilot; he served in the Main Directorate of fighter aviation air defence of the USSR. In Saratov, he was employed as a specialist to intercept reconnaissance aircraft. Shapochka had five night air victories to his account. Along with this specialist, a specially upgraded La-5 fighter was also delivered to the city, on which were pinned high hopes. It was equipped with an experimental turbocharger, an American sight and had an increased shell capacity. At the same time, the plane did not have armour and was as light as possible. The Russians built small batches of similar fighters created specifically to attack reconnaissance planes. In Saratov, the 'terminator' Vasily Shapochka and his plane fully met the expectations of the Soviet military leadership.

During the chase, Captain Kovzun fell behind the leader and returned to the airfield. At 12.15 the La-5 intercepted a target at an altitude of 7,300m in the Sosnovka area. Entering from the sun, Major Shapochka attacked in a dive, firing two long bursts at his quarry from 500m. The pilot managed to release 344 rounds of 20mm calibre, after which the Ju 88 D-5 disappeared into the clouds. Unlike his inept colleagues, Major Shapochka turned out to be a real sniper; he shot down the reconnaissance plane with the first attack, achieving many hits. At 12.23, the fatally damaged Ju 88 D-5 '4N+NK',

Experimental fighter La-5 M-71.

Major Vasily Shapochka.

crashed in Schirokiy Karamysh area (50km south-west of Saratov). Two crew members (pilot Walter Jobtfinke and navigator Oberleutnant Werner Trabert) baled out and were captured.

More mysterious is the 'military fate' of the radio operator Gefreiter K.H. Hammer and flight gunner Unteroffizier F. Mathey. They jumped out of the falling plane with parachutes but disappeared without a trace. Both are still missing. They probably tried to reach the front line but were killed. Such a tragic ending could be the result of many different reasons. German pilots could simply be killed by local residents, they could be attacked by wild animals (bears or wolves), they could drown in a reservoir or simply die of starvation. Their remains could be lost without trace in the vast Russian expanses.

On 29 June, a Ju 88 D reconnaissance plane from 2.(F)/100 was supposed to fly from Zaporozhye to Saratov. The crew commander was navigator Unteroffizier Wastlom. Initially, the plane was supposed to leave at 15.23, but soon after take-off the navigator felt ill. He needed an urgent visit to the toilet, so the Ju 88 D returned at 17.30. At 18.00, after the navigator had made a short visit to the toilet, his problem was solved and the aircraft took off again. However, this time the aircraft failed to reach the target because its oxygen unit failed during the ascent to a high altitude.

As a result, the flight took place only on 30 June at 08.35. Radio operator Feldwebel Max Lagoda was part of the crew of the reconnaissance aircraft. He recalled:

> The route went far in the direction of Saratov, and then back over the railway line. When crossing the front line, Russian fighters tried to intercept us. But we had sufficient altitude and were already flying home. Several bursts from the Otto side gunner from the paired MG forced our Russian fighters to withdraw. As we climbed higher, Wastlom and I also took to our MGs, but we didn't have to do anything. We were madly happy and thought: 'Thank God', they wanted to shoot us down, but we are still flying. With about an hour to go before landing, there was no immediate threat. At an altitude of 3,000 metres, we took off our oxygen masks and then started smoking cigarettes. Then we ate chocolate or cookies.[26]

However, they did not have an uneventful return. The radio operator received a coded message that Zaporozhye air base had just been attacked by three Russian bombers. Hence, the reconnaissance plane first circled the base to assess the situation on the ground. At the end of the runway, the burning wreckage of a plane was visible. As it turned out, it was a downed Soviet bomber. Then red flares were fired from the airfield. This meant that all vehicles coming in to land should be careful. At 12.35, the Ju 88 D landed safely. It turned out that the Russians had managed to cause some damage to the base. One of the bombs exploded near a shelter for ground technical personnel, killing one person.

The last days of June in the Volga Region were spent waiting for new Luftwaffe air attacks. Russian air defence units were quickly receiving new guns and planes, and MPVO soldiers were learning how to extinguish heavy incendiary bombs. Sand reserves were deposited in the surviving factories, additional fire reservoirs were dug and shelters were built. In the ruins of bombed out workshops, workers were sorting through the rubble, trying to find any surviving equipment. However, large-scale reconstruction work had not yet begun because they were afraid of the resumption of raids. And these fears were well founded. The Luftwaffe command, intoxicated with success, planned to continue the destruction of the Soviet military industry. Lists of new priority goals were drawn up but at the end of June all staff received an encrypted message that Operation *Zitadelle* was finally scheduled for 5 July. As a result, it was decided to give all crews a week's rest. Summer nights over the Volga had finally become quiet.

The complete fiasco of Stalin's air defence

The end of the Luftwaffe bombing raids on the Volga Region allowed the Soviets to assess the less than impressive results in countering them that amounted to a complete failure of Stalin's air defences.

Saratov

During the repulse of night raids on the city of Saratov and adjacent important targets from 12 to 27 June, the pilots of the 144th Fighter Aviation Division performed 179 sorties. Soviet interceptors claimed to have taken part in twenty-two air battles and downed three aircraft. Anti-aircraft artillery units claimed twelve downed German bombers. In fact, the Luftwaffe lost only three aircraft, including one reconnaissance aircraft, while four other bombers were severely damaged but were able to return to their territory. Anti-aircraft searchlight groups carried out 188 searches and illuminated twenty-nine targets. However, the lighting lasted for just a short time and the anti-aircraft artillery did not have time to go from barrage to aimed shooting. As a result, across all nine raids the anti-aircraft gunners fired at only five lit targets.

Yaroslavl

The Yaroslavl divisional air defence district claimed twelve downed aircraft, including seven attributed to anti-aircraft artillery, four night fighters and one barrage balloon. In fact, Luftwaffe losses amounted to eight bombers, including those shot down en route to the target and back. Another four German planes were badly damaged but reached their territory. One of these had crashed, while a second had burned after an emergency landing near German troops.

Results of combat work of the Yaroslavl air defence divisional district in June 1943

Date	Number of bombers involved in the raid	Downed bombers according to Soviet data	Loss confirmed by Luftwaffe[27]
9/10 June	109	5	3
20/21 June	90	7	6
In total	199	12	9

Gorky

The results of the struggle of the Gorky corps area of air defence against the Luftwaffe cannot be called brilliant. Anti-aircraft artillery claimed twenty-four downed aircraft, while it expended 170,000 shells. Pilots of the 142nd Fighter Aviation Division carried out 201 sorties and claimed six downed German bombers. The 142nd Fighter Aviation Division's own losses were four night fighters.

In fact, the Luftwaffe lost only six bombers during the Gorky raids, including those shot down on the way to the target and on the way back to their bases. At the same time, German data confirmed that at least two aircraft were victims of night fighters. Another three bombers were damaged, but were able to return to base. Russian searchlight operators reported they had illuminated ninety aircraft, but the effect of this painstaking work was insignificant. The reasons for the poor performance of searchlights were as follows:

First, the June nights were very bright and the bombers were clearly visible against the sky even without lighting. Secondly, it was not possible to establish a clear interaction between searchlight 'seekers' and searchlight 'escorts'. Search searchlights had to find the enemy aircraft with a beam. The beam could break from the plane, so other searchlights – escorts – picked up the plane in the intersection of the beams, highlighted it, then the anti-aircraft artillery came into action. The searchlight escorts could not accompany the targets for a long time and lost thirty-six aircraft out of ninety that were illuminated by the seekers. As a result, anti-aircraft artillery fired at only three illuminated German aircraft.

Results of combat work of the Gorky corps area of air defence in June 1943

Date	Number of bombers involved in the raid	Downed bombers according to Soviet data	Losses confirmed by Luftwaffe[28]
4/5 June	168	-	-
5/6 June	128	2	1
6/7 June	154	6	1
7/8 June	20	7	-
10/11 June	86	10	1
13/14 June	92	5	2
21/22 June	85	1	1
In total	733	31	6

Actions of night fighters

Soviet night fighters were traditionally the weakest link in the air defence system. The reasons for their disastrously low efficiency generally coincide with the main congenital malformation of other components of air defence. Let us list some of them:

1. There was no interaction between aviation and anti-aircraft artillery. Often night fighters were fired at by their own anti-aircraft guns. Often the guns had to stop firing to avoid hitting their night fighters. Thus, instead of mutual assistance, these means of air defence created interference and confusion for each other.
2. Night fighters were poorly guided to the target using ground radar data. Russian pilots had to rely on luck and a sharp eye.
3. Night fighter pilots were unable to determine the distance to the detected targets, as a result of which they usually opened fire from long distance and this did not have any effect.
4. Stalin's Falcons often tried to ram the bombers, not even expending any ammunition. Their motives can be easily explained. The fact is that this method of attacking an enemy bomber guaranteed glory and high rewards from the commanders. However, only two ramming attempts were successful, and only one German plane was brought down in this way.

5. Many German crews reported visual contact with the 'night hunters', but without coming under attack. German pilots from KG 55 'Greif' later noted that the Soviet night fighters, despite the favourable conditions created by the light nights, were not only unable to intercept the attacking bombers, but simply could not detect them.

All the above evils were only a consequence of the total backwardness of the Soviet armed forces and the associated tendency to ignore technical culture and military education. The Soviet air force, unlike Germany and Great Britain, did not have any special programmes and schools for training night fighter pilots. The Germans took at least two years to train a professional in this specialty! Their training course included 'blind' flights, studying radar, practising take-off and landing at night (with zero visibility), and much more. In the USSR, a 'night' pilot differed from a 'day' pilot only in that he took off on alert at night and slept during the day.

In addition, the Luftwaffe and RAF night squadrons were equipped with twin-engine aircraft specially equipped for operations in the dark. The Soviet 'night hunters' flew conventional single-engine fighters.

Disappointing overall results

In total, the Russian air defence units defending the Volga Region claimed that they shot down fifty-seven German aircraft from 4 to 27 June. In fact, the Luftwaffe lost sixteen bombers (including fifteen crews)[29] and one reconnaissance aircraft during the operation to destroy Soviet industrial centres. Another twelve aircraft were damaged in various ways, but were able to reach German territory. In addition, one bomber was lost by the Germans over the Caspian Sea.

The greatest damage was sustained by KG 27 'Boelcke', which lost eight bombers along with their crews. Another three aircraft from this Kampfgeschwader were damaged and made emergency landings on their own territory. KG 1 'Hindenburg' lost three bombers, while two more of its planes made emergency landings on German territory. KG 3 'Blitz', I./KG 100 and KG 55 'Greif', which participated in almost all the raids (II. and III./KG 55 made 300 sorties from 4 to 25 June), lost only one crew each. II./KG 4 'General Wever' lost two crews. Luftwaffe losses were less than 2 per cent of the bombers involved in the raids. Since flights at night are always associated with risk, this percentage is almost the same as the average operational losses of bomber aircraft. Thus, the bitter truth is that even if the Soviet air defence was completely absent, the German bombers would have suffered about the same losses due to technical failures, bad weather and crew errors.

Separately, we can sum up the results of Luftwaffe mine installations carried out by I./KG 100. According to Russian observation posts, from 29 April to 26 June, 409 bottom mines were dropped into the Volga, of which eighty-four fell on the shore and exploded when they hit the ground. All this seriously hindered the movement of ships, especially oil caravans. Tugs and barges were forced to move along the waterway only in the daytime, at a low speed, carefully avoiding dangerous areas. As a result, 751,000 tons of oil products were transported along the Astrakhan–Saratov section in June, which is less than in May. In the Caspian Sea, bombers from I./KG 100 sank two minesweepers and a floating fish factory, and damaged two large oil barges and the boat *Sea Hunter*.

Chapter 7

'One Hundred Days'

'Aerial photos of targets showed the devastating impact of dropped bombs'

The Luftwaffe command was fully satisfied with the results achieved. In the period from 4 to 28 June 1943, German Kampfgeschwader carried out nine air attacks on Saratov, seven on Gorky and two on Yaroslavl. In addition, raids were carried out on Astrakhan, Rybinsk, Uglich, Konstantinovsky, Syzran, Balashov and Kamyshin. As a result of these raids, about thirty large, medium and small enterprises were put out of action, including the completely destroyed No. 736 Yaroslavl tyre plant, Gorky Molotov automobile plant, No. 718 Engine of the Revolution plant, Saratov Aviation plant No. 292, Kirov oil cracking plant and several other important sites of Soviet industry.

Aerial photography showed that all the intended targets were hit and received maximum damage. The most extensive destruction was caused to the Molotov plant. According to German data, the Luftwaffe …

> completely destroyed two large assembly workshops, a blacksmith shop, the main foundry, stamping production and a certain number of melting furnaces. Four large assembly buildings, the main warehouse, the main electrical substation, the main test stand for tanks, an engine-building workshop, lathe workshops and a foundry for fittings were also severely damaged. Here the effects of prolonged bombing were such that a long-term interruption in production could be expected, which even with the pronounced ability of the Russians to improvise could not be quickly eliminated.

According to the Germans, 'empty space' remained on the site of the barracks town, which served as a place of residence for thousands of workers. The human losses were estimated at 15,000 people, with this information allegedly taken from an intercepted 'Russian message'. According to German intelligence data on the Gorky plant, '800 T-34 tanks were destroyed, which came off the assembly line and stood in full readiness'. That is, allegedly, the full weekly production of the plant was lost. The final conclusion read: 'As a result of this attack the Gorky automobile plant 'Molotov' was completely paralysed for six weeks, so no Russian tank attack could have followed at this time.'[1]

The report of KG 4 'General Wever' on the raids on Yaroslavl and Gorky stated:

> Aerial photos of the targets showed the devastating impact of the dropped bombs. The tank factory and rubber plant have suffered extensive destruction, and this important part of the military industry has been put out of action for a long time.[2]

Despite the dubious reliability of some German data (as we have already stated, the Molotov plant did not produce T-34 tanks), it can be stated that the largest strategic operation of the Luftwaffe on the Eastern Front (the first stage of which was called *Carmen II*) was a complete success. As already noted, encouraged by the success achieved, the Germans wanted to continue to continue to carry out major air attacks on Russian military industry. At the end of June, a new list of targets was prepared in the cities of Gorky, Rybinsk, Tambov, Kuibyshev and other large and medium-sized industrial centres. However, the large-scale operations planned by the Luftwaffe command had to be cancelled due to Operation *Zitadelle*, which began on 5 July.

Meanwhile, as the German raids ceased, the Russians were gradually coming to their senses and they began to realise with horror the terrible scale of the disaster that had befallen them. At the Molotov plant, thirty-four of the forty-four workshops were damaged significantly. In July, the plant's director, I.K. Loskutov, compiled a secret report to the State Defence Committee and Central Committee of the Bolshevik party on the consequences of enemy bombing. It reported:

> As a result of the actions of enemy aircraft on the automobile plant 'Molotov', most of the production workshops were damaged, including completely destroyed: the main assembly line, montage workshop, assembly workshop, woodworking workshop No. 2, several warehouses (including a significant number of finished products).[3]

Out of the total number of mechanical, press, forging, foundry, lifting and transport equipment (excluding power) available at the plant, 5,944 units were damaged and 350 units were permanently destroyed. Some important workshops had almost lost their production base. In the press workshop, 543 out of 546 pieces of equipment were disabled, in the wheel workshop 305 out of 323 and in the chassis workshop 1,788 out of 1,799![4]

Loss of equipment in the workshops at the Molotov plant

Workshop	Number of units equipments	Destroyed
Blacksmith workshop	340	184
Grey cast iron foundry	654	544
Malleable iron foundry	292	170
Press workshop	546	543
Body workshop	423	375
Wheel workshop	323	305
Motor workshop No. 2	1,897	1,130
Chassis workshop	1,799	1,788

In addition, 8,000 electric motors of various capacities and types, 14,000 electrical appliances (including 12,000 destroyed), and more than 300 welding machines needed to be replaced or be subject to major repair. As a result of the attacks, almost all the compressors were disabled or destroyed, which left the plant without compressed air. Some 100km of various pipelines, 9km of conveyors and transporters, and twenty-eight bridge cranes were put out of operation. Ten power substations that supplied electricity to the following plant facilities were destroyed: the 1st body workshop, 2nd body workshop, forge, foundry workshop, press workshop, spring workshop, machine assembly workshop No.1, mechanical assembly workshop and wheel workshop. In the warehouses of the GAZ supply department, 264 tons of coal, 58 tons of valuable alloys, 15,712 tons of rolled ferrous metals and steel and 21.5 tons of copper burned. The railway workshop of the plant suffered serious losses. Three locomotives, four freight cars and thirty-four railway platforms were destroyed or damaged. The vehicle section of the plant lost sixty cars and twenty-five trucks. In addition, 365 tyres burned in the warehouse of the automobile workshop.[5]

General view of the destroyed Gorky Molotov automobile plant (GAZ)

Destroyed foundry.

Vehicle production was particularly hard hit, as the main workshops were destroyed: the chassis workshop, the gearbox department, the engine workshop, the malleable iron workshop, the wheel workshop, the steam forge and the main assembly line. According to official data from the plant, the production of tank components was not paralysed, but the failure of the electric melting furnaces, and most importantly the furnace in the malleable iron shop, significantly complicated the production of armour. As a result, it was necessary to apply a 'new method' of 'high-speed melting' in gross violation of all the rules and regulations of metallurgy. The use of such 'bypass technologies' became a daily reality for the plant. The estimated amount of damage to the plant was 191 million rubles ($36 million at the exchange rate of 1943), which at that time was a huge amount.

Serious losses were caused to the housing and communal services. Forty-two wooden houses and five warehouses were completely destroyed. Thirty-nine stone and 109 wooden houses, a clubhouse, baths and other structures were damaged to varying degrees. In the residential village, two-thirds of the housing stock needed significant or major repairs. Many houses and barracks had their walls and supporting beams askew, their broken window frames and door jambs knocked out, and their roofs torn off. In total, it was necessary to restore 6,400sqm of housing stock and build 10,000 sq m to replace destroyed homes. High-explosive bombs and fires destroyed 6km of high-voltage lines, more than 7km of low-voltage power lines and 1.3km of water supply pipes. Some 5,000sqm of roads were destroyed.[6]

Facilities located in the immediate vicinity of the automobile plant also received significant damage, to the point of complete destruction. Severe damage was caused to the No. 466 aircraft engine plant on the Molotov plant site. The marshalling yard located north-west of GAZ was almost destroyed. The secret tank repair plant (aka 'repair base No. 97'), where American and British tanks supplied to the USSR under Lend-Lease were being conserved and repaired, was ruined. A large amount of American and British military equipment located there was destroyed.

Losses among the workers and civilian population were significant. According to the reports of the Russian rescue service (MPVO) for June 1943, in Gorky, as a result of air attacks, about 400 people were killed and 864 were injured. The largest number of casualties occurred on the seventh raid (on the night of 22 June), when the Luftwaffe bombed five districts of the city at once. The actual number of victims remained unknown due to grossly negligent accounting. The reports counted only the dead whose bodies were found immediately after the raid. Those who died and remained under the rubble or simply disappeared during the explosions were not recorded. The Russian reports did not include the term 'missing persons', and this made it impossible to account for all the victims. Even considering the Soviet disdain for accounting for human casualties, we can say that the Luftwaffe bombed the Russian cities 'accurately'! These were not terror air attacks, but strikes on military targets. Civilian casualties were minimal.

The destruction of the Molotov plant and other enterprises caused huge damage to the entire Soviet military industry. The rate of production of all types of weapons, from shells and machine guns to tanks and aircraft, decreased significantly. The most effective was not direct, but indirect, damage. GAZ supplied hundreds of parts and components for medium and heavy tanks, including gears for gearboxes, parts for side clutches and chassis. In the industry correspondence of the People's Commissariat of tank industry it stated the reduction of the production of tanks in June 1943. For example, the No. 200 Kirov plant in Chelyabinsk (the main manufacturer of tanks for the Red Army, nicknamed Tankograd) fulfilled the plan for heavy tanks KV by only 64 per cent, for the T-34 by 70 per cent. Tank factory No. 174 in Omsk delivered only 59 per cent of the planned production to the Red Army front.[7] Production of the new T-80 light tank, which was scheduled to begin in June 1943, was completely disrupted by German bombing. This model of armoured vehicles was a victim of Luftwaffe attacks.

In addition, the Germans, without knowing it, completely stopped the production of American diesel engines in the USSR.

Military historian Mikhail Svirin explained:

> In 1942, specifically for the needs of the tank industry, a licence was purchased in the United States for a GMC diesel engine with a capacity of 210–230 horsepower, which was planned to be installed in light tanks, self-propelled artillery units, armoured personnel carriers and tractors, the development of which was carried out at the tank enterprise. Particularly high hopes were raised by the possible installation of the specified diesel engine in T-50 or improved T-70 light tanks (instead of the GAZ-203 engine, also, by the way, American) …Production of the GMC diesel engine was planned to be undertaken at the Molotov plant in Gorky and the Yaroslavl automobile plant. But there was an obstacle in the way that no one could have predicted. The name of this obstacle is Luftwaffe action. On 5 June, during the mass bombing of the city of Gorky, the main blow fell on the GAZ engine workshops, and the experimental workshop where GMC production was organized was put permanently out of order… the Yaroslavl automobile plant, which had mainly wooden structures, suffered especially hard after the bombing with 'lighters'…[8]

At the Krasnoye Sormovo No. 112 shipyard in Gorky (the plant was not the target of Luftwaffe attacks), the planned production of T-34 tanks in June was 355 but only about fifty were produced. The reason for this was the termination of deliveries of parts from the Molotov plant and gearboxes from machine tool factory No. 113. The workers tried to improvise, with some of the parts made the 'artisanal' way, but the plan was still thwarted. Subsequently, in the annual report on the work of the Krasnoye Sormovo shipyard for 1943, the following is stated: 'All this created extremely difficult conditions, led to the disruption of the June programme and did not allow us to deploy even better work in July and subsequent months.'[9]

In May, Soviet factories produced a total of 2,303 tanks of all types. In July, the output was 1,481, 30 per cent fewer. In total, due to the raids on the cities in the Volga Region, the Red Army was short of about 2,500 tanks. In addition, the growth of production was significantly slowed in the second half of 1943.

Despite the fact that, contrary to German data, the Molotov plant did not produce '800 T-34 tanks per week', the goal of the Luftwaffe operation, to partially paralyse the production of tanks, was achieved indirectly.

According to the Russian rescue service MPVO, 1,000 high-explosive bombs and 5,000 different incendiary bombs were dropped on Saratov and surrounding targets during June 1943. As a result of air attacks, the Kirov oil cracking plant, Saratov Aviation Plant No. 292, and the Uleshovskaya and Uvek oil storage facility were destroyed, and the GPZ-3 ball-bearing factory was severely damaged. In addition to the Stalinsky district of the city, the bombing damaged the villages of Knyazevka, Yurish, Krasnaya Sloboda, and Mochinovka. A total of 306 houses and barracks were destroyed in Saratov.[10] The destruction of the Kirov oil cracking plant and the adjacent oil storage facilities created a critical situation with the supply of fuel and lubricants and petrol to the front. As a result of the raids, 31,000 tons of fuel were burned, and due to the cessation of oil processing, the Red Army did not receive 22,000 tons of fuel on the eve of the battle for Kursk. This was approximately equal to all the fuel reserves available by 5 July on five fronts – Zapadniy, Bryansk, Zentralniy, Voronezh and Stepnoy – 28,491 tons. Of these, only 13,975 tons were Russian made, and the rest was supplied by the Allies. To get out of the current crisis, the Soviets had to cut fuel consumption limits, limiting the mobility of troops. In the future, the Russians compensated for the lack of fuel by using their own reserves and Lend-Lease supplies.

The damage caused to the Yaroslavl tyre plant No. 736 amounted to 50.7 million rubles ($9.4 million). The overall picture of destruction there was so terrible that at first the plant staff were unsure if production could be resumed.

'There is no electricity, almost no dishes, food goes bad …'

Factories lay in ruins and the Soviet military industry was in deep crisis. This happened on the eve of the grandiose German offensive at Kursk, which was only a few days away. It was necessary to take urgent measures to restore production. First of all, the attention of Stalin and the Soviet leadership was focused on the Molotov plant. Experts concluded that it would take about two years to fully restore the enterprise! However, Stalin was not satisfied with such a prospect. He ordered GAZ to be resuscitated as soon as possible and to use all available resources for this purpose.

On 24 June, the State Defence Committee ordered construction and installation work on GAZ without listing projects and making cost estimates. It also decided to spend 2 million rubles ($377,000) on assistance to workers injured during air raids and their families. At the same time, the State Defence Committee ordered the immediate allocation of 100 million rubles ($18.8 million) for the restoration of the Molotov plant. By 1 July, 2,500 conscripts unfit for combat service were mobilised and sent to help with the work. Materials, products, metals and equipment needed for the restoration of workshops and the reactivation of production were to be reserved and allocated preferentially, and subject to urgent delivery.[11] The restoration of the factory's workshops was originally planned to be completed between 15 July to 15 August. However, these deadlines were obviously impossible. The chief curator and organiser of the recovery work was the People's Commissar of internal affairs and Stalin's chief executioner, Lavrentiy Beria.

As already noted, a special state construction and installation concern (OSMCH), Stroygaz No. 2 Construction Company, was entrusted to raise the Molotov plant from the ashes. Employees of the Stalkonstruktsiya, Tsentralektromontazh and other corporations were sent urgently to Gorky, and these actually became subcontractors of the Construction Company.

Active work to restore the plant began immediately after the start of Operation *Zitadelle*. On 5 July, German army groups Central and South struck in converging directions on the Kursk salient. On the ground, fierce battles began with the use of thousands of tanks and guns. From the air, all available aviation forces joined the fray. Under these conditions, it became clear that the Germans would not be able to resume air attacks on the rear in the near future.

However, despite the redoubtable orders of the bloody dictator, the recovery work did not go according to plan at first. The fact is that the system of state capitalism created in the Soviet Union, despite the large number of virtual slave labour, did not function very effectively. State planning was carried out in complete disregard of all economic laws. Completely incompetent in the field of economics, Stalin set impossible tasks for state enterprises. The heads of factories and even entire industries were forced to invent clever ways under the threat of death in order to at least formally carry out the orders of the ruthless Stalin and his executioner Beria. Often they had to resort to red tape, simplification of technology and hard labour, which led to the fall of the already poor quality of military products to almost zero.

On 8 July, the director of the Molotov automobile plant, I.K. Loskutov, in a letter to the head of the regional office of the NKVD, Vasily Ryasnoy, noted the 'failure of priority deliveries of metal necessary for recovery, failure of the repair plan for electric motors'. There was a tendency to avoid unscheduled deliveries to the automobile plant under the pretext of implementing the state programme and other reasons. For example, the Krasnoye Sormovo No. 112 and metallurgical plant in Kulebaki brazenly engaged in such sabotage. Loskutov wrote:

> There is a desire by some plants to delay the organisation and execution of orders for the automobile plant, to wait for the end of the month, quarter and consider their obligations for deliveries null and void (Vyksa metallurgical plant), to refer to the lack of a resolution (People's Commissariat of ferrous metallurgy of the USSR) and so on.[12]

Implementation of the delivery plan of the necessary materials was only 23 per cent. A special difficulty was represented by the repair of electrical equipment. The plant's management had to organise new workshops, staff them with low-skilled labour and start producing complex electrical equipment and electrical repairs. Due to the lack of specialists, lack of ball-bearings and roller bearings, the work was very slow and of poor quality. As a result, the plan to repair electrical equipment was fulfilled only by 27 per cent.

Despite the fact that almost a month had passed since the first air attacks, the management of Stroygaz No. 2 did not start preparatory and recovery work at a pace that would ensure the implementation of the decisions of the State Defence Committee. The Construction Company was supposed to start work on twenty-four sites at once, but its managers considered only five priority operations (mechanical assembly building, foundry building, wheel workshop, press and body workshop and the main logistics warehouse of related parts). Part of the work was started on 30 June–1 July (for workshops No. 5, 8, press-body workshop and thermal and power station). In total, by 1 July, Stroygaz No. 2 and its subcontractors had 9,756 workers at their disposal.

Forty-seven support trusses had to be installed in the foundry building (site No. 1), but in fact only five had been installed by the beginning of July. Of the 15,400sqm of roof, 4,640 were made. Clearing rubble on an area of 13,000 sq m in the mechanical assembly building was particularly difficult. By the beginning of July, less than a third of this laborious work had been completed. Repair work on the destroyed roof of the building with an area of 62,500sqm

Workers in the destroyed shop.

was at the initial stage, and had only been carried out on an area of 2,700 sqm. Only 272 damaged metal structures had been dismantled out of the 600 planned. The organisation of work at the initial stage was at a low level: there were many instances of employees being absent from their workplaces without permission, causing unnecessary downtime. For example, on 27 June, only four of the fourteen workers who were required to work in the wheel workshop on carpentry jobs were actually present. Recovery work on the workshop had only just begun, although it had been in ruins for three weeks. The working day was formally twelve hours, but construction crews were poorly provided with welding machines and tools for gas cutting. There were not enough winches, gloves and work suits. For the vast mass of people brought in to work, the most basic things were missing: tables, stools, boilers, water tanks and drinking mugs. Some of the workers on site No. 1 worked without shoes. In the Russian reality, such 'methods' of work were commonplace.

Director Loskutov constantly pointed out the failure of deliveries and the violation of work schedules. In desperation, he literally filled up the postbox of the chief of the regional office of the NKVD, Colonel Rjasnogo. Loskutov wrote in another message:

> Water transport: not only extraordinary, but also in general delivery of goods to the address of the automobile plant is not secured. Most cargo is unloaded at the city port, not near the automobile plant. Currently, the port has 1,000 tons of necessary metal. These cargoes are criminally delayed, and the plant is forced to pay large sums for their storage in the port.

Suppliers sabotaged the supply of shoes, glass, and other materials and components.[13] Fuel deliveries were delayed. On 6 July, the barge *Anadyr* sailed from Astrakhan with fuel oil for plants No. 92, 112, 176 and the Molotov plant. However, the cargo never reached the consumers. The ship was stopped by enterprising officials at the mouth of the Kama River and actually looted! Some 6,000 tons of fuel oil was 'taken' by the Rechflot company, with the rest sent to the Molotov (Perm) region. As a result, all these plants were left without fuel. As a result of the Luftwaffe attacks, fuel was in short supply in the Soviet Union, and various state-owned companies were literally hunting for it!

Functionaries of the regional office of the Bolshevik Party suggested reviving the plant by the method of Shturmovshchina – a common Soviet practice of frantic and overtime work at the end of a planning period in order to fulfill the planned production target. The practice usually gave rise to products of poor quality at the end of a planning cycle. But there were neither the necessary human resources, nor the equipment or building materials. The Stroygaz No. 2 management had its own plan for how to conduct recovery work. At the end of the first stage of emergency work, which ensured the normal operation of individual workshops of the plant with the remaining intact equipment, the builders began restoration work on priority equipment. The order of construction and installation work was established for individual workshops. For example, mechanical assembly building No. 1 with its four main workshops was divided into four stages: 1st – engine workshop No. 2, 2nd – heat treatment workshop, 3rd – main conveyor, 4th – chassis workshop. This made it possible to concentrate human and material resources on a narrow area of priority work and ensure the commissioning of individual workshops and units sequentially, in parts, without waiting for the completion of work on all buildings as a whole.

Taking into account the need for the rapid recovery of the plant and the inability to carry out construction and installation work on all the equipment at once, first of all the focus was only on the recovery of production areas. Repair work on sections of workshops that had auxiliary, household and service functions was only carried out secondarily.

The main task of the teams of builders in the first period of recovery work was to ensure the protection of workshops from rain and to install industrial wiring associated with the operation of technological equipment. The following order was used:

1. General construction works, including recovery and installation of the main load-bearing structures of floors with the roof device;
2. Electrical installation works, including recovery of workshops substations and power supplies to them;
3. Industrial ventilation: installation of air ducts to stoves, hoods;
4. Plumbing installation and industrial wiring (oil pipeline, steam pipeline, storm sewer, heating, fecal sewer).

The minimum working day was eleven hours, but in many cases the builders worked for fourteen to fifteen hours, and often stayed overnight on the construction site in order to take up an urgent task at dawn.

However, the terms of work did not suit the Soviet bosses. On 13 July, the Bureau (presidium) of the regional office of the Bolshevik Party discussed the implementation of the resolution of the State Defence Committee to restore the Molotov plant workshops. Those present stated that 'the work is going unsatisfactorily'. By 9 July, out of twenty-four objectives in the first stage, construction work had been organised on only five. The schedule was carried out with a large backlog, there was massive downtime and non-compliance with standards. Party functionaries noted:

> The Party and the Stroygaz No. 2 economic leadership did not take measures on expanding the construction works, do not know how to coordinate the management of subcontractors, allowed the confusion in the distribution of objects… By the decision of the city committee of defence the roof of the blacksmith's housing should have been repaired by July 15, but by July 10 only preparatory work was underway (dismantling of the damaged structures). For the wheel workshop, the completion date was set as July 25, however on 10.07 only work on recovery of reinforced bearing concrete elements of the building were carried out. The planned volume of restored metal structures is 597 tons, at 8.07 only 5 tons were recovered.

In July, the automobile plant was visited by People's Commissar for construction S.Z. Ginzburg, and the chief Stalin executioner Lavrentiy Beria also visited regularly. He constantly frightened the leaders of the plant's recovery work with reprisals. Beria even threatened them with the immediate death penalty, and during meetings ostentatiously put his loaded pistol on the table. Thus, the tension increased and the Soviet bosses, scared of death, began to act according to a typical pattern, which consisted of increasing the number of people involved in the recovery of the Molotov plant. As a result, more and more teams of workers and emergency recovery units arrived at the construction site.

However, the registration and placement of labour was unsatisfactory. One group arrived on 25 June from the city of Arzamas but did not commence work until the beginning of July, while another group from the Pavlovskiy district, Gorky region, arrived on 22 June, but only started work on 1 July. At the same time, barracks for housing workers were not built. A large number of people were placed in the unfinished barracks of the Novo-Zapadnogo settlement in Gorky. There they slept on piles of construction debris or on planks. The dormitories and barracks were in an unsanitary state. There was not enough food or bedding, and sleeping workers were attacked by countless swarms of lice and bedbugs. There were not enough spoons and plates in the dining rooms. Workers who came to the plant from different parts of the country were amazed at the conditions there. As a result, the Turkmens who worked on the construction area No. 2 wrote a letter about poor household and medical services to the Supreme Council of the Republic of Turkmenistan: '... the food was organised on a one-time basis, i.e. a hot lunch once a day, the hostel was not prepared for housing. Around is dirt, darkness, and so on.' The letter soon had an effect, and the Turkmens were placed in a comfortable hostel (a two-storey wooden house) and provided with bedding, clothing and other supplies. The subject of 'special pride' for these colleagues from Soviet Asia was the presence in the dormitories of portraits of the leaders, Bolshevik slogans and posters!

Despite all the efforts, the optimistic work schedules were hopelessly disrupted, and on 26 July the deadlines for recovery of the workshops (15 July–15 August) were pushed back.

The most deadline work at the Gorky plant occurred at the end of July–September 1943. All divisions of the Construction Company – the central concrete plant, reinforcing workshop, workshop of precast concrete slabs, sawmill, woodworking workshop, workshop of alabaster-sawdust plates and other enterprises – worked in constant tension. Stroygaz No. 2 carried outwork based on the principle of simultaneous construction, installation and special works, which made it possible to speed up the commissioning of products.

The clearing of the debris of the ruined buildings was carried out by excavators, mobile cranes, tractors and by hand. Recovery work then began immediately on the cleared areas. This often brought great difficulties and complex technical solutions. For example, in the wheel workshop, the installation of metal structures was performed using a huge mast and several swinging masts. The 24m span was restored using a specially installed two-span cable crane with a medium swinging mast, manufactured by the Stalkonstruktsiya construction company directly on the site. The complex structure was assembled in twelve days and installed within ten. The trusses were assembled outside the workshop, from two ends, then transported by cable crane to the installation site and lowered on reinforced concrete columns. The installation period was only twenty-five working days.[14]

When restoring the mechanical assembly building, due to a lack of metal for replacement, many original trusses and girders were straightened using hydraulic and mechanical presses. Deformed trusses were raised by jacks to the previous position by connecting posts, and at high altitude by special metal towers. Then they were fixed in the desired position. Deformed parts

Recovery of the wheel workshop.

Russian workers work and eat among the ruins.

were cut out and new elements were inserted. The correction of columns deformed near the bottom was performed by replacing the deformed part with a new segment. During the replacement, the adjacent part of the wall was supported by posts and struts, so the weight was removed from the columns.[15]

Due to the extremely wide variety of damage to reinforced concrete structures of various types, it was impossible to find a common method for their restoration. In each case, they had to make an individual decision, depending on the extent and nature of the damage. Before restoration, damaged sections of reinforced concrete elements were cleared, and concrete that had lost strength as a result of fire or breakage was removed to a depth where its strength was not in doubt.[16] Due to the lack of iron and reinforced concrete, metal flooring made of corrugated iron was used for the roof, and some workshops used reinforced concrete roof slabs.

Plumbing works were carried out by department No. 4 of the separate construction and installation part No. 102 (OSMCH-102). Electrical installation work was performed by section 3 of the No. 5 Centrjelektromontazh special design and installation department. The works were carried out in two main directions:

1. Recovery of main power cables and linear feeders from the heat and power plant to the workshop substations and restoration of power main lines inside the workshops;
2. Running all undamaged machine tools in newly created technical groupings.

Works on recovery of ventilation systems were carried out by installation department No. 2 of the separate construction and installation part No. 48 (OSMCH-48). The installation sites were divided between teams of workers who worked on individual items to be repaired. During the recovery period, 124 ventilation systems were installed and put into operation for 608,000 rubles ($114,000).

A huge amount of material and semi-finished products (bricks, mortar, concrete, reinforced concrete slabs, thermal insulation materials, metal flooring and so on) had to be raised in a very short time. This required a large number of cranes. The lack of time to manufacture complex cranes forced the builders to take the path of using the simplest design known since the Roman Empire. One of them was a lifting block, which uses two racks mounted with a slight slope to the wall of the workshop and connected by cross ties. A bar was placed on the upper platform, and a block and tackle was fixed at the cantilever end. A cable was threaded through the block, to one end of which a lifting platform was attached, and the other was attached to an electric winch. In addition, skip hoists, belt conveyors, etc, were used.[17]

No less difficult was the recovery of a significant number of residential and cultural buildings damaged as a result of the bombing. A typical example was four-storey residential buildings made of silicate bricks. A typical problem faced by the builders was the longitudinal stratification of brickwork caused by shock waves. In addition to the stratification, the action of the blast wave caused vertical deviations of up to 10cm in the longitudinal walls of houses, with a break in the masonry in the places where the longitudinal walls adjoined the average transverse walls and the walls of staircases. Recovery teams had to practically reinstall the roof of the building, make metal ties that held together damaged walls, replace masonry in many places, and fill the seams with concrete.

The design of all works was carried out directly on the construction site by the Promstroyproekt team, which allowed for close and operational coordination of the work of designers and production workers, technologists and builders. Designs and production methods were selected in accordance with the resources available on the site. This also allowed the use of new structures made from local materials (for example, asbestos slabs) and new methods in the production of buildings. During the recovery, many pre-war errors were corrected, in particular, all wooden floor structures were replaced by structures made of fire-resistant materials.

In order to speed up the work, all the load-bearing reinforced concrete structures in the destroyed workshops were replaced by metal ones, and only the workshops with reinforced concrete columns that had minor damage were left in the same form. The number of light aperture (windows) had to be reduced by 30 per cent, and these were closed using iron sheets and asbestos plywood. The wooden elements of the roof were replaced by corrugated iron, the production of which was organised in a mechanized way in the press workshop of the automobile plant. The most primitive materials were used as thermal insulation: alabaster with sawdust, cement with ash, peat with clay and even alumina slabs. All materials were tested for fire resistance to incendiary bombs and anti-tank flammable liquid before use.

Recovery of huge areas of the roofs of buildings meant more than 1,500 storm funnels were needed. The lack of cast iron forced the use of 'auxiliary materials', such as parts of the box of the rear axle of trucks and the noses of aviation bombs produced at the Molotov plant.

On 25 August, the Bolshevik Party meeting of Stroygaz No. 2 Construction Company was held. The activists who spoke at it stated:

> Information about the progress of restoration work on the second site: labour discipline is unsatisfactory. The programme for 20 days in August was 62 per cent completed. The deadline for delivery of objects on August 25 has been disrupted. Low labour discipline. On 23 August, 721 people did not show up for work, and the working day starts 30–40 minutes late. On the eve of the working day, the task is given only to a few teams, the rest receive it at the beginning of the working day.

As a result of the meeting, the head of the second site, Romanov, was threatened with a very dangerous punishment – expulsion from the Party.

The total demand for labour at the beginning of construction was approximately 9,500 workers. According to the plan, 12,800 people were supposed to be involved in the work, but this total - was never fulfilled. By 1 October 1943, 10,000 people were working on the recovery of the Gorky automobile plant (according to the lists). To accommodate this huge mass of people, a significant living area was required. However, many homes in the area were destroyed and there was not enough space for the GAZ workers themselves. Schools, unfinished residential buildings, clubs and simple tents had to be used for housing. In addition, frame-filled barracks and earthhouses were hastily constructed.

In total, 10,000sqm of space was adapted for temporary housing. By August, to feed the huge number of workers, twenty canteens and distribution points were opened. But that was not enough. The level of comfort in the hastily constructed 'summer cafes' left much to be desired. During the inspection conducted on 17 July in dining room No. 7, it turned out that there was no order: 'There is no electricity, almost no dishes, food goes bad. Workers wait for hours to get dinner, because of the lack of lighting, not everyone is given bread.'

At the end of July, the progress of work was seriously hampered by the beginning of prolonged rain and downpours. In early August, among those workers forcibly driven to restore the Gorky Molotov automobile plant, the number of those dissatisfied with the disgusting working conditions was growing. Despite the fear of severe punishment, mass absenteeism of workers began. Some people escaped from the site and simply disappeared into the vast expanses of Russia. As a result, the average daily number of people engaged in recovery works decreased by 1,500 people. There was a complete lack of supervision of labour safety. The number of accidents increased, especially on the cranes.

The work was carried out with a constant lack of transport. Initially, the Stroygaz No. 2 Construction Company had only sixty-four trucks of various types, of which only twenty-seven were in working condition! It was also possible to use thirty-six horses as a draft force. In the second half of July, seventy-five ZIS-5 trucks with a capacity of 5 tons were allocated for repair work. However, even for those trucks that were in working order, there was a chronic shortage of fuel. Gas-generating trucks were idle due to the lack of wood chips, as the workshop for their production had burned down during the bombing. There were not enough drivers and mechanics. The management of Stroygaz No. 2 had to organise short-term driving courses for truck drivers on the spot, preparing twenty-eight new drivers in a short time. Mechanics showed real heroism, restoring trucks literally from nothing. As a result, drivers made an average of thirty-three trips a day, transporting goods to a variety of sites.[18] During the same period, water transport, which was at the disposal of Stroygaz No. 2, transported 23,500 tons of cargo. The rest of the construction materials were delivered by rail and the wood was floated down the river.

However, the course of recovery works was particularly affected by the chronic shortage of wood and concrete. The situation was complicated by the consequences of the German bombing, which completely burned down the Stroygaz No. 2 concrete factory, woodworking plant, blacksmith workshop, machine workshop and sawmill. All these facilities for the production of scarce construction materials had to be repaired first. Repair workers, despite bad weather and fatigue, worked around the clock, and simultaneously with the restoration of these enterprises, production began. On the second day after the start of work, the concrete plant produced the first concrete! And this was without water and a constant supply of electricity. Water was transported by car, and electricity was supplied through a temporary cable. At the height of the recovery works, the company produced 230m³ of concrete per day, although this was still not enough.

It was decided to build a new woodworking plant on the bank of the Oka River, on the site of the surviving sawmill No. 1. First a carpentry workshop was built, which immediately began to produce beams, boards, trusses, scaffolding, etc. Instead of recovering concrete products from the works, finished roofing and building slabs were supplied. In total, from July to November, the Stroygaz No. 2 plant produced 3,374m³ of concrete, 7,350m³ of cement mortar, 9,920sqm of reinforced concrete roofing slabs, 500m³ of foam concrete, 60,661sqm of alabaster-sawdust slabs, 200 tons of rebar, etc. However, the quality of these products, manufactured with a chronic lackof technology, was extremely low.

Bolshevik propaganda and reality

The amount of work performed by Stroygaz No. 2 and its subcontractors can be determined by the following figures. From 1 July to 1 October, 2.7 million bricks and 128,170sqm of bitumen sheets were laid, 3,400 tons of metal structures were installed, almost 43km of pipelines were laid, 32.6km of high-and low-voltage cable and another 50km of various wires were laid, 3,500 electric motors were connected to machines, and 2,640 electric outlets and 348 heaters were installed.[19] Most of the work was done in a temporary manner with low quality. For example, the glazing of windows and light apertures, in addition to glass, was carried out with plywood and roofing iron. In total, 79,800sqm were 'glassed' in this way.

By 1 October 1943, the production capacity of the Molotov plant had generally been restored. The first five vehicles produced using simplified

GAZ-MM truck comes off the Assembly line in the open air.

Autumn of 1943. A column of armoured vehicles of BA-64 leaves the gates of the recovered Gorky automobile plant 'Molotov'.

technology were released by the plant on 25 July. In August, the first 100 BA-64 armoured vehicles came off the conveyors, in October the first GAZ-67 jeeps. Assembly of American trucks was carried out in the open. However, the deadline for completing the work (15–30 September) was again unfulfilled. On 6 October, the State Defence Committee rescheduled this again, to 15 October–15 November. This deadline only concerned the main production facilities; auxiliary structures were only supposed to be recovered by 20 December 1943. According to the acceptance certificates, most of the workshops were put into operation between 21 and 30 October.

On 28 October, the staff of GAZ and the Stroygaz No. 2 Construction Company compiled a report to the Red 'Tsar' Joseph Stalin in the form of a photo album. It said:

> We are extremely happy to be able to report to you today, great leader, on the completion of the recovery and smooth operation of all workshops and productions of Gorky automobile plant 'Molotov'. We are especially happy that this coincides with the victorious offensive of our valiant Red Army. The Nazis tried to destroy our native factory. But never will the black enemy pack break our will to fight and win, or shake our confidence in the near triumph of our just cause. The factory has lived and will live. October 28, 1943.

The report was signed by 27,567 people, the first to sign being the director of the automobile plant, I.K. Loskutov.[20]

However, this was false propaganda. The order for the plant dated 30 November noted:

> … still not repaired: the main store of related parts, the pumping station with water pipes and ammunition storage. Until now, the construction of a warehouse for rubber and a diesel station has not been completed. The repair of the thermal and power station, car workshop, locomotive depot, and automatic machine workshop is not completed. The reconstruction of the housing stock started only on 10.11 and was completed in the amount of 5 per cent.

In December, Stroygaz No. 2 continued to work on the following facilities: foundry No. 1, foundry No. 3, wheel workshop, body workshop, main logistics warehouse of related parts, heat and power plant, water supply, mechanical assembly workshop No. 1, locomotive depot, housing stock and forge.[21]

All recovery activities took place under the close attention of the Soviet press. The field editorial office of the *Pravda* newspaper worked at the plant for 120 days, producing four issues of the newspaper 'Everything for the front!', 246 newspaper sheets 'lightning', fourteen 'Pravda windows', and many photo newspapers, technical sheets and posters. For propaganda purposes, it was announced that 'automobile plant 'Molotov' was completely restored in 100 days'. In fact, given that GAZ was deactivated after the first air attack on the night of 4 to 5 June, before the stated deadline restored – 28 October – it took almost five months or more than 150 days! Moreover, the automobile plant was still far from a complete 'rebirth' at that time. This historical example shows that even the Russians, who are prone to improvisation and fanaticism, could not restore a completely destroyed factory in just six months. However, the actual recovery time of the plant beat even the most optimistic estimates of the Luftwaffe command.

No less ambitious in scale than in the Molotov plant, recovery work at the Yaroslavl tyre factory was also was underway. In the summer and autumn months of 1943 the Volga Region turned into a huge construction site, recalling the years of Stalin's 'industrialisation'. On 24 June, the State Defence Committee issued a resolution to restore the Yaroslavl plant as

The first batch of T-70 light tanks produced after the bombing of Gorky automobile plant 'Molotov'.

soon as possible. This company was the main supplier of rubber products for the Red Army, military industry and transport in the country. A special construction and installation Department No. 3 of Mospromstroy under the leadership of I.A. Dorokhov was selected as the general contractor. By order of Stalin, workers, vehicles and a huge amount of construction materials from all over the country were sent to the ruins of the enterprise. According to the government's decision, the Yaroslavl workers were to be provided with enhanced nutrition and improved supplies throughout the recovery period.

By the beginning of July, more than 1,000 people, mostly farmers from the Yaroslavl region, were mobilised to restore the plant. Workers and employees of city enterprises and institutions were set to work clearing the rubble. Scientists and engineers headed by such specialists as the Major General of engineering troops, doctor of technical sciences, Professor V.M. Keldysh,[22] doctor of technical sciences Professor Onishek and others were sent to determine the total amount of destruction, and determine the order and methods of recovery of the plant. Keldysh made a valuable suggestion about the procedure for restoring load-bearing concrete columns without disassembling them and replacing them with new ones, having suggested strengthening them with metal clips, which saved a lot of time.[23]

To speed up the work on restoring the affected facilities they were divided into two queues. At first, along with major work on the restoration of reinforced concrete floors in buildings 'I' and 'A', it was planned to install temporary structures and protective brick walls in buildings 'V', 'B', 'G', 'D' and in the saved part of building 'A'. This made it possible to resume the operational activities of workshops 1, 2, 3 and 4 in parallel with the repair and recovery work. The second stage included works related to the complete restoration of the production workshops of the Yaroslavl tyre plant, in particular, the recovery of the entire area of the building 'I', the first floor of the building 'A', and household and administrative premises in the five-storey extensions of the main entrance.

In total, 2,000 workers and employees of the plant and more than 1,000 mobilised farmers and urban residents took part in the work to clear the ruins from 10 June to 15 July. This work was carried out around the clock in two shifts of twelve hours. At the same time, site managers, foremen and foremen did not leave their sites for days, sleeping and eating on the premises. As a result, by 7 July, the damaged reinforced concrete floors had been broken up and disassembled on an area of up to 8,000sqm, and more than 24,000 tons of rubble and debris had been removed. In total, 65,000 tons of rubble, reinforced concrete and debris were removed.

The recovery of technological equipment was extremely complex mechanical work that required a lot of experience and knowledge in the field of mechanical engineering. This mission was carried out by about 200 members of staff from the mechanical service of the plant. During the period from 10 July to 1 December 1943, 200 units of heavy and medium equipment were restored and installed. It was extremely difficult to restore power equipment and communications for steam, electricity, industrial water, high and low hydraulics, heating, lighting, alarm systems and telephone networks. The electrical equipment and communications of the plant were most affected by incendiary bombs and fires.

The destruction of the energy sector of the Yaroslavl plant was so great that, under normal conditions, it would have taken at least a year and a half to repair it. However, the team of power engineers from the plant managed to complete the major work to restore the energy base for production in four months. Often it was necessary to use frankly artisanal methods, repairing most of the power grid in the spirit of improvisation. For example, in the bid to shorten the start-up time of the equipment, the energy service team, at the suggestion of chief power engineer Migulin and chief of the electrical laboratory Shcherbin, produced five starting boxes for synchronous electric motors according to a 'simplified scheme'. This ensured the launch of several rubber mixers significantly ahead of schedule.

Part of the production of semi-finished products had to be organised to be completed on the equipment of other factories of the Soviet rubber industry: plants No. 766, 739 and 151. In addition, workshops 1 and 2 were put into operation during the recovery process. As a result, at the end of June, production of aviation tyres, rubber-rimmed for tank wheels and for artillery gun tyres partially resumed.[24] Although the Director of the Yaroslavl plant, P.F. Badenkov, and chief engineer Lubashevsky reported on the 'full recovery' of production in October, in fact, the rebuilding work continued until the end of the year, and the planned production volume was still far away. The Russians were able to work quickly and fanatically, ignoring technology, but they were not wizards. The technological base of Soviet industry has always been based on technologies purchased or illegally borrowed from developed countries. However, during the war, buying German technology was impossible, and borrowing technology from other industrialised countries was difficult.

To restore Saratov Aviation Plant No. 292, all the forces of the People's Commissariat of Aviation Industry were thrown in. Numerous construction teams arrived in the city, and unused equipment was transferred from other enterprises. Director Isaac Levin recalled that the plant's staff 'with the huge help of the Central Committee of the Bolshevik Party, local offices of the Bolshevik Party and People's Commissariat of Aviation Industry' managed to restore the factory in eighty days. However, such 'round' figures, which were very popular with the Soviets, never reflected an objective picture. It was almost impossible to restore a factory razed to the ground in two and a half months, even in the Soviet totalitarian system.

Against the background of large enterprises, recovery work at mid-level factories went quite 'unnoticed'. They were not subject to the high-profile resolutions of the State Defence Committee and Stalin, and correspondents of the central newspapers did not visit the ruins. However, their workers overcame no less difficulty during their activation than their counterparts working on the restoration of the giant factories.

On 28 July, the Director of the No. 718 Engine of the Revolution plant, Nikitin, wrote to the People's Commissariat:

> Despite a number of measures taken by me to quickly restore the destruction after the enemy bombardment, the recovery works is extremely slow due to the lack of construction workers, which threatens to disrupt the restoration of the plant's workshops by the beginning of the cold snap.

At least 500 workers were needed on the construction sites, but in fact only sixty-nine were still working.

Just to restore the main workshops of the Engine of the Revolution plant, 50,000 bricks, 10 tons of bitumen, 3,100sqm of glass, thirty-eight electric motors and hundreds of metres of cable, etc, were needed. But where could this be found if all the available resources were being absorbed by the neighbouring Molotov plant? On 9 August, Nikitin wrote to People's Commissar of mortar weapons Parshin: 'At the moment, the light openings are closed, part of the shop buildings have been restored, the power supply has been partially repaired, and some damaged machines have been repaired. However, the main labour intensive work is extremely slow. There are not enough vehicles, not enough building materials.'

As a result, construction work stretched into the winter. In October, the rubble on the site of the former logistics warehouse was cleared. The housing stock of the enterprise was generally abandoned to its fate, and residents who had lost their apartments had to be resettled with the families of those residents whose houses survived.

'Factories are stopped'

The Russian military industry was much more vulnerable than the Germans thought. It was like a thick but stretched steel cable that crackled with tension and could break at any moment. The Russians were chronically short of equipment and technology, and their production process was extremely primitive. Transport, logistics and energy were working with huge overloads and had no reserves of capacity. As soon as a strong blow was struck at the vulnerable points of this system, the entire supply chain and cooperative relationships between enterprises began to collapse like a house of cards.

On 20 August, the Director of the Molotov automobile plant, Ivan Loskutov, and the chief of the regional office of the Bolshevik Party, Mikhail Rodionov, received a telegram from the authorised State Defence Committee for arming. It said: 'Yaroslavl tyre plant is idle due to the lack of wheels, the artillery factories have difficulties in completing the guns and sending them to the front.' The next day, Loskutov received a much more threatening telegram from the People's Commissar of the NKVD, Lavrentiy Beria: 'For 14 days in August, there were no deliveries to the Yaroslavl and Omsk tyre plants. The wheels are no longer rubberised. Factories are stopped.'

On 5 November, People's Commissar of medium machine building Sergey Akopov was angry at the employees of the Molotov plant for not implementing the programme. In a telegram, he wrote: 'During the third quarter and October 1943, 70 per cent of automobile parts were not delivered to plant No. 183, as a result of which the production of tanks was disrupted at this plant.'

On 26 December, GAZ received a new telegram from Beria:

> The task of producing parts for the M-13 and M-30 rockets has been disrupted. November plan 40,000 – produced 21,600. Until December 20, 13,700 were manufactured with a plan of 45,000 parts. As a result, plan not completed at plants No. 26 of the aviation industry, ZIS, No.172, and No. 70 of the People's Commissariat of ammunition and the plan of assembly of M-13, M-20 and M-30 projectiles plant No. 586 of the People's Commissariat of ammunition was not fulfilled.

But it was not just businesses that had suffered from air attacks that disrupted the component supply programme. For example, in the third quarter of 1943, Chelyabinsk plant No. 701 did not ship any semi-finished products to the plant of aircraft airscrews (propellers) No. 467 in the city of Pavlov. Plant No. 95 in the city of Sverdlovsk unsatisfactorily supplied the same enterprise with partly finished blades for screws. Despite the July plan of 3,500 pieces, only 504 were received, and in August there were no deliveries at all! Saratov ball bearing factory GPZ-3, also affected by German air raids, supplied plant No. 467 with only a quarter of the required number of bearings. As a result of all this, the production of aircraft propellers was paralysed.

Sverdlovsk metallurgical plant completely disrupted the supply of calibrated rolled products. In July, not a single kilogram was received from it! Weapons factory No. 2 in Kovrov disrupted the delivery of 20 mm aviation guns to Gorky Aviation Plant No. 21. In July, instead of 2,300 guns, only 700 were delivered. Plant No. 212 did not get the steel it needed. Plants No. 808 and 765 (Rybinsk city) did not fulfil the plan to supply 120mm mine shells to chemical plant No. 80 in Dzerzhinsk. The August plan was 119,000 pieces, and 51,000 were actually delivered. The production output was completely disrupted at weapons factories No. 187 and No. 176 in Tula. At Sverdlovsk plant No. 76, instead of 30,000 shells for mortar mines, only 2,900 were produced. At Plant No. 326 (Kirov), instead of 30,000 pieces, production was just 3,900. In August and September chemical industry plants delivered unsatisfactory amounts of paint and varnish products to aviation plants. As a result there was a lack of putty, aviation lacquer, enamels and solvents for the brake assembly of aircraft.

Even the food industry experienced supply disruptions. For example, all the flour milling plants in Gorky were idle due to the lack of raw materials, completely disrupting the shipment of grain for the Western Front and Leningrad. By 16 September, only 7 per cent of the planned amount of raw materials was being delivered to the flour milling plants.

The No. 718 Engine of the Revolution plant had not been able to cope with the production programme since mid-June. By 15 June, instead of 255 mortars, ninety-one were issued, and the plan for projectiles for M-8 and M-31 rocket mortars was thwarted generally. Since July, the production of 120mm mortars had to be completely stopped. The workshops had only been making individual parts for them, but they did not succeed in this. The production plan was not fulfilled due to the lack of rubberised wheels for GAZ-AA trucks from Yaroslavl tyre plant No. 736 and parts of the hub device from the Molotov plant. After the air attacks and the resulting destruction, the casting of crankcases for the T-34 tank's gearshift box had to be moved from the No. 718 Engine of the Revolution plant to a nearby machine tool factory. Even the abridged plan for the production of rockets for Katyusha mortars was not fulfilled. Instead of 121,000 pieces, the Red Army received only 60,500 pieces, half the planned total. Due to the bombing and recovery works, the construction of the thermal processing department of the tool workshop and its equipment remained incomplete. It had to be moved in 1944.[25] It should also be noted that as a result of the repeated air attacks (the No. 718 Engine of the Revolution plant was first damaged in November 1941), one of the best Soviet factories built using German technology was deactivated until the end of the war. It degraded to the level of a small factory, which did not play a large role in providing the Red Army with military equipment.

Russian engineers and party bosses could not work miracles, but Soviet propaganda was good at it! At the end of 1943, Gorky's Molotov automobile plant – the main victim of the Luftwaffe – officially reported 'overfulfilling' the annual production plan! The same 'fantastic achievements' for propaganda purposes ('in spite of the Nazis'!) were reported by the heads of other businesses affected by the attacks. If you believe these figures, it turned out that before the bombing, production schedules were chronically unfulfilled, and after them, production went up sharply (to unprecedented 'success').

In fact, the production plan for GAZ in 1943 for the main types of products was: 50,000 cars, 6,200 T-70 tanks, 4,800 BA-64 armoured vehicles, etc. But the annual final report of the plant said that it produced 18,800 cars, 3,346 T-70 tanks and 1,100 BA-64 armoured vehicles. That is one and a half to four times fewer than planned.[26] Moreover, these figures are in doubt, as the managers of the Molotov plant had to resort to outright fraud with their production figures. How then was it possible to 'exceed' the production plan? Elementary! After the air attacks, the plan was constantly revised, and by the end of the year just adjusted to the actual release. All this was in the spirit of the duplicitous essence of the Soviet state, which has always skilfully manipulated figures and statistics.

The situation was similar in other military enterprises. In May 1943 (before the German bomber raids) Saratov Aviation Plant No. 292 produced 286 fighters. In June (or rather until 23 June), the factory managed to deliver 173 aircraft to the air force. In July, fifty-seven fighters were produced, but these were semi-finished products collected in the field from previous reserves. However, even this figure is clearly doubtful. In August, with great difficulty, it was possible to produce 115 Yak-1s, and in September, 242. And only by the end of October did it formally almost reach the previous level of production – 280 aircraft per month. But these 'fighters', which even before the attacks of German bombers were notable for their poor-quality assembly, were only conditionally suitable for combat.

The last voyage of the *Karl Liebknecht*

In addition to air attacks on industrial facilities, the Soviets suffered serious problems from the bottom mines dropped by Luftwaffe bombers in the summer of 1943 along the entire course of the Volga River from Saratov to Astrakhan. Although much of the waterway was quickly cleared, dozens of German mines still lay at the bottom, waiting for their victims. The threat of mines made it difficult to conduct oil tankers and made navigation on the river very dangerous. The need to avoid dangerous areas and slow down significantly reduced cargo turnover, and caused the sailors, navigators and captains to be in constant tension. They expected an explosion and the death of the ship and crew at any moment.

In June and July, in order to increase the number of ships available for trawling, it was necessary to withdraw all new vessels from cargo transportation, which were already sorely lacking. By 1 July, the Volga military flotilla had 165 minesweepers, and a month later 203! By 1 September, the minesweeper flotilla had 213 units, and the number of trawls of various types reached 317. There was no such anti-mine fleet even in the Baltic Sea! In July–August, the number of mine monitoring posts increased to 956.[27] By the end of September, the number of anti-aircraft guns in the Volga military flotilla, the air defence task force of the transport service of the Volga basin, reached 427, with 1,320 machine guns and 189 searchlight stations. All these forces were controlled from the flagship command post on the staff ship *Zheleznodorozhnik*, which was located near Stalingrad. It received data on the situation in the entire operational zone from Astrakhan to Saratov, including reports of German aircraft appearing in the Volga Region. However, all these 'great achievements' were no longer needed by the summer of 1943. The only serious problem the mines, including those left over from 1942.

In August, the front line began to rapidly roll back to the west, and it became clear that the Luftwaffe would not be able to resume mining the Volga. Therefore, further mobilisation of transport vessels for conversion to minesweepers was suspended. By autumn, the minesweepers conducted a controlled trawling of the waterway, then repeated trawling using magnetic acoustic trawl barges and depth charges. The entire length of the Volga coast was surveyed. By the end of the exercise, the minesweepers had raked an area of 112 sqkm fifteen times and had trawled 176,761km. With the help of trawls, sixty-seven bottom mines were destroyed, and twenty-two were destroyed by depth charges. Another twelve mines found on the shallow sections of the river were defused by sappers. Most of the mines – 242 – were neutralised, but several dozen were not detected. At the same time, action was carried out to demagnetise dry cargo, oil-loading and passenger vessels.

All these large-scale measures produced results, and the loss of ships on the Volga became rare. But the ships continued to explode after the exposure of German bottom mines. For example, at the end of July, near Stalingrad, the tugboat *Tajikistan* blew up and sank. Some other river vessels also met with a similarly sad end.

At the end of August, the passenger steamer *Karl Liebknecht*, under Captain Leonid Gudovich, arrived in Astrakhan after another journey. After disembarking the passengers, the crew learned that their ship was being demagnetised. The steamer went to the area of Durnovsky Island and anchored there. With the help of the bow and stern anchors, the ship was placed across the river, strictly according to the compass, with the axis in the direction from north to south. By order of the engineers, the crew members loaded a huge arc of copper wire into the ship's boat and encircled the hull with this wire. They hung a wire on hemp ropes at each porthole and ran an electric current through it. On command, the wire was alternately submerged and removed from the water. The engineers kept turning on some portable devices, and then again and again forced the wire to be submerged in water, alternately raising it above the surface to a single height along the entire almost 200m length. This tedious, hard work took six hours. After that, the captain was told that the ship was now insured against mines. Then the *Karl Liebknecht* returned to port, where it took on board 500 passengers, and set off up the Volga.

On the evening of 8 September, the steamer reached the Cherniy Yar pier, where Captain Gudovich received orders to take a large empty wooden barge in tow and pull it to Stalingrad. When it began to get dark, the ship went further upstream. At night, the weather turned bad, a strong wind blew, and the sky almost merged with the river. The buoys that marked the waterway with their dim lights were almost invisible. The steering of the vessel deteriorated greatly, as the barge attached to the side did not have a steering system, and its length was one-and-a-half times that of the

Karl Liebknecht. The captain was nervous: 'They gave me a burden! A freak, not a ship!'

Slowly rolling from wave to wave, the steamer went through the fog to Stalingrad. Passengers mostly rested in their cabins, sailors smoked on the decks, and occasionally the murky water was lit up by cigarette butts falling into it. The steamer had already passed the shallow part of the river, when suddenly it was shaken by a strong explosion. One of the ship's crew later recalled:

> For a long time I could not sleep, involuntarily listening to the strained roar of overloaded diesels, to the whistle of the wind and the splash of water outside the window, under the side. Only, it seems, I fell asleep, as the ship was hit by something with an unimaginable crash and roar. Together with the wreckage of the stateroom, I flew in the dark for some time and finally fell into the cold water.

The ship began to list rapidly to port, its forward superstructures failing, and clouds of steam and smoke rose above the almost invisible deckhouse. The passengers who managed to get on deck immediately began to jump overboard into the dark river water. The vessel was sinking fast, however, in the shallow water it did not completely sink, and the top awning remained above the water.

Fortunately, at the time of the accident, the steamship *Manychstroy* was just a few kilometres from the steamer. Immediately after the explosion, Captain Shitov gave up the tow of his own caravan and hurried to the scene. The team managed to rescue about 100 passengers who were on a half-sunken wooden barge. Several dozen more people managed to swim to the shore. A total of 350 people drowned, including almost the entire crew and many of the deckhands. Captain Gudovich was seriously injured.[28] Bodies were removed from the river for another ten days after the tragedy. The commission investigating the loss of the ship concluded that the cause of the sinking of the *Karl Liebknecht*, the flagship of the Volga passenger fleet, was an acoustic mine with a multiple fuse. This was the last victim collected by German bottom mines on the Volga. However, in the following years, all rivermen were wary of passing the section between Saratov and Astrakhan.

In total, according to Soviet data, from April to September 1943, thirteen ships were blown up by bottom mines, that is, 0.2 per cent of all ships that passed. The mining of the Volga by bombers from I./KG 100 made it much more difficult to navigate the river and transport oil products. In July, 1,100,000 tons of oil were transported along the Astrakhan–Saratov section, 1,155,500 tons in August, and only 965,000 tons in September.

At the end of the navigation, the Volga military flotilla began to gradually disarm. Armoured boats, minesweepers and patrol vessels were sent to the Dnieper, the Sea of Azov and Lake Peipus. Seventy-five previously taken vessels were disarmed and returned to the river transport and fishing fleets. But it was decided not to completely disband the flotilla in 1943. By 18 October, the Volga military flotilla still had six gunboats, eighty minesweepers, thirteen patrol boats, five mortar boats, thirty-five speedboats, two floating batteries, five staff ships, and thirty towed trawl barges.

Chapter 8

Recipe for the Collapse of the Luftwaffe – Göring Psychosis

Ephemeral flourishing in anticipation of death

This book tells the story of the time that became a period of prosperity for Luftwaffe bomber aviation, at least on the Eastern Front. The 'Blitz' over the Volga in June 1943 proved to be one of the most successful Luftwaffe operations of the Second World War, and one of the few examples of the use of He 111 and Ju 88 bombers against strategic targets. With minimal losses, the German Kampfgeschwader caused serious damage to the Soviet military industry and reduced its potential for a considerable time. It is in Russia that the most favourable conditions developed for the use of bomber squadrons. Long-term training of the bomber elite and optimal combat experience allowed the creation of a sufficient number of aces, leading inexperienced newcomers. The belated transition of German industry to increased production of military products by 1943 gave excellent results in the production of bombers, although these were types that were obsolete on the Western Front, but shockingly effective on the Eastern. Hitler's talentless leadership had already led to a number of disasters at the front, but the experience and intelligence of the German generals who had not yet been dismissed by Hitler (in particular Manstein) had so far compensated for the Führer's total incompetence. The situation on the Western Front, where the Allies were still concentrating forces and gaining experience, made it possible to provide the Luftwaffe with everything necessary, primarily fuel. The collapse of the Russian air defence, which merely created very bright pyrotechnic performances over the attacked cities consisting of separate 'shows' of searchlights, anti-aircraft gunners and night fighters, gave experienced German pilots the opportunity to demonstrate their brilliant bombing skills with almost impunity.

But there is a reasonable question: why did these effective air attacks did not affect the Soviet offensive in the summer and autumn of 1943? Why did the German army fail and be forced to retreat hastily to the 'the Panther' line located along the Dnieper River?

In operations on the Eastern Front, the middle and lower levels of the Luftwaffe command at the level of tactical control of bomber aviation proved to be brilliant. Such a conclusion cannot be drawn about the highest levels of Luftwaffe command, where, against the background of a strange contrast in the actions of Göring, darting between outright adventurism and complete helplessness, his closest deputies showed inflexibility and template planning, along with a complete lack of a clear strategy for the use of bomber squadrons on the Eastern Front. In this regard, the bomber aviation performed the function of supporting the ground forces and only accidentally, under favourable circumstances, was an independent force capable of having a strategic impact on the course of the war on the Eastern Front.

So, when planning bombing attacks on the Volga Region, the Luftwaffe high command made the following serious miscalculations and mistakes.

First, if such air attacks had been carried out at the end of 1941 or in the middle of 1942, they could still have seriously undermined the military potential of the Soviets and prevent German catastrophes on the Eastern Front, or at least reduce their scale. It is worth emphasizing that the Volga Region industrial enterprises were a kind of Soviet analog of the Ruhr region of Germany. But by the fall of 1943, the Volga Region factories were no longer as important in supplying the Red Army with equipment, ammunition, and equipment as they were at the end of 1941 and the first half of 1942. Allied aid under Lend-Lease and the work of evacuated enterprises in the Urals (where German bombers could not fly) gained such momentum that the Red Army, at least for a while, could do without the Gorky Molotov automobile plant, Yaroslavl tyre plant, Saratov Aviation Plant No. 292 and other important enterprises.

Secondly, the pause in the battles on the Eastern Front (with the exception of the Kuban bridgehead), which lasted from April to June 1943, played an ambivalent role. On the one hand, it allowed the Third Reich to free up its 'flying artillery'– twin-engine bombers – for strategic missions. On the other hand, in the absence of attritional fighting, the Russians were able to significantly replenish stocks of their military equipment and accumulate large reserves. Therefore, despite a sharp reduction in the production of tanks, vehicles and guns, the Soviets still had all these in sufficient quantity.

Third, not all available targets were attacked. The Molotov plant was completely destroyed after three air attacks. However, there were several other important targets in this city: Gorky Aviation Plant No. 21 (produced La-5 fighters), Gorky artillery factory No. 92 Stalin (produced 76mm guns), and the Krasnoye Sormovo No. 112 shipyard (produced T-34 tanks). But none of these objects were attacked for some reason! Instead, for four raids, the Luftwaffe continued to bomb already deactivated production facilities and secondary targets.

Fourth, the main vulnerable link of Soviet industry was the electric power industry. All power plants and thermal and power stations with hydrocarbon fuel worked with heavy overloads. To save electricity, councils had to turn off about a third of consumers (mainly hospitals, homes and other social facilities). At the same time, the majority of power plants operated turbines and aggregates of German production (mainly Siemens). There was nothing to replace this equipment during the war. German intelligence was aware of these facts. The Luftwaffe had detailed aerial photographs of power facilities, transmission lines and substations. But for some reason these extremely vulnerable targets were not given priority! The destruction of such facilities as the Molotov plant had strategic consequences, but they were shortterm and not fatal to the Soviets. In contrast, the destruction of energy facilities in the European part of the Soviet Union could have had long-term, catastrophic consequences.

The idea of an air attack on Russian power plants and thermal and power stations only arose in late 1943. It was initiated by Reichsminister Speer and Professor of electrical engineering Steinmann. As targets, they selected eleven heat and power plants in Gorky, Balakhna, Yaroslavl, Shatura, Kashira, Stalinogorsk and other cities. These stations generated 60 per cent of the electricity in central Russia, and their deactivation would have brought most military enterprises to a standstill. But during this period, the Kampfgeschwader was completely tied up in endless gruelling missions to overcome crisis situations at the front. And the front itself was gradually moving away from the Russian industrial centres. In the autumn of 1944, the German bomber force was effectively disbanded, with only a few Geschwader remaining. There was no one left to carry out strategic missions…

The order for an air attack against Soviet power plants was signed by Hitler only in January 1945! At that time, only the Mistel composite strike aircraft could perform such a mission. Operation *Eisenhammer* was designed and carefully planned. At that time, the distance from the German air bases in the Berlin area to the farthest goal – the power plant in Gorky – was already 2,250km! Mistels and their accompanying pathfinders had to fly for eight hours to get there. It was a very risky, but really doable task! Even if only 30 per cent of the Mistels reached the targets, they would surely be able to hit most power plants and thermal and power stations in the vicinity of Moscow. But the order to start the mission was not received. However, even if Operation *Eisenhammer* had taken place, in 1945 it no longer made sense.

The discussion of the role of aviation in the Second World War is a typical topic of modern research. Numerous works by historical researchers usually describe secondary reasons for the collapse of the Luftwaffe, the discussion of which further confuses an already difficult situation. Many authors single out the lack of strategic (four-engine) bombers in Germany as one of the main reasons for Germany's defeat in the war. Indeed, German bombers never achieved the power shown at the end of the war by the armadas of allied four-engine Lancasters, Flying Fortresses, and Liberators. However, the authors of this book, written on the basis of years of research, have presented in previous chapters a lot of evidence of the effectiveness of German twin-engine bombers and their ability to perform strategic missions, at least in the first years of the Second World War.

However, even in this period of prosperity, there were already clear signs of the imminent collapse of German bomber aviation. It is the human, not the technical, factor of this shameful collapse that we will discuss further.

Hitler's mad heir

To find out the reasons for the strategic impotence of the Luftwaffe, we will focus special attention on the top management of German aviation, and specifically on Hermann Göring. Only he, as the second man in the Third Reich and the official heir of Hitler, could make the most of his influence over the Führer in promoting the interests of military aviation. However, even during the failure of the Battle of Britain, and especially after the Stalingrad disaster, the Luftwaffe, and especially its leadership in the person of Göring, became the object of universal ridicule and mockery from the army and the leadership of the Third Reich. Moreover, more and more often, at first covertly, and then more and more clearly, frank accusations of the chief of aviation not only of inefficiency, but even of cowardice and treachery, began to be heard. Let us emphasise that these accusations, as history has shown, had quite clear grounds.

In our opinion, the answers to all these questions should be found in the mental organisation of Luftwaffe leaders, and first of all, in the mental state of the creator and official of the Luftwaffe – Reichsmarschall Hermann Göring. At the same time, as a theoretical basis for analysing the natural and social features of this individual the authors use the approaches formulated by the scientific school of psychoanalysis.

Psychoanalytic interpretation of the biography of the chief of German aviation in full accordance with the idea of the unconscious mind Freud must begin with an analysis of his childhood and the features of child–parent relations in the family.

Childhood. Two fathers

On 12 January 1893, near Rosenheim, Germany, in the family of an official, a sturdy baby was born, the future German Reichsmarschall. The father (Ernst Göring) was not present at the birth of his second son from his second marriage because of his absorption with the affairs of the German colonies. His young wife, Francisca, gave birth in the presence of a close friend of the Göring family – the doctor Hermann Epenstein. We have not accidentally mentioned this interesting person in all respects: a successful entrepreneur, a lover of women and ancient castles, and also prone to risky adventures. The fact is that it was Hermann Epenstein, seemingly an outsider, who was destined to play a very important role in the fate of Hermann Göring. He also became the godfather of the future creator of the Luftwaffe and may have given it his name.

It is very difficult to understand the relationship of the triangle formed by the Göring couple and Epenstein. There seems to have been more than friendship between Franziska Göring and Hermann Epenstein. We can only assume who was the real biological father of the two sons of Franziska Göring. At least, this role could well be claimed not only by Ernst Göring, but also by Epenstein. In any case, when comparing photos of Hermann's younger brother, Albert, you can see some similarities with the mysterious patron of the Göring family. It is only safe to say that this man became the second father of Ernst Göring's sons. Moreover, Epenstein was very warm to Hermann, constantly took care of his godson, and even left a considerable inheritance to him.

The Göring family situation was complicated by the fact that the formal head of the family not only knew about the close relationship between his wife and a family friend, but also apparently took this fact calmly and even extracted financial benefits from this strange relationship. We can also assume that Epenstein was attracted not only by his young wife, but also by the fact of his friendship with Ernst Göring. The fact is that Epenstein, being a passionate patriot of the German Empire, suffered all his life from the false contradiction between his origin and his beliefs imposed by the social environment. A maniacal fan of all things German, he knew that he had Jewish blood in his veins. Apparently, in order to somehow resolve the contradiction instilled in him by the social environment, this financially successful man bought a German knighthood along with an old castle and officially became known as Hermann Epenstein Ritter von Mauternburg. And the strange friendship with Ernst Göring, which had grown, in fact, into full financial support for the entire Göring family, receives in this case quite a plausible explanation. Apparently, communication with the ruined colleague of Bismarck, and the fact he was completely dependent on Epenstein, brought this admirer of all things German pleasant satisfaction.

Soon after the birth, the mother left the young Hermann in the care of their friends, and the boy first saw Ernst only at the age of three, when he retired and returned with his wife from the German colonies to their homeland. Due to the innate features of the nervous system, Hermann grew up a difficult child. From the first days of his life, such qualities as hyperactivity, aggression and stubbornness gave his teachers and parents a lot of trouble. Hermann was the ringleader of all the risky children's games and was completely devoid of a child's usual fear of heights.

At training in elementary school, Hermann's innate pathological tendencies became particularly obvious. Violations of good behaviour were pronounced; there was total insubordination to teachers and aggression towards peers. Parents had to repeatedly transfer their violent son from one school to another. Endless fights, escapes, and even strike action became familiar episodes of young Hermann's training. The Göring couple was forced to place their son in a special boarding school for difficult teenagers, but even such extreme measures could not quell the furious temper of the future Reichsmarschall.

Eventually, the situation was resolved with the help of Epenstein, who, thanks to his connections, arranged for his godson to attend an elite cadet school in Karlsruhe. It is here that the natural aggressiveness and irrepressible temper, combined with complete fearlessness, finally found a constructive application. As a result, Hermann's terrible behaviour and academic performance improved somewhat. At the age of sixteen, young

Göring graduated from the cadet school and soon entered the main military school in Lichterfeld. It is clear that the son of a German official in the German Empire, where everyone raved about the idea of world domination, could expect only one worthy application – a career in the professional military. Since then, the military uniform, and, most importantly, the military environment, became an integral part of Göring's life.

In March 1911, at the age of eighteen, he graduated with honours from the Berlin military school, received the Kaiser's own congratulations, and was promoted to second lieutenant. At the same time, it is not necessary to think that military education somehow changed the psychopathic traits that were so clearly manifested in Hermann in elementary school. He still continued his hooligan antics in order to attract attention. However, in the military officer environment, where people with similar characteristics such as hypertrophied aggression, a thirst for glory and a complete lack of moral standards were concentrated, such manifestations were interpreted as entirely approved signs of military valour and bravery.

The main feature of the emerging character of Göring was a maniacal desire to attract attention to his person at any cost. This hypertrophied feature makes it possible to assert with a high degree of probability that the future Reichsmarschall had a character deformity, which was designated by the term hysteria among specialists in minor psychiatry. Accordingly, the individual psychopath, the bearer of such a trait, can be designated by the term hysteroid. The predisposition to the development of psychopathy has an innate basis, and this mental feature gets its direct form during the life of the individual, being transformed under the influence of the surrounding social environment.

The authors do not know from which of the two fathers Hermann inherited hysterical features, however, it is safe to say that the samples of irrepressible luxury, which he later in a manic hypertrophied form embodied in the Palace of Carinhall, he saw and adopted in the castle and behaviour of Epenstein. But with the man whose last name he bore, the young Hermann did not develop a relationship at all. We can only assume that the possible cause of this discord was excessive severity and perhaps even corporal punishment applied by Hermann's father. Despite the fact that Göring lost his father at a young age, the image of a cold, domineering and overly strict father remained with him forever.

Meanwhile, Göring's military career continued to develop. In the elite 112th Infantry Regiment, he led the unruly life of pampering fate, interspersing friendly drinking with many romantic adventures with the opposite sex. It is clear that the only thing that the handsome young officer lacked to demonstrate his prowess was a good war. To the general satisfaction and even joy of all Europe, two stupid dreamers of military glory, Russian Tsar Nicholas II and German Kaiser Wilhelm II, soon organised a world war.

The dashing officer met the beginning of the war with manic enthusiasm and immediately plunged into military adventures. Completely ignoring orders, Second Lieutenant Goring performed many senseless feats, thoughtlessly risking the lives of his subordinates, for which he was awarded the Iron Cross 2nd Class. It was with this award that the countless collection of orders of the future Knight's Cross of the Iron Cross began. However, the war soon passed into a stagnant and boring trench phase, completely incompatible with the ambitions and maniacal activity of Göring. In addition to the mental discomfort associated with the inability to realise his hysterical tendencies, Hermann experienced physical problems associated with rheumatism. The way out of this situation was suggested by his old friend from the 112th Infantry Regiment – Bruno Loerzer, who opened a completely new guaranteed path to glory – aviation! However, the main 'weapon' of the two friends and adventurers who demonstrated similar hysterical traits of character was a photographic camera installed on the plane. We have to admit that the fearless young officers Göring and Loerzer really gained fame by providing the German command with valuable photos of enemy positions, for which each deservedly received the Iron Cross 1st Class.

However, the first successes were devalued by the sluggishness of the gunners, to whom Göring reported valuable information obtained in the course of a risky aerial reconnaissance. Routine and dependence on primitive inhabitants in military uniforms soon bored the ambitious fan of military glory, and he decided to become a fighter pilot.

After graduating from flight school brilliantly, Göring had a new tool in his hands for the first time in his life – the controls of a fighter plane, which allowed him to receive glory and attention in almost unlimited quantities. It was with aircraft that Göring was inseparable for many years of his life, but only as long as they were a means of attracting attention. As soon as he mastered his next tool, politics, the planes were forgotten. An interesting fact is that at the end of his life, as the chief of the Luftwaffe and the second person in the state, Göring hated to fly and moved exclusively by car or, which was more preferable for him, in a personal train – a mobile palace.

In the status of a fearless pilot, he performed numerous brilliant feats. In one of the adventures, Goring was seriously wounded in the hip and after recovering went to show off to his already only father – Hermann Epenstein. He stood before him in a magnificent uniform, festooned with battle honours, glittering in the glory so necessary to a psychopathic hysteroid. It was a demonstration that he had fulfilled all the hopes of his godfather, and possibly his biological father, to the full.

The next ambitious goal for Göring was to win the competition with the famous 'Red Baron', Manfred von Richthofen. This rivalry shows that the future Reichsmarschall set the bar for its achievements incredibly high. Many of the less well-known competitor pilots Göring was able to catch up with quickly enough and received the award Pour le Mérite from the hands of the German Kaiser himself. However, despite all the valour and bravery, comparing the number of enemy aircraft shot down, he could not even come close to the results of the aviation legend of the Great War. However, life itself, in the form of an accidental bullet that killed the Red Baron, removed the last obstacle to the culmination of the young aviator's military career. It was Göring, despite the presence of other, more worthy candidates, who became the commander of the Manfred von Richthofen fighter squadron.

However, defeat and the collapse of the German empire brought Göring back from heaven to earth. Suddenly it turned out that yesterday's hero was not needed in the new peaceful conditions. The former Captain Göring was forced to start a difficult life as an unemployed pilot, for which he was completely unprepared. The plane, which was previously a means of achieving fame for Göring, has become a boring means of earning daily bread.

Third father. The voice, the master

After long wanderings and boring work as an air taxi pilot, Göring returned to his homeland in Germany, where he decided to try his luck in another gamble that promised glory – political struggle. Here, in November 1922, he met Adolf Hitler, and finally found a master and idol in one person. Note that this odious character in German history became a father figure for Hermann Göring. He could not only curb the frenzied temper of Goring, but also cause him to panic in terror. It is almost impossible to explain this strange fact based on the analysis of conscious representations. Indeed, the relevant question is how the puny Gefreiter Hitler, who was only four years older than Göring, was able to completely subdue the headstrong captain, who was distinguished by a rabid temper?

And it is not, of course, the magical influence of the future German Führer on people or the hypnosis of the Nazi ideology created by him. The facts show that these factors are nothing more than a myth. Let us emphasise that Göring was never seriously interested in the primitive and confused Nazi ideology. It is clear that a logical interpretation of such a strange phenomenon can only be found in the realm of the unconscious mind. According to Freud, the answer is hidden in the analysis of the characteristics of parent–child relationships. But, since the reader already knows about the existence of two fathers, the question arises, what kind of father was replaced by the evil psychopathic fanatic Hitler in the unconscious mind of hysteroid Göring? Obviously, we cannot talk about the kind and fun-loving Epenstein. We can only recall the image of the domineering and cruel Ernst, who inspired little Hermann with panic terror. We must not forget that under the guise of a dashing and fearless warrior and the creator of the Luftwaffe, an infantile individual was hiding, demonstrating all the attributes of a child, namely suggestibility, dependence on parents, emotional instability and even tearfulness. That is why Göring until the end of his days could only accept the opinion of his Führer and believed it without limit, just as he once believed and panicked in fear of his dead father Ernst.

Wound and caricatured physical appearance

The physical image of Göring is no less recognisable than that of Hitler. Thick and thin, good and evil, funny and frowning, these two complementary characters became remembered symbols of Nazi Germany. The simplest explanation for Göring's fullness comes from his pyknic physique, and hence his predisposition to fullness. This bodily constitution, against the background of prolonged immobility during a prolonged recovery from injury and the absence of dietary restrictions, led to predictable results.

There is another explanation, also related to the body, or rather to a serious injury to the body of the future Luftwaffe chief. It was boundless trust in the Führer that brought Göring to the streets of Munich, where he received his famous wound in the hip and groin area. The severe injury not only increased the future Reichsmarschall waistline to an incredible size, but also made him much more unstable mentally. This bullet, which ricocheted off the paving stones, led to the creation of a caricature image of the fat man Göring, hung with medals like a Christmas tree.

However, we are more interested in the psychological explanation of the peculiarities of the Reichsmarschall's corporeality. To begin with, it is customary in various books to discuss Hitler's physical defects in the area of the male genitals, but the greatest grounds for such discussion are in relation to Göring. The fatal bullet not only made Göring barren, but also dealt a terrible blow to his hypertrophied self-esteem. In our opinion, it was the painful psychological feeling of losing a body part that led to Göring hating himself and seeking to commit suicide in various ways. He chronically destroyed his body with drugs, and during the acute crisis made repeated attempts to kill himself through strangulation and by falling from a great height. In an even more sophisticated way, he tried to kill his mental identity – becoming a long-term patient of a psychiatric clinic and rightly receiving a terrible diagnosis– psychosis.

It is no secret that Hitler unconsciously, and to some extent consciously, gathered in his environment a lot of people with various mental disorders (psychopathy). There were also those who rightfully deserved to be in a clinic for the mentally ill. One of these characters was undoubtedly Hermann Göring.

Although time had somewhat blunted the terrible mental wound of Göring, all his subsequent luxury and the immense power of Nazi No. 2 could not compensate for his loss of love for himself, and the mental trauma constantly reminded him of his existence by the exacerbation of chronic drug addiction and psychosis.

The chief of the Luftwaffe. Professional unfitness

Now that the reader is sufficiently aware of the psychological characteristics of Hermann Göring, the authors will attempt to answer the question about his personal role in the collapse of the Luftwaffe. In principle, it is important to consider whether such a pathological person could lead his brainchild somewhere other than to death?

Usually, when discussing the professional fitness of an individual to perform important managerial functions, one emphasises the importance of abilities. First of all, one would analyse the degree of expression of the universal ability to solve problems – intelligence. In many books written about Göring, he is quite rightly accused of many of his inherent sins: hypertrophied vanity, corruption, extravagance, drug addiction, pathological lies, and so on. However, for some reason, it is customary to declare his undoubtedly high intelligence. At the same time, authors who write confidently about the mind of Göring usually do not bother with deep proofs, referring to a number of well-known facts, namely: excellent grades in English and French and horseback riding, obtained by Göring while at a military school; training at the university; the allegedly successful recreation of German military aviation; his appointment by Hitler to the high position of Commissioner for the four-year plan (Beauftragter für den Vierjahresplan). Also, as the most serious and direct argument in favour of a high mind, the results of the notorious test of intelligence, conducted by an American psychologist on Göring during the Nuremberg Tribunal, are usually cited.

The authors of this book have a different explanation for these facts. Excellent grades in certain subjects and university education during a period of total crisis in Germany may not have a direct bearing on Göring's mental abilities. The success in the post of Commissioner for the four-year plan is also very doubtful. The direct management of the German economy by the very energetic but not very clever Göring was accompanied by very strange and comical facts. For example, it is worth mentioning a direct order given to German chemists, strongly recommending that they synthesize butter oil from hard coal.

It is more difficult to refute the results of the American test, but it should be emphasised that the test, which was performed with such enthusiasm by Göring, did not determine the level of intelligence as such, but showed the overall level of mental development. Thus, the composite IQ index included features of such mental processes as memory, attention, perception and temperament, and Göring was sanguine; that is, the owner of a strong nervous system. And, finally, do not forget that the test was not subjected to a locksmith or janitor, engaged exclusively in manual labour, but a person engaged in desk work. Thus, a fairly high level of IQ obtained by Göring rather indicates an innate high motivation to achieve success and this is borne out by his professional activity.

An analysis of his performance as head of the Luftwaffe provides facts that inexorably indicate Göring's low intelligence. Unable to understand the needs of the advanced branch of the armed forces, he created a complex and complicated Luftwaffe leadership structure – a viscous bureaucratic swamp in which all sound ideas were drowned, and mistakes, on the contrary, continued to be implemented by inertia.

Being an incompetent leader, he surrounded himself with equally incompetent, but personally pleasing protégés. The consequences of his personnel decisions appeared quickly enough and continued to grow until the complete collapse of German aviation. The top management of the Luftwaffe has been divided into many warring clans since its inception. Many of the top officers and deputies of Göring openly hated each other and dreamed of overthrowing their competitors. The situation of internal conflicts arising from the very manner of Göring's leadership was complicated by its increasing disregard for its direct functions. The Luftwaffe chief's desire increased throughout the war to pass on to others the solution of the most pressing problems related primarily to the definition of the strategy for the development and application of the Luftwaffe increased throughout the war. Under the facade of the Blitzkrieg's success, there were objectively existing problems associated with the outright adventurism underlying the creation of the Luftwaffe. And the longer the war dragged on, the more acute were the strategic mistakes that were originally laid in the foundation of the Göring brainchild. The quickness of creating a new kind of troops, the deliberate exaggeration of the power of German aviation, the desire to borrow technical and tactical experience from the more developed aviation powers, primarily Britain and the United States, gave rise to chronic insecurity among the senior management of the Luftwaffe, hidden under the false veil of 'large' figure Hermann Göring.

We must admit that the Luftwaffe, for all its ostentatious brilliance, suffered from an acute inferiority complex. Striking symptoms of this complex was the obsessive comparison of fighters and bombers with British aircraft, and not in favour of the German type, which was not always actually true. The idea of the Luftwaffe top management fix was to create strategic bombers on the model of British and American four-engine aircraft. On this disastrous story, the Germans spent a lot of effort and money, endlessly reworking and refining already ready-made, but completely unsuccessful projects. The same situation was repeated in the design and production of a heavy fighter, in fact, also copies of British and American aircraft. For all this intense, but absolutely meaningless activity, the Luftwaffe leadership overlooked and failed miserably to develop its jet aircraft.

It should be said that the chief of German military aviation not only failed to build a strategy, and therefore to reconcile the numerous groups in the leadership and clans of aircraft designers who hated each other, but on the contrary, his incompetent actions sowed chaos and confusion in his already troubled department.

The collapse of the Hitlerite Reich and the end of the life of the hysteroid

The death of Hitler, symbolising the final collapse of the Third Reich, was perceived by the former Reichsmarschall in a completely childish way, i.e. with confusion and tears, almost like the death of his father Ernst. Hermann Göring – a pathological liar and traitor – never changed his patron, continuing to protect him until his death.

The life of a man who always tried to be the centre of attention at all costs could not end in the arms of a rough rope. The death rattle and the executioner's frowning smile seemed to the former Luftwaffe chief too boring and devoid of theatrical effect as an accompaniment. Hermann Göring was true to his ugliness of character to the last breath, even a stupid death from cyanide of potassium served the purpose of attracting the last universal attention to his pitiful and absurd person.

References and Sources

Balke, U., *KG100. History*, Stuttgart: Motorbuch Verlag. 1981.

Chadaev, J.E., *The economy of the USSR in the Great Patriotic War*. Moscow: thought, 1985.

Chenakal, D.D., *Military sky of the Volga region*. Saratov, 1986. p. 131.

Dierich, W., *Kampfgeschwader 55 'Greif'*. Stuttgart: Motorbuch Verlag, 1994.

Efimov, A.N., *Over the battlefield*. Moscow: Voenizdat, 1976. p. 113.

Fritzsche, K., *Air shooter. Through anti-aircraft fire*. Moscow: Yauza-Press, 2009. p. 69.

Frolov, D.F., *Feat saratovtsev in the Great Patriotic War*. Saratov, 1972.

Ginzburg, S.G., *About the past for the future*. Moscow: Politizdat, 1990.

Gorkov, Yu A., *State Defence Committee decides*. Moscow: OLMA-Press, 2002.

Gundelach, K., *Kampfgeschwader 'General Wever' 4*. Stuttgart: Motorbuch Verlag, 1978.

Häberlen, K., *Davongekommen. Als Kampfflieger über der Fronten*. Vaizendorf: VDM Verlag, 2001.

Kiehl, H., *Kampfgeschwader 'Legion Condor' 53*. Stuttgart: Motorbuch Verlag, 1996.

Kington, John A.& Selinger, Franz, *Wekusta: Luftwaffe Meteorological Reconnaissance unit and operations 1938–1945*. Flight recorder publications, 2006.

Lagoda, M., *Ein Blick in die Vergangenheit. Kriegsernnerungen eines Fernaufklarers aus Russland und dem Orient*. Helios, 2011.

Loktionov, I.I., *The Volga military flotilla during the Great Patriotic War*. Moscow: Voenizdat, 1977. p. 99.

Manstein, E., *Lost victories*. Smolensk: Rusich, 1999.

Morokhin, V.N., *Through the fire of the great battle*. N. Novgorod, 1995. p. 112.

REFERENCES AND SOURCES

Nauroth, H., *The Luftwaffe. From the North Cape to Tobruk. 1939–1945.* Schiffer Military History, USA, 1991.

Okorokov, V.N., *Over the roof of your house. Documentary essay on air defence during the Great Patriotic War.* N. Novgorod, 1992.

Panteleev, Y.A., *Sea front.* Moscow: Voenizdat, 1965. p. 251.

Rastrenin, O., *Split sky. May–June 1943.* Moscow: Eksmo; Yauza, 2007. p. 231.

Sojm, V.M., *Soviet counterintelligence in the years of the Great Patriotic War.* Moscow: Kraft+, 2005. pp. 102–103.

Svetlicic, N., *Air defence forces of the country in the Great Patriotic War.* Moscow: Nauka, 1979.

Svirin, M.N., *Stalin's Steel fist. History of the Soviet tank. 1943–1945.* Moscow: Yauza, Eksmo, 2006. p. 173.

Waiss, W., *Chronic Kampfgeschwader Nr. 27 Boelcke. Teil IV. 01.01.1943–31.12.1943.* Helios Verlag, Aachen, 2007.

Zarembo, N.P., *Volzhsky ples.* Moscow: 1970. p. 124.

Zefirov, M.V., *Aces of the Luftwaffe: Bomber aviation.* Moscow: AST, 2002.

Air defence forces of the country in the Great Patriotic War. Moscow: Voenizdat, 1968. p. 174.

Air defence forces of the country in the Great Patriotic War. Moscow: Voenizdat, 1981.

Oblivion is not subject to: pages of Nizhny Novgorod history (1941–1945). N. Novgorod, 1995. p. 530.

One hundred Stalin's Falcons. In the battles for the Motherland. Moscow: Yauza, Eksmo, 2005. pp. 156–157.

Saratov region during the Great Patriotic War (1941–1945). Archival document. Saratov, 2005. pp. 43–44.

Soviet river transport in the Great Patriotic War. Moscow: Nauka, 1979. p. 111.

Yaroslavl region for 50 years. 1936–1986. Essays, documents, materials. Yaroslavl, 1986. p. 234.

Yaroslavl tyre plant. Collection of documents and materials. Yaroslavl, 1968. p. 81.

Fliegerbuch Hans Georg Bätcher
Fliegerbuch Helmut Abendvoth
Fliegerbuch Hans Grotter

Archives

Archiv KG 27 'Boelcke'.

Central archive of the Ministry of Defence of the Russian Federation (TSAMO RF)
TSAMO RF Foundation 13626. Inventory 20293. Case 7. The sheet 46, 48.
TSAMO RF. Foundation 566 Shap. Inventory 36584s. Case 11. Sheet 331.

State socio-political archive of the Nizhny Novgorod region (GOPANO)
GOPANO. Fund 3. Inventory 1. Case 3275. Sheet 9–14.
GOPANO. Foundation 2518. Inventory 1. Case 9. Sheet 15.
GOPANO. Foundation 2518. Inventory 1. Case 6. Sheet 15–19.
GOPANO. Foundation 2518. Inventory 1. Case 9. Sheet 24–27.
GOPANO. Foundation 2518. Inventory 1. Case 9. Sheet 15–19.
GOPANO. Foundation 2518. Inventory 1. Case 9. Sheet 17–18.
GOPANO. Foundation 2518. Inventory 1. Case 9. Sheet 19.
GOPANO. Foundation 2518. Inventory 1. Case 9. Sheet 20–21.
GOPANO. Foundation 2518. Inventory 1. Case 9. Sheet 20–21.
GOPANO. Foundation 2518. Inventory 1. Case 9. Sheet 36.
GOPANO. Foundation 2518. Inventory 1. Case 9. Sheet 37–39.
GOPANO. Foundation 2518. Inventory 1. Case 9. Sheet 37–39.
GOPANO. Foundation 2518. Inventory 1. Case 9. Sheet 31–32.
GOPANO. Foundation 2518. Inventory 1. Case 9. Sheet 55–56.
GOPANO. Foundation 3. Inventory 1. Case 3275. Sheet 9–14.
GOPANO. Foundation 2518. Inventory 1. Case 9. Sheet 55–56.
GOPANO. Foundation 3. Inventory 1. Case 3308. Sheet 106–125.
GOPANO. Foundation 2518. Inventory 1. Case 9. Sheet 73–83.
GOPANO. Foundation 2518. Inventory 1. Case 9. Sheet 93, 93a.
GOPANO. Foundation 2518. Inventory 1. Case 9. Sheet 155–166.

GOPANO. Foundation 2518. Inventory 1. Case 9. Sheet 155–166.
GOPANO. Foundation 2518. Inventory 1. Case 9. Sheet 153–154.

State institution Central archive of the Nizhny Novgorod region. (GU TSANO)
GU TSANO Foundation 2435. Inventory 8. Case 64. Sheet 82.
GU TSANO. Foundation 6146. Inventory 3. Case 4. Sheet 11.
GU TSANO. Foundation 6146. Inventory 3. Case 4. Sheet 13.
GU TSANO. Foundation 6146. Inventory 3. Case 4. Sheet 19.
GU TSANO. Foundation 6146. Inventory 3. Case 4. Sheet 16.
GU TSANO. Foundation 6146. Inventory 3. Case 4. Sheet 23.
GU TSANO. Foundation 6146. Inventory 3. Case 4. Sheet 26.
GU TSANO. Foundation 126. Inventory 5. Case 35. Sheet 9–14.
GU TSANO. Foundation 126. Inventory 5. Case 35. Sheet 9–14.
GU TSANO. Foundation 2816. Inventory 4. Case 166. Sheet 1–6.
GU TSANO. Foundation 2518. Inventory 1. Case 9. Sheet 80–91.
GU TSANO. Foundation 126. Inventory 5. Case 35. Sheet of 10–14.
GU TSANO. Foundation 2435. Inventory 8. Case 66. Sheet 40–45.
GU TSANO. Foundation 2435. Inventory 8. Case 66. Sheet 61, 65.
GU TSANO. Foundation 2435. Inventory 1. Case 180. Sheet 79.
GU TSANO. Foundation 2435. Inventory 8. Case 66. Sheet 4.
GU TSANO. Foundation 15. Inventory 4. Case 234. Sheet 5.
GU TSANO. Foundation 2435. Inventory 8. Case 65. Sheet 47–48.
GU TSANO. Foundation 2435. Inventory 8. Case 65. Sheet 36–37.
GU TSANO. Foundation 2435. Inventory 8. Case 65. Sheet 38.
GU TSANO. Foundation 2435. Inventory 8. Case 65. Sheet 31–34.
GU TSANO. Foundation 2435. Inventory 8. Case 65. Sheet 35–37.
GU TSANO. Foundation 2435. Inventory 8. Case 65. Sheet 35–37.
GU TSANO. Foundation 2435. Inventory 8. Case 65. Sheet 57.
GU TSANO. Foundation 6146. Inventory 3. Case 4. Sheet 62.
GU TSANO. Foundation 6146. Inventory 3. Case 4. Sheet 64.
GU TSANO. Foundation 6146. Inventory 2. Case 7. Sheet 1.
GU TSANO. Foundation 2435. Inventory 8. Case 65. Sheet 143.
GU TSANO. Foundation 126. Inventory 5. Case 35. Sheet 1–17; Case 18. Sheet 201–207.
GU TSANO. Foundation 2435. Inventory 1. Case 180. Sheet 106–114.

Endnotes

Chapter 1: The Führer's Nazgûl

1. Manstein, E., *Lost victories*, Smolensk: Rusich, 1999. p. 490.
2. The Ford V8 family of cars was produced in the United States from 1932 to 1942. It included sedans, phaetons, pick-ups, coupés and roadsters. Häberlen drove a Roadster, the most luxurious version. It was a true legend of the American automobile industry and was the basis for the Russian GAZ-M1. The Ford V8 is also known for the fact it was used by the famous bank robbers Bonnie and Clyde.
3. Kurt Pflugbeil, commander of Fliegerkorps IV.
4. Häberlen, K., *Davongekommen. Als Kampfflieger über der Fronten.* Vaizendorf: VDM Verlag, 2001. p. 136.
5. Häberlen, K., *Davongekommen. Als Kampfflieger über der Fronten.* Vaizendorf: VDM Verlag, 2001. p. 138.
6. Gundelach, K., *Kampfgeschwader 'General Wever' 4*. Stuttgart: Motorbuch Verlag, 1978. p. 224.
7. Gundelach, K., *Kampfgeschwader 'General Wever' 4*. Stuttgart: Motorbuch Verlag, 1978. p. 229.
8. Boelke archive.
9. *Soviet River Transport in the Great Patriotic War*. Moscow: Nauka, 1979. p. 111.
10. Fliegerbuch Hans Georg Bätcher. pp. 146–147.
11. Fliegerbuch Hans Georg Bätcher. pp. 148–149.
12. Loktionov, I.I., *The Volga Military Flotilla During the Great Patriotic War.* Moscow: Voenizdat, 1977. p. 99.

Chapter 2: New Goal

1. Gundelach, K., *Kampfgeschwader 'General Wever' 4*, Stuttgart: Motorbuch Verlag, 1978. pp. 230–231.

2. Dierich, W., *Kampfgeschwader 55 'Greif'*, Stuttgart: Motorbuch Verlag, 1994. p. 298.
3. Häberlen, K., *Davongekommen. Als Kampfflieger über der Fronten*, Vaizendorf: VDM Verlag, 2001. p. 134.
4. Gundelach, K., *Kampfgeschwader 'General Wever' 4.*Stuttgart: Motorbuch Verlag, 1978. pp. 234–235.
5. Dierich, W., *Kampfgeschwader 55 'Greif'*. Stuttgart: Motorbuch Verlag, 1994. pp. 304–305.
6. *Oblivion is not subject to: pages of Nizhny Novgorod history (1941–1945)*. N. Novgorod, 1995. p. 530.
7. Central archive of the Ministry of Defence of the Russian Federation (TSAMO RF). Foundation 13626. Inventory 20293. Case 7. Sheet 46, 48.
8. GOPANO. Fund 3. Inventory 1. Case 3275. Sheet 9–14.

Chapter 3: Two Deaths Carmen

1. Fliegerbuch Hans Grotter. pp. 102–103.
2. Gundelach, K., *Kampfgeschwader 'General Wever' 4,*Stuttgart: Motorbuch Verlag, 1978. pp. 228, 238.
3. Dierich, W., *Kampfgeschwader 55 'Greif'*. Stuttgart: Motorbuch Verlag, 1994. p. 306.
4. Archiv KG27'Boelcke'.
5. Fliegerbuch Helmut Abendvoth. pp. 70–71.
6. In 1938–39, he was the head of the school of bomber aviation, and then in April 1940, led the training and combat Geschwader LG 1. In June the same year, his Ju 88 was shot down over France and Oberst Bulowius, wounded, was captured. After the surrender of France, he was released and spent another four months in hospital. After that, Bulowius led the bomber and assault aviation schools. In July 1942 the new commander of Luftflotte 4, Generaloberst Richthofen, appointed him commander of the tactical air command 'Nord', whose tasks were to support the fighting of the 2nd Army on the Don and cover the left flank of the group moving along the Don to Stalingrad. In November 1942, Generalmajor Bulowius was appointed commander of Fliegerdivision 1. On 26 June 1943, he became commander of Fliegerkorps II.
7. Former 1st Squadron Aufkl.Gr.Ob.d.L.
8. The Ju 88 D, which had flown out to investigate the weather, went unnoticed by the air surveillance posts. But one of the GAZ workers

281

women later recalled that around 15.00, leaving the factory after the end of the shift, all the workers saw a black plane flying over the city at a high altitude.

9. This refers to the commander of 5./KG 27.

10. This refers to the penultimate letters in the codes of the He 111s, meaning a specific aircraft inside the Staffel. Thus, the sequence of take-off was as follows: '1G+AN' (Staffelcommander), '1G+CN', '1G+PN', '1G+EN', '1G+FN', '1G+BN', '1G+SN', '1G+ON', '1G+MN', '1G+NN' and '1G+KN'.

11. Archiv KG 27 'Boelcke'.

12. Fliegerbuch Helmut Abendvoth. pp. 70–71.

13. Fliegerbuch Hans Grotter. pp. 102–103.

14. At that time, the Moscow air defence front (MF PVO) consisted of fifteen anti-aircraft artillery divisions (ZenAD), three anti-aircraft machine-gun divisions, four anti-aircraft searchlight divisions, and two VNOS divisions. They were armed with 1,447 guns, including 1,256 large and 191 small calibre, thirty guidance stations for gunfire.

15. GOPANO. Foundation 2518. Inventory 1. Case 9. Sheet 15.

16. GU TSANO. Foundation 2435. Inventory 8. Case 64. Sheet 82.

17. Dierich, W., *Kampfgeschwader 55 'Greif'.*Stuttgart: Motorbuch Verlag, 1994. p. 307.

18. Archiv KG 27 'Boelcke'.

19. Fachwerk – a type of building structure in which the bearing base are vertically mounted load-bearing pillars, which are, along with spacer inclined beams, the supporting structure of the building. These supporting pillars and beams are visible from the outside and give the building a distinctive look. The space between the beams is filled with adobe material, brick, sometimes wood.

20. GU TSANO. Foundation 6146. Inventory 3. Case 4. Sheet 11.

21. *Air defence forces of the country in the Great Patriotic War*. Moscow: Voenizdat, 1968. pp. 243–244.

22. *Air defence forces of the country in the Great Patriotic War*. Moscow: Voenizdat, 1968.p. 126.

23. Dierich, W., *Kampfgeschwader 55 'Greif'*. Stuttgart: Motorbuch Verlag, 1994. p. 307.

24. GOPANO. Foundation 2518. Inventory 1. Case 6. Sheet 15–19.

25. It was named after the American engineers involved in the construction of GAZ.

26. It was evacuated from Moscow in 1941. Now it is called the 'Heat Exchanger' plant.
27. GOPANO. Foundation 2518. Inventory 1. Case 9. Sheet 24–27.
28. Archiv KG 27 'Boelcke'.
29. Fliegerbuch Helmut Abendvoth. pp. 70–71.
30. Fliegerbuch Hans Grotter. pp. 102–103.
31. Archiv KG 27 'Boelcke'.
32. GOPANO. Foundation 2518. Inventory 1. Case 9. Sheet 15–19.
33. GU TSANO. Foundation 6146. Inventory 3. Case 4. Sheet 13.
34. GOPANO. Foundation 2518. Inventory 1. Case 9. Sheet 17–18.
35. GOPANO. Foundation 2518. Inventory 1. Case 9. Sheet 19.
36. GOPANO. Foundation 2518. Inventory 1. Case 9. Sheet 20–21.
37. GOPANO. Foundation 2518. Inventory 1. Case 9. Sheet 20–21.

Chapter 4: Missions on Schedule

1. Fliegerbuch Helmut Abendvoth. pp. 70–71.
2. Archiv KG 27 'Boelcke'.
3. GU TSANO. Foundation 6146. Inventory 3. Case 4. Sheet 19.
4. GU TSANO. Foundation 6146. Inventory 3. Case 4. Sheet 16.
5. GOPANO. Foundation 2518. Inventory 1. Case 9. Sheet 36.
6. Archiv KG 27 'Boelcke'.
7. Fliegerbuch Helmut Abendvoth. pp. 70–71.
8. Of these, twenty-eight did not explode.
9. GOPANO. Foundation 2518. Inventory 1. Case 9. Sheet 37–39.
10. GOPANO. Foundation 2518. Inventory 1. Case 9. Sheet 37–39.
11. GOPANO. Foundation 2518. Inventory 1. Case 9. Sheet 31–32.
12. Archiv KG 27 'Boelcke'.
13. Fliegerbuch Helmut Abendvoth. pp. 70–71.
14. Archiv KG 27 'Boelcke'.
15. GU TSANO. Foundation 6146. Inventory 3. Case 4. Sheet 23.
16. GU TSANO. Foundation 6146. Inventory 3. Case 4. Sheet 26.
17. *Oblivion is not subject to: pages of Nizhny Novgorod history (1941–45).* N. Novgorod, 1995. pp. 379–380.
18. In fact, the death toll was much higher. The summary included only the primary data received by the morning of 7 June. At the same time, the figure of seventy-three means the number of bodies found at that time on the territory district. Attention is drawn to the lack of any data on missing persons.

19. Gundelach, K., *Kampfgeschwader 'General Wever' 4*. Stuttgart: Motorbuch Verlag, 1978. p. 236.
20. GOPANO. Foundation 2518. Inventory 1. Case 9. Sheet 55–56.
21. Historian Vladimir Okorokov in his book *Over the roof of your house* solemnly wrote on this occasion: 'the Pride of the fascist air force, the vaunted Fw 200, engulfed in flames, abruptly went toward the ground.'
22. Archiv KG 27 'Boelcke'.
23. Fliegerbuch Helmut Abendvoth. pp. 70–71.
24. GOPANO. Foundation 3, Inventory 1. Case 3275. Sheet 9–14.
25. Gundelach, K., *Kampfgeschwader 'General Wever' 4*. Stuttgart: Motorbuch Verlag, 1978. pp. 236–237.
26. GOPANO. Foundation 2518. Inventory 1. Case 9. Sheet 55–56.
27. Despite this, in the post-war years Boris Tabachuk often boasted of his only aerial victory. In an interview published on 13 April 1986 in the newspaper *Leninskaya Smena*, to the question of the journalist 'Did you see the result of the ram?' Tabachuk replied evasively: 'We tried, but did not. I only know that Gorky was not bombed that night.' Further, he claimed that he personally thwarted an air attack on the city, as he shot down a 'special aircraft designator' (pathfinder), and therefore the rest of the 'bombers' did not find the target. Forty-three years after the ram, Tabarchuk advised the 'red trackers' (a children's political organisation that searched for the remains of soldiers who went missing during the war) to look for the crash site of the German plane, after talking with local residents. But, of course, no one has ever found any wreckage.
28. Years later, his memory again failed Tabarchuk, and he forgot from whom he received his first order: 'and a few days later someone from the high military authorities came to the airfield, took off the Order of the Red Banner and awarded it to me.'
29. Fliegerbuch Hans Grotter. pp. 104–105.
30. Efimov, A.N., *Over the battlefield*. Moscow: Voenizdat, 1976. p. 113.
31. Russian nickname for a Bf 109.
32. Efimov, A.N., *Over the battlefield*.Moscow: Voenizdat, 1976. p. 114.
33. Rastrenin, O., *Split sky. May–June 1943*. Moscow: Eksmo; Yauza, 2007. p. 231.
34. Efimov, A.N., *Over the battlefield*. Moscow: Voenizdat, 1976. p. 115.
35. Russian nickname for the Il-2.
36. Rastrenin, O., *Split sky. May–June 1943*.Moscow: Eksmo; Yauza, 2007. p. 234.

Chapter 5: The Entire Volga Region is on Fire

1. GOPANO. Foundation 3. Inventory 1. Case 3308. pp.106–125.
2. He later became the commander of the 784th ZenAP.
3. Okorokov, V.N., *Over the roof of your house*. Documentary essay on air defence during the Great Patriotic War, N. Novgorod, 1992. p. 101.
4. *Air defence forces of the country in the Great Patriotic War*. Moscow: Voenizdat, 1968. p. 247.
5. Archiv KG 27 'Boelcke'.
6. Archiv KG 27 'Boelcke'.
7. Angle from 5° to 20° in the direction of the target.
8. Angle of 15° in the direction of the target.
9. 15km north-east of Moscow.
10. Willi Ebbinhaus was captured.
11. Archiv KG 27 'Boelcke'.
12. Calender – a press with horizontally arranged shafts, between which the rubber is passed in the form of rolls or sheets to increase its density and improve smoothness.
13. Yaroslavl tyre plant. Collection of documents and materials. Yaroslavl, 1968. pp. 74–75.
14. GOPANO. Foundation 2518. Inventory 1. Case 9. Sheet 73–83.
15. Angle from 60° to 90° towards the target.
16. Angle from 5° to 20° towards the target.
17. TSAMO of the Russian Federation. Foundation 566 Shap. Inventory 36584s. Case 11. Sheet 331.
18. Rastrenin, O., *Split sky May–June 1943*. Moscow: Eksmo; Yauza, 2007. p. 261.
19. John A. Kington, Franz Selinger. Wekusta. *Luftwaffe Meteorogical Recconaissance unit and operations 1938–1945*. Flight recorder publications, 2006. pp. 76–77.
20. In addition, it accounted for over 200 destroyed railway trucks and one heavy artillery battery. On 9 October 1943 commander 9./KG 27 Oberleutnant Grasemann was awarded the Knight's Cross.
21. *Saratov region during the Great Patriotic War (1941–1945)*. Archival document. Saratov, 2005. pp. 43–44.
22. *Air defence forces of the country in the Great Patriotic War*. Moscow: Voenizdat, 1968. p. 174.
23. Chenakal, D.D., *Military sky of the Volga Region*. Saratov, 1986. p. 131.
24. Fliegerbuch Helmut Abendvoth. pp. 72–73.
25. Now Kanavinsky bridge.

26. GU TSANO. Foundation 126. Inventory 5. Case 35. Sheet 9–14.
27. GU TSANO. Foundation 126. Inventory 5. Case 35. Sheet 9–14.
28. GU TSANO. Foundation 2816. Inventory 4. Case 166. Sheet 1–6.
29. GU TSANO. Foundation 2518. Inventory 1. Case 9. Sheet 80–91.
30. GOPANO. Foundation 2518. Inventory 1. Case 9. Sheet 93, 93a.
31. Archiv KG 27 'Boelcke'.
32. None of the Soviet pilots saw the circumstances of Belousov's death. In many post-war publications he was credited with ramming a German bomber, and this was described in great detail. For example, in S. Makarenko's article 'the Enemy over the city', published in the *Leninskaya Smena* newspaper on 18 February 1969, it was written as follows: 'Having gained the set height, Mikhail started searching. Suddenly, bluish fireflies appeared ahead. As they passed, Mikhail saw that they were the exhaust of a twin-engine plane. There was no doubt that a heavily loaded fascist vulture was going to bomb Gorky … Belousov opened fire with cannon. But the shells did not reach their goal. The pilot repeated the attack. Failure again. And the earth is getting closer. Without losing sight of the Heinkel, Mikhail pressed the trigger again. The guns were silent: they had run out of ammunition. What to do? The pilot decides to ram. The impact hit the upper part of the tail, and the He 111 crashed down.'
33. Fliegerbuch, Helmut Abendvoth. pp. 72–73.
34. Chenakal, D.D., *Military sky of the Volga Region*. Saratov, 1986. p. 136.
35. Fritzsche, K., *Air shooter. Through anti-aircraft fire*. Moscow: Yauza-Press, 2009. p. 69.
36. Angle from 20° to 40° in the direction of the target.
37. The name of the area literally was translated from Russian, bear ravine.
38. Fritzsche, K., *Air Shooter. Through Anti-aircraft Fire*, Moscow: Yauza-Press, 2009. pp. 70–71.
39. Sojm, V.M., *Soviet Counterintelligence in the Years of the Great Patriotic War*, Moscow: Kraft+, 2005. pp. 102–103.
40. Fliegerbuch Helmut Abendvoth. pp. 72–73.
41. Fliegerbuch Helmut Abendvoth. pp. 72–73.
42. Fritzsche, K., *Air shooter. Through anti-aircraft fire*. Moscow: Yauza-Press, 2009. p. 72.
43. The German nickname for the He 111.
44. Fritzsche, K., *Air shooter. Through anti-aircraft fire*. Moscow: Yauza-Press, 2009. pp. 73–74.
45. Fritzsche, K., *Air shooter. Through anti-aircraft fire*. Moscow: Yauza-Press, 2009. p. 75.

46. Fliegerbuch Helmut Abendvoth. pp. 72–73.

47. On 10 May 1943, the Stroygaz No. 2 Construction Company had 2,178 workers and 147 engineers (a total of 2,706 people).

Chapter 6: The Finishing Blow

1. Dierich, W., *Kampfgeschwader 55 'Greif'*. Stuttgart: Motorbuch Verlag, 1994. pp. 250–252.

2. Fritzsche, K., *Air shooter. Through anti-aircraft fire.* Moscow: Yauza-Press, 2009. p. 77.

3. Fritzsche, K., *Air shooter. Through anti-aircraft fire.* Moscow: Yauza-Press, 2009. pp. 78–79.

4. Fritzsche, K., *Air shooter. Through anti-aircraft fire.* Moscow: Yauza-Press, 2009. pp. 79–80.

5. Panteleev, Y. A., *Sea front.* Moscow: Voenizdat, 1965. p. 251.

6. Fritzsche, K., *Air shooter. Through anti-aircraft fire.* Moscow: Yauza-Press, 2009. pp. 80–81.

7. *One hundred Stalin's Falcons. In the battles for the Motherland.* Moscow: Yauza, Eksmo, 2005. pp. 156–157.

8. *One hundred Stalin's Falcons. In the battles for the Motherland.* Moscow: Yauza, Eksmo, 2005. p. 157.

9. Archiv KG27 'Boelcke'.

10. *Yaroslavl region for 50 years. 1936–1986.* Essays, documents, materials. Yaroslavl, 1986. p. 234.

11. Archiv KG 27 'Boelcke'.

12. Archiv KG 27 'Boelcke'.

13. GOPANO. Foundation 2518. Inventory 1. Case 9. Sheet 155–166.

14. Characteristically, the chief of staff of MPVO Gorky, Major Antropov, and NKVD Colonel Zverev, in their reports to their superiors, tried to downplay the damage in every possible way. In particular, the latter openly lied to Stalin's Minister Lavrentiy Beria that the foundry shop No. 3 was 'caused minor damage'. In reality, the value of the losses just from those two bombs were subsequently estimated at 583,785 rubles!

15. GU TSANO. Foundation 126. Inventory 5. Case 35. Sheet of 10–14.

16. The plant was founded in 1896, named after the Etna volcano, and renamed by the Bolsheviks on 7 November 1922 as the Krasnaya Etna metallurgical plant.

17. GOPANO. Foundation 2518. Inventory 1. Case 9. Sheet 155–166.
18. GOPANO. Foundation 2518. Inventory 1. Case 9. Sheet 153–154.
19. *Oblivion is not subject to: pages of Nizhny Novgorod history (1941 –1945).* N. Novgorod, 1995. pp. 380-381.
20. Angle from 20°to 40° in the direction of the target.
21. Angle from 5° to 20° in the direction of the target.
22. Chenakal, D.D., *Military sky of the Volga Region.* Saratov, 1986. p. 139.
23. Sojm, V.M., *Soviet counterintelligence in the years of the Great Patriotic War.* Moscow: Kraft+, 2005. p. 103.
24. Morokhin, V.N., *Through the fire of the great battle.* N. Novgorod, 1995. p. 112.
25. According to one of the Soviet legends, in July 1943, the director of the already defunct aircraft factory No. 292, Isaac Levin, flew on a business trip to the front. There, General F.I. Tolbukhin arranged for him to meet an unidentified captured German pilot, the 'deputy commander of the Geschwader that bombed the factory'. An interesting conversation took place between the participants. Tolbukhin, who presented to the captured German the current factory director, expressed his doubt that the aviation plant in Saratov had been 'wiped off the face of the earth'. But his argument could not convince the stubborn 'nazi bomber'. The prisoner logically objected to his interlocutor that 'the director may be alive, but the plant is not, it was completely demolished'. Then Levin tried to prove to the offender that the plant still produced aircraft, and would produce even more! The Luftwaffe pilot, who flew in the bombing raid and witnessed the results, insisted: 'This can't be, your factory is completely destroyed.'

    In his rewritten post-war memoirs, when the events of the past war were seen in a different perspective, Levin recalled the consequences of the air attack on the night of 23/24 June 1943 without much enthusiasm. He admitted that '70 per cent of the capacity and 60 per cent of the equipment were put out of action, and the buildings turned into piles of rubble'.
26. Lagoda, M., *Ein Blick in die Vergangenheit. Kriegsernnerungen eines Fernaufklarers aus Russland und dem Orient.* Helios, 2011. p. 116.
27. Including those shot down on the way to the target and on withdrawal outside the area of action of the Yaroslavl air defence divisional area.
28. Including those shot down on the way to the target and on withdrawal outside the area of action of the Gorky corps area of air defence.
29. At least one of these crews was killed due to technical reasons.

Chapter 7: 'One Hundred Days'

1. Dierich, W., *Kampfgeschwader 55 'Greif'*. Stuttgart: Motorbuch Verlag, 1994. p. 308.
2. Gundelach, K., *Kampfgeschwader 'General Wever' 4*.Stuttgart: Motorbuch Verlag, 1978. p. 235.
3. GU TSANO. Foundation 2435. Inventory 8. Case 66. Sheet 40–45.
4. GU TSANO. Foundation 2435. Inventory 8. Case 66. Sheet 61, 65.
5. GU TSANO. Foundation 2435. Inventory 1. Case 180. Sheet 79.
6. GU TSANO. Foundation 2435. Inventory 1. Case 180. Sheet 79.
7. GU TSANO. Foundation 2435. Inventory 8. Case 66. Sheet 4.
8. Svirin, M.N., *Stalin's Steel fist. History of the Soviet tank. 1943–1945*. Moscow: Yauza, Eksmo, 2006. p. 173.
9. GU TSANO. Foundation 15. Inventory 4. Case 234. Sheet 5. In July, the Krasnoye Sormovo No. 112 shipyard barely released 178 T-34 tanks, again underperforming the already reduced plan. At the same time, all this manufactured military equipment was of extremely low quality due to the notorious 'bypass technologies'. Krasnoye Sormovo built 2,962 tanks in 1943, onlyslightly more than in 1942. Thus, the company was not able to meet the annual production plan for military products.
10. *Saratov region during the Great Patriotic War (1941–1945)*. Archival document. Saratov, 2005. pp. 66–67.
11. GU TSANO. Foundation 2435. Inventory 8. Case 65. Sheet 47–48.
12. GU TSANO. Foundation 2435. Inventory 8. Case 65. Sheet 36–37.
13. GU TSANO. Foundation 2435. Inventory 8. Case 65. Sheet 38.
14. GU TSANO. Foundation 2435. Inventory 8. Case 65. Sheet 31–34.
15. GU TSANO. Foundation 2435. Inventory 8. Case 65. Sheet 35–37.
16. GU TSANO. Foundation 2435. Inventory 8. Case 65. Sheet 35–37.
17. GU TSANO. Foundation 2435. Inventory 8. Case 65. Sheet 57.
18. GU TSANO. Foundation 6146. Inventory 3. Case 4. Sheet 62.
19. GU TSANO. Foundation 6146. Inventory 3. Case 4. Sheet 64.
20. GU TSANO. Foundation 6146. Inventory 2. Case 7. Sheet 1.
21. GU TSANO. Foundation 2435. Inventory 8. Case 65. Sheet 143.
22. Professor Keldysh, a teacher at the military engineering academy, was one of the originators of the method of calculating reinforced concrete structures. He was a participant in the design, examination and acceptance of many great construction projects, including the Moscow–Volga canal, the Dnepropetrovsk aluminum plant and the Moscow metro.

23. Yaroslavl tyre plant. Collection of documents and materials. Yaroslavl, 1968. p. 81.
24. Yaroslavl tyre plant. Collection of documents and materials. Yaroslavl, 1968. pp. 82–83.
25. GU TSANO. Foundation 126. Inventory 5. Case 35. Sheet 1–17; Case 18. Sheet 201–207.
26. GU TSANO. Foundation 2435. Inventory 1. Case 180. Sheet 106–114.
27. Zarembo, N.P., *Volzhsky ples*. Moscow: 1970. p. 124.
28. In the future, Captain Gudovich was sent to the hospital in Gorky, where he died of his wounds.

Index

Teckelmann, Unteroffizier Hans, 15
Third Reich, 1, 4, 34, 37, 149, 263, 265, 275
Typhoon, Operation, 44

USAAF, viii
USSR, 28, 33, 42–3, 48, 81, 112, 116, 136, 139, 188, 213, 220–1, 227, 233–4, 237

Volga Region, 10, 28–30, 32–3, 55, 78, 132, 150, 153, 186–8, 213, 219, 223–4, 227, 235, 251, 258, 263
Volga River, 32, 39, 48–9, 58, 60, 64, 136, 139, 155, 157, 172, 175, 183, 185, 214–18, 220, 258
von Greim, Generaloberst Robert, 10, 36–7, 114
von Manstein, Generalfeldmarschall Erich, 2–4, 7, 9, 262
von Richthofen, Manfred, 6, 270

Wehrmacht, 3, 7, 20, 36–7, 53, 189–90
Wetterer, Major Wolf, 35

Winkel, Leutnant Eberhard, 5–6
Wunderwaffe, 1

Yakovlev,
Yak-1, 10, 12–13, 15–16, 18, 28, 42, 47, 122, 124–6, 151, 155, 173–5, 179, 199, 214–16, 218, 221, 257
Yak-7, 12–13, 15, 28, 47, 122, 124–6, 134, 137–8, 151
Yak-9, 53–5
Yaroslavl, 43, 55, 132–40, 169, 184, 188, 198, 200–203, 224–5, 229–30, 234, 236, 251–53, 255–6, 263–4

Zayets, Lieutenant, 13
Zementbomber, 118, 123, 125, 150–1, 153
ZenAP, 46, 49, 64, 67, 71, 80, 100, 102, 109, 115, 131, 154, 158, 215
Zitadelle, Operation, ix, 36, 190, 224, 230, 236